THE CINEMA OF DANIÈLE HUILLET AND JEAN-MARIE STRAUB

LEGENDA

LEGENDA is the Modern Humanities Research Association's book imprint for new research in the Humanities. Founded in 1995 by Malcolm Bowie and others within the University of Oxford, Legenda has always been a collaborative publishing enterprise, directly governed by scholars. The Modern Humanities Research Association (MHRA) joined this collaboration in 1998, became half-owner in 2004, in partnership with Maney Publishing and then Routledge, and has since 2016 been sole owner. Titles range from medieval texts to contemporary cinema and form a widely comparative view of the modern humanities, including works on Arabic, Catalan, English, French, German, Greek, Italian, Portuguese, Russian, Spanish, and Yiddish literature. Editorial boards and committees of more than 60 leading academic specialists work in collaboration with bodies such as the Society for French Studies, the British Comparative Literature Association and the Association of Hispanists of Great Britain & Ireland.

The MHRA encourages and promotes advanced study and research in the field of the modern humanities, especially modern European languages and literature, including English, and also cinema. It aims to break down the barriers between scholars working in different disciplines and to maintain the unity of humanistic scholarship. The Association fulfils this purpose through the publication of journals, bibliographies, monographs, critical editions, and the MHRA Style Guide, and by making grants in support of research. Membership is open to all who work in the Humanities, whether independent or in a University post, and the participation of younger colleagues entering the field is especially welcomed.

MOVING IMAGE

Legenda/Moving Image publishes cutting-edge work on any aspect of film or screen media from Europe and Latin America. Studies of European-language cinemas from other continents, and diasporic and intercultural cinemas (with some relation to Europe or its languages), are also encompassed. The series seeks to reflect a diversity of theoretical, historical, and interdisciplinary approaches to the moving image, and includes projects comparing screen media with other art forms. Research monographs and collected volumes will be considered, but not studies of a single film. As innovation is a priority for the series, volumes should predominantly consist of previously unpublished material.

Proposals should be sent with one or two sample chapters to the Editor, Professor John David Rhodes, Corpus Christi College, Cambridge CB2 1RH, UK.

APPEARING IN THIS SERIES

1. *Spanish Practices: Literature, Cinema, Television*, by Paul Julian Smith
2. *Cinema and Contact: The Withdrawal of Touch in Nancy, Bresson, Duras and Denis*, by Laura McMahon
3. *Cinema's Inter-Sensory Encounters: Krzysztof Kieślowski and Claire Denis*, by Georgina Evans
4. *Holocaust Intersections: Genocide and Visual Culture at the New Millennium*, edited by Axel Bangert, Robert S. C. Gordon and Libby Saxton
5. *Africa's Lost Classics: New Histories of African Cinema*, edited by Lizelle Bisschoff and David Murphy
6. *Agnès Varda Unlimited: Image, Music, Media*, edited by Marie-Claire Barnet
7. *Thinking Cinema with Proust*, by Patrick ffrench
8. *Blanchot and the Moving Image: Fascination and Spectatorship*, by Calum Watt
9. *Chantal Akerman: Afterlives*, edited by Marion Schmid and Emma Wilson
10. *Screening Work: The Films of Christian Petzold*, by Stephan Hilpert and Andrew J. Webber

Managing Editor
Dr Graham Nelson, 41 Wellington Square, Oxford OX1 2JF, UK

www.legendabooks.com

The Cinema of
Danièle Huillet and Jean-Marie Straub

❖

EDITED BY MARTIN BRADY AND HELEN HUGHES

l

LEGENDA

Moving Image 14
Modern Humanities Research Association
2023

Published by Legenda
an imprint of the Modern Humanities Research Association
Salisbury House, Station Road, Cambridge CB1 2LA

ISBN 978-1-83954-058-5 (HB)
ISBN 978-1-83954-059-2 (PB)

First published 2023

Copy-Editor: Charlotte Wathey

CONTENTS

❖

Acknowledgements   ix

Notes on the Contributors   x

Introduction: Incendiary Films   I
MARTIN BRADY AND HELEN HUGHES

1   'Nor do I seek out difficult postures': Huillet's and Straub's Intellectuals   25
    NICOLAS HELM-GROVAS

2   Part and Whole: On Some Uses of Landscape in the Films of Huillet
    and Straub   45
    SAM MCAULIFFE

3   The Incarnation of Language in Quotation: The Böll and Bruckner Films
    of Huillet and Straub   61
    MARTIN BRADY

4   History in the Visible: Memory Through Landscape in *Fortini/Cani*   77
    CHRIS GROENVELD

5   'The noise, the air, and the wind': Sound and Stratification in the Films
    of Danièle Huillet, Jean-Marie Straub, and Harun Farocki   91
    LAURA LUX

6   'Guardami!': *Sicilia!* and the Claim on Attention   109
    BRENDAN PRENDEVILLE

7   Into the Woods: The Green Spaces of Huillet and Straub's *Workers,
    Peasants* and *The Return of The Prodigal Son — Humiliated*   123
    JANE MADSEN

8   Jean-Yves Petiteau, *Itinerary of Jean Bricard*: Three Documents   141
    TRANSLATED BY RICARDO MATOS CABO

9   Communist Photosynthesis   166
    RASTKO NOVAKOVIĆ

10 Relocating Kafka in Jean-Marie Straub's *Jackals and Arabs* (2011)   182
    HELEN HUGHES

11 Interview with Danièle Huillet and Jean-Marie Straub apropos *The Death
    of Empedocles* and *Black Sin*: 9 April 1990, Goethe-Institut London   196

Filmography   210
Bibliography   213
Epilogue   222
Index   224

ACKNOWLEDGEMENTS

❖

This book emerged from lively discussions during and after the complete retrospective of the films of Danièle Huillet and Jean-Marie Straub in London from March to June 2019 curated by Ricardo Matos Cabo. That retrospective would not have been possible without the financial and organisational support of the Goethe-Institut, in particular the film coordinator in London, Maren Hobein, and Head of the Culture Department, Melanie Bono.

We are particularly grateful to Barbara Ulrich at BELVA Film for providing material and for letting us reproduce images from the films of Huillet and Straub. Christophe Clavert kindly arranged access to the digital files for us. Many thanks also go to Erik and Lou Petiteau for allowing us to publish a translation of their father's *Itinerary of Jean Bricard* and related documents. Misha Donat, long-time translator for Huillet and Straub and expert commentator on their music films, very generously allowed us to use the image that appears on the cover of this volume; we are also grateful to him for permission to draw on his subtitles for *Itinerary of Jean Bricard*. We would also like to thank the journal *La furia umana* for permission to translate Jean-Yves Petiteau's text 'Apropos Jean-Marie Straub and Danièle Huillet: *The Itinerary of Jean Bricard*' and Giorgio Passerone for allowing us to reproduce his script for *O somma luce*.

It has been a pleasure to transcribe and translate the interview between Huillet, Straub, and Julian Petley at the Goethe-Institut in April 1990 and we are grateful for the permission of Margaret Deriaz, film coordinator of the 1990 retrospective at the London Goethe-Institut, and of Julian to publish the interview.

Stimulating discussions at the workshops preceding this publication were attended by a number of people who are not otherwise represented in this volume. We are grateful to all of them for their contributions and would also like, in particular, to thank Erica Carter and Emma Wilson for their encouragement to submit the proposal for this volume in 2020.

At Legenda, Graham Nelson, John David Rhodes, and Charlotte Wathey supported us throughout the project and were unwaveringly patient.

It was with great sadness that we learnt of the death of Jean-Marie Straub on 20 November 2022 as this book was in production. We hope that these essays and documents will stimulate lively debate about the films that he and Danièle Huillet made across six decades and in four languages.

Martin Brady and Helen Hughes, March 2023

NOTES ON THE CONTRIBUTORS

❖

Martin Brady is Emeritus Reader in German and Film Studies at King's College London. He has published on European film (documentary, GDR cinema, Brechtian and experimental film, Wenders, Straub-Huillet), music (Schoenberg, Dessau, Larcher, Krautrock), philosophy (Adorno), literature (Böll, Handke, Jelinek), Jewish exile architects, the visual arts (Beuys, Kiefer), disability (thalidomide), foraging, and ordinariness. He translated Victor Klemperer's *LTI (The Language of the Third Reich)*, has interpreted for Alexander Kluge, Michael Haneke, Ulrich Seidl, and Edgar Reitz, and also works as a visual and performance artist.

Ricardo Matos Cabo is an independent film programmer. Recently he has organized film series on the work of Tsuchimoto Noriaki, Haneda Sumiko, and Claudia von Alemann. He collaborates regularly with the Open City Documentary Film Festival and the Essay Film Festival in London and the Courtisane Film Festival, in Ghent, Belgium. He teaches Film Exhibition Histories at the Elías Querejeta Film School in San Sebastian.

Chris Groenveld is a CHASE scholar and PhD candidate at the University of Sussex, working on the spatial turn in contemporary Holocaust memory. Her creative and critical practice is concerned with notions of posthuman or prosthetic memory. In 2018 she undertook an MA in Ethnographic & Documentary Film at University College London. Her dissertation film, *Workshop*, explores personal memory and re-enactment during a filmmaking workshop for adults at a centre for independent living.

Nicolas Helm-Grovas is a writer and curator. His writing — on histories of radical cinema, experimental film and video, film theory and contemporary art — has appeared in *Oxford Art Journal*, *Radical Philosophy*, *Moving Image Review & Art Journal*, and various books and catalogues. He has taught at Arts University Bournemouth, Oxford Brookes University, King's College London, and Royal Holloway, University of London. With Oliver Fuke he has co-curated several exhibitions related to the work of Laura Mulvey and Peter Wollen, most recently at Camera Austria in Graz.

Helen Hughes is Senior Lecturer in German and Film Studies at the University of Surrey. Her research has engaged with documentary studies, German-language cinema, and environmental humanities. She is the author of *Radioactive Documentary* (Intellect, 2021), *Green Documentary* (Intellect, 2014), co-editor of *Documentary and Disability* (Palgrave Macmillan, 2017), co-translator of *History and Obstinacy*, (Kluge, Negt, 2014) and has also published several chapters and articles in journals such as *Screen*, *Continuum*, and the *Historical Journal of Film, Radio and Television*. She is currently working on a project about the GDR filmmaker Annelie Thorndike with the working title *Red Documentary*.

Laura Lux is a PhD candidate in the German Department at King's College London. Her PhD research analyses the early films, video practices, and texts of the German essay filmmaker Harun Farocki in the context of the West German 1968 student movement and the media. Between 2018 and 2020 she worked for the GSSN project 'Circulating Cinema' and taught as a Graduate Teaching Assistant at King's College London. In 2021 she was invited to deliver the annual Sylvia Naish Research Student Lecture by the Institute of Modern Languages Research in London and has held presentations at the annual BAFTSS conference and Visible Evidence.

Jane Madsen is a filmmaker whose work includes artist's 16mm film and video, installation, and essay documentary. Her work is experimental and interdisciplinary. She has written and published on film, art, and architecture exploring the themes of home, place, space, territory, landscape, absence, and poetics. She has a practice-based PhD from the Bartlett School of Architecture, UCL, with practice supervised at the Slade. She has taught at the University of the Arts London for many years and is Senior Lecturer and researcher at the London College of Communication.

Sam McAuliffe is a Lecturer in Visual Cultures at Goldsmiths, University of London, where he works in the fields of modern European philosophy and critical theory, with particular emphasis on questions of image, language, and the politics of aesthetic experience. Recent publications have focused on the fiction of Raymond Queneau and René Daumal, and he is currently writing a monograph on the culture of *ressentiment* in modernist literary practice, organized around the motif of self-accusation and the 'turn against oneself'.

Rastko Novaković is a writer and filmmaker who has authored or co-authored sixty moving image works. He has worked on video activist and DIY media projects with a feminist antimilitarist group (Women in Black, Serbia), a climate justice group (Climate Camp, UK), and London Indymedia. He is currently coordinator of the Activist Media Project, based at the MayDay Rooms in London.

Jean-Yves Petiteau (1942–2015) was a French sociologist, researcher at the CNRS (Centre national de la recherche scientifique), at the National School of Architecture in Grenoble, and at the National School of Architecture in Nantes. He worked particularly on art and anthropology, on staging in public space, as well as on the relationship between image and narrative. He is particularly known for his 'itinerary' method, an investigative approach which questions the place given to words and images in sociology. As well as publishing numerous itineraries, his books include *Nantes: récit d'une traversée* (Nantes: Story of a Crossing, 2013).

Brendan Prendeville is Senior Lecturer in the Department of Visual Cultures at Goldsmiths, University of London. His research centres on aspects of phenomenology, with particular reference to painting, and to aspects of realism; he has published articles and chapters on Maurice Merleau-Ponty, Henri Bergson, and Michel Henry, with reference to painting, and on Géricault, de Hooch, Velazquez, Francis Bacon, Seurat, Agnes Martin, and Caravaggio, dwelling particularly on the phenomenology of embodiment. His *Realism in 20th Century Painting* was published in 2000, and he is currently writing a book on painting and phenomenology.

INTRODUCTION

❖

Incendiary Films

Martin Brady and Helen Hughes

The Kabbalah tells a legend: At the beginning God said: 'Let There Be Light'.
Out of space a flame burst out. God crushed that light to atoms. Myriad of
sparks are hidden in our world, but not all of us behold them.
— ARNOLD SCHOENBERG, *Kol Nidre*

For us fiction matters because if you combine it with documentary images or
a documentary situation you get a contradiction where sparks can fly. Fiction
is crucial to start the fire.
— DANIÈLE HUILLET[1]

The films of Danièle Huillet and Jean-Marie Straub have provoked fierce debate
ever since their debut, *Machorka-Muff*, was screened out of competition at the West
German Short Film Festival in Oberhausen in 1963. Attacked by German critics,
who complained for example about the sympathetic portrayal of its titular character
(a 1950s West German general with fascist leanings), it was defended in the French
journal *Cahiers du cinéma*, where it was announced as the first post-war German
auteurist film and described as 'the most violently anti-militarist film that has ever
been made'.[2] For those who have valued the filmmakers' methods and politics, their
works have consistently been welcomed as an alternative practice to celebrate and
defend. Indeed, their iconic status is such that the leftist, Brechtian wing of post-war
European cinema, one of Peter Wollen's 'two avant-gardes', became known by the
moniker 'Godard-Straub'.[3]

The more militant critical reception and appropriation of Huillet and Straub's
cinema has frequently adopted the rhetoric and vocabulary of ignition and
explosion. In a much-quoted essay of 1976 in the journal *ça Cinéma*, Jean-André
Fieschi describes the films of Huillet and Straub as shot through with 'shock, the
sign of the fissure, the euphoria of destruction'; these explosive forces produce
'works of rupture' in service of political transformation.[4] Whilst commentators are
in general agreement about the explosive or 'deconstructive' nature of the work,
they have interpreted the resulting gaps and fissures in radically different ways.[5] For
Fieschi and others such ruptures — elsewhere he refers to them as 'confrontations',
'resistances', and 'displacement' — were, in the mid-seventies, a rich source of
Brechtian estrangement, weapons in the armoury of political modernism. As Louis
Séguin once neatly put it, Huillet and Straub 'belong to a non-hierarchical and

frontier-less clan of rebels, stateless persons and social misfits, and the challenge of their cinema matches this permanent irreducibility'.[6] As the recent surge of interest in the films of Huillet and Straub has amply demonstrated, their films, made in four European countries and four languages, have 'stood the test of time' and continue to inspire new generations of audiences, scholars, and film and media practitioners.

The heated nature of the early reception of the films and their status as part of the practice of an alternative, political modernist school of filmmaking is now a significant chapter in the history of European cinema. In his two-volume work on the film journal *Cahiers du cinéma*, Daniel Fairfax has reconstructed the conditions in which audiences found the art of Huillet and Straub 'explosive' during the late sixties and early seventies. More recently, the films have been undergoing reassessment, not only for their formal innovation, but also in relation to the filmmakers' ostensibly idiosyncratic choice of texts, music, and paintings as raw material for their films. The reasoning behind specific aesthetic and political choices is still full of interest to fiction, documentary, and essay filmmakers as well as those working in expanded media and film research as practice.[7]

Spearheading this reassessment is Jacques Rancière who, in a thoughtful essay in the collection *The Intervals of Cinema*, first published as *Les écarts du cinéma* in 2011, sought to situate them within a broader landscape of political filmmaking.[8] For film scholars and cinephiles Rancière makes a number of points which have encouraged renewed engagement with the political cinema of the Cold War, considering both where it came from and how it feeds into contemporary alternative film practices. The most contentious of these points, perhaps, has been his identification of a 'post-Brechtian' cinema that continues the formal practices of European political cinema of the sixties and seventies, but which has moved away from affirming a Marxist understanding of why there is political injustice in the world, preferring to point to the difficulties and ambiguities of revolutionary failure.[9] Rancière picks out the cinema of Huillet and Straub as an example of 'the Brechtian paradigm', which he defines as 'an art that replaces the continuities and progressions of the narrative and empathetic model with a broken-up form'.[10] He goes on to argue that their cinema becomes 'post-Brechtian' with *From the Cloud to the Resistance* (1979), their adaptation of Cesare Pavese's *Dialogues with Leucò* (*Dialoghi con Leucò*) and *The Moon and the Bonfires* (*La luna e i falò*). The change is not one of film form, but one which marks a turn from 'the exposure of mechanisms of domination' towards 'the study of the aporiae of emancipation'.[11]

$$\star \quad \star \quad \star \quad \star \quad \star$$

Rancière's argument is, on the face of it, a simple invitation to film scholars to revisit the films of Huillet and Straub and to consider the development of the *œuvre* across six decades. This process has been helped in recent years by a number of full retrospectives in the US (MoMA) and France (Pompidou Centre) in 2016, in Germany in 2017, and then in the UK in 2019. There have also been major surveys in Spain (Madrid) and Japan (Tokyo). For English audiences and scholars, the translation of a number of works has helped to bring the films into new contexts.

This new wave of activity began with a valuable overview of their career edited by Ted Fendt and in tandem with the MoMA retrospective, followed by the translation of the collected *Writings* of Straub and Huillet, a substantial monograph on cinematic and poetic realism by Benoît Turquety in translation from French, and, most recently, an extensive and engaging collection of essays derived from the 2017 exhibition and retrospective in Berlin *Tell It to the Stones*.[12]

The new perspectives provided by these recent contributions to Huillet and Straub scholarship have begun to revise established ideas about how their cinema is to be read. Along with essays on their films published in the British film journal *Screen* in the 1970s, book-length studies by Richard Roud (regrettably entitled just *Jean-Marie Straub*, 1971) and Barton Byg (*Landscapes of Resistance*, 1995) led discussion of Huillet and Straub's work amongst English-speaking film scholars until well after Huillet's death in 2006.[13] This meant that weight was given to the early and German-language films — Byg indeed explicitly brackets out all those in French and Italian. The proximity of the early work to the dramatic film and media theory of Bertolt Brecht also played a major role in this emphasis, encouraged by articles, interviews, and screenplays in *Screen* and in the wake of lively debate throughout the sixties and early seventies in French-language journals, most notably *Cahiers du cinéma*, as already observed, and *Positif*.

This rather limited view of their work as German and Brechtian has been revised through the lens of Rancière's concept of a 'post-Brechtian' cinema and also through greater attention being paid to the later works and to those made in French and Italian. A simple tally reveals, after all, that the number of films in which French, German, or Italian is spoken is roughly equal. The balance was redressed in part by *Tell It to the Stones* and the present study aims to continue this work.

This volume, like its Berlin predecessor, derives from a retrospective — the complete survey of the films of Huillet and Straub held between March and June 2019 at a range of venues in London, including the BFI Southbank, the Goethe-Institut London, the Institute of Contemporary Arts (ICA), King's College London (KCL), the Birkbeck Institute for the Moving Image (BIMI), Close-Up Film Centre, and the Whitechapel Gallery. It was curated by Ricardo Matos Cabo in collaboration with and funded by the Goethe-Institut.[14] As had been the case in Berlin two years previously, a 'hardcore' of enthusiasts met again and again at the sixty or more screenings. Out of this 'enthusiasm' — the term was weighed up as a possible title for the retrospective in homage to the journal of that name edited by Andi Engel in 1974 — a working group emerged that met in late 2019 and early 2020 at KCL to continue engaging with the treasures that had been unearthed in the retrospective. Cut short by the Covid-19 pandemic which broke out in England in March 2020, the face-to-face meetings focused on landscape, nature, and Marxist ecologism (November 2019), and on language and voice (February 2020).

These two focal points have become the basis for the diverse responses in this volume to the challenge of reassessing the cinema of Huillet and Straub, notionally kick-started by Rancière and his thesis proposing an interpretation of their work as 'post-Brechtian' political cinema. The chapters which follow are not only held together by a thread of ecological thinking discerned in the films (the colour green, wind, sunlight, mountains, deserts, woodland), they also engage with a further overarching and more formal set of questions posed by scholars working on the languages of adaptation.

From the discussions in the post-retrospective workshops, it became clear that there was considerable interest amongst the participants in the films that emerged from the later phase of the collaborative films of Huillet and Straub and those of Straub alone from 2006, in particular the works that came from their protracted engagement with the Teatro Francesco di Bartolo in the Buti region of Tuscany. Eight joint films and five by Straub alone resulted from this collaboration. Debate in the two workshops was animated by very different views — some enthusiastic, some critical — of Rancière's provocative assertion in interview that these films and the Friedrich Hölderlin adaptations that preceded them in the 1980s marked a radical shift from cosmopolitan Brechtian Marxism to a pastoral, even mystical green alternative:

> I would say that the film that is the turning point is *From the Cloud to the Resistance*, a film from 1978 [*sic*] adapted from Pavese [...]. We move to a peasant or ecological communism, opposed to the communism of Soviet engineers. [...]
> What is certain is that it is a matter of going back to a religion of the earth that existed under diverse forms during the Romantic era. The Straubs' Marxism has more and more of a tendency to move towards Heidegger and to distance itself from the Brechtianism of thirty or forty years ago.[15]

Although not the subject of a separate essay here, the Hölderlin films are key to the alleged shift in thinking that has been identified in the films of Huillet and Straub. Again and again, commentators on their films and the filmmakers themselves return to the speech of Empedocles on the slopes of Mount Etna in the first version of Hölderlin's drama which appears in no fewer than six films if one counts the four separate versions of *The Death of Empedocles* (1987, Figure I.1). Quoted in *Cézanne: Conversation with Joachim Gasquet* (1990) and subsequently in *Communists* (2014), this extraordinary passage of verse has become, not only for Huillet and Straub but also for many interlocutors, a political programme like no other, a kind of utopian, green-red manifesto for the Anthropocene with all its political and ecological crises. The centrality of this passage from Hölderlin's unfinished drama justifies lengthy citation as it appears in the film, in Barton Byg's subtitles:

> So venture it! what you have inherited, what you have acquired,
> what your father's mouth has told you, taught you,
> law and custom, the names of the ancient gods,
> forget it boldly and raise, as newborn,
> your eyes to godly Nature,
> as then the spirit is kindled on the light
> of the heavens, a sweet breath of life will
> drench your bosom as if for the first time,
> and full of golden fruits the woods will rustle
> and springs out of the rock, when the life
> of the world seizes you, its spirit of peace and
> like a holy cradle song stills your soul,

FIG. I.I. Danièle Huillet and Jean-Marie Straub, *The Death of Empedocles* (1987, courtesy of BELVA Film).

then out of the bliss of a beautiful dawning
the green of the earth will glisten from anew for you
and mountain and sea and clouds and stars,
the noble powers, like heroic brothers,
will come before your eyes so that your breast,
as of weapon bearers, beats toward deeds,
and a beautiful world of your own, then reach one another your hands
again, give the word and share the goods,
o then you dear ones — share deed and glory,
like true Dioscuri; let each one be
as all, — as upon slender pillars, rest
upon righteous ordinances the new life
and let the law affirm your bond.
Then o you geniuses of wandering
Nature! then you serene ones
who take joy out of the depths and the heights
and as grief and happiness and sunshine and rain,
bring it from a far strange world
to the hearts of narrowly bounded mortals,
the free people will invite you to its feasts,
friend to guests! pious! for lovingly
the mortal gives of the best, if his bosom is not
closed and narrowed by servitude.

This remarkable passage provides not only a rich resource for scholars of their film-making, but also, for the filmmakers themselves, amounts to a political declaration of intent.

The essay filmmaker, and 'student' of Huillet and Straub, Harun Farocki made a short 'film-tip' for television to promote *The Death of Empedocles* in which he interviewed the film's leading player Andreas von Rauch (see Chapter 5). Rauch's detailed and revealing comments on the protracted rehearsal stage and the attention paid by the directors to the minutest details of pacing, rhythm, intonation, and breathing demonstrates how the red-green thinking behind Straub-Huillet's aesthetics and their politics — inseparable, of course, as might be expected of any credible political modernism — cannot be extricated from the constitution of the human body itself, from its inspirations and exhalations (see Chapters 3 and 9).

This provides us with our second focus in the current volume: language, voice, and embodiment. This focus embraces questions of translation and adaptation, of recitation, of authorial voice, or performance, dialect, and of technology (the recording apparatus required to capture the sound waves, see Chapter 5). These questions, together with the aporia of ecology already mentioned, run through the essays. Again, the focus shifts towards the later works, including those of Straub alone — *O somma luce* (2010, see Chapter 9), *Jackals and Arabs* (2011, see Chapter 10).[16] Earlier, in Chapter 3, we have an investigation of the origins of the engagement with text, recitation, quotation, and embodiment in the German-language films of the 1960s, the adaptations of texts by Heinrich Böll and Ferdinand Bruckner. But already this analysis of Huillet and Straub's most overtly and incontrovertibly 'Brechtian' films demonstrates that it will be impossible to subdivide their sixty or so works into different colours of Marxism. The programme is already fully developed in 1963.

This is perhaps the very point Straub was making when in 2013, after five decades of filmmaking, he not only revisited the title of the 1972 Brecht adaptation *History Lessons* for an incisive reflection on contemporary Europe (*Concerning Venice (History Lessons)*, 2014) but also quoted in it a full scene from his and Huillet's 1968 Bach film, *Chronicle of Anna Magdalena Bach*. The Straub-Huillet *œuvre* is uniquely consistent or resolute — the untranslatable German term *konsequent* comes closer to capturing the essence of it — in its aesthetics and its politics. Times change and celluloid prints decay and deteriorate, this is the lesson of Straub's extraordinary installation at the 2015 Venice Biennale of a digital fragment (filmed by Amir Naderi) of the final minutes of a dirty, scratched, bleached magenta copy of an English-subtitled print of *History Lessons* accompanied by documents and photographs relating to the original film. What this installation, *Homage to Italian Art!*, shows us is not so much the demise or obliteration of the film and its urgent ideological message, but rather its preservation, transformation, remediation, and revitalization.[17] *Homage to Italian Art!* is a politically incisive act of (self)citation and recycling of the kind Brecht would very much have approved of.[18] Recycling and citation bring us back to the two main threads of this volume once again: ecology and language(s).

Huillet and Straub's first longer film, *Not Reconciled, or Only Violence Helps Where Violence Rules* (1965), begins, at the end of the credit sequence, with a quotation from Brecht that serves as a motto for all their works right through to Straub's final solo film, *France Against Robots* (2020): 'Instead of wanting to create the impression that he is improvising, the actor should rather show what the truth is: he is quoting'.[19] All of Straub-Huillet's films quote. Many of them — *The Bridegroom, the Actress and the Pimp* (1968), *Introduction to Arnold Schoenberg's Accompaniment to a Cinematographic Scene* (1973), *Fortini/Cani* (1976), *Too Early, Too Late* (1981), *Cézanne: Conversation with*

Joachim Gasquet, Corneille – Brecht (2009), *Communists*, for example — layer literary, musical, documentary, and film quotations in horizontal and vertical montage. This brings us to another concept which ties together the diverse arguments in this volume, and a concept which is discussed explicitly in a number of them — what Brecht termed 'the separation of the elements'. Unlike a conventional drama, an 'epic' work can, he claimed with a nod to novelist Alfred Döblin, be 'cut up with scissors into individual pieces that all remain perfectly viable' (*BFA* XXII.I: 108).[20] In his famous table of the characteristics of dramatic and epic (that is Brechtian) theatre, drawn up in the context of his opera with Kurt Weill, *Rise and Fall of the City of Mahagonny* (1930), Brecht distinguishes, to put it at its simplest, between the action, engagement, linearity, and suspension of disbelief of the Aristotelian stage and the narrative, reflection, fragmentation, and estrangement of his own theatre. As he notes following the famous table of 'shifts of accent' (*Gewichtsverschiebungen*): 'when the epic theatre's methods begin to penetrate the opera the first result is a radical *separation of the elements*'.[21]

All of the essays in this volume, in one way or another, explicitly or implicitly, engage with this separation of the elements: of words, images, music, sounds. This means the splitting apart of a linear narrative in the manner advocated by Walter Benjamin in his two most frequently quoted essays, 'The Work of Art in the Age of Mechanical Reproduction' ('Das Kunstwerk im Zeitalter seiner technischen Reproduzierbarkeit') and 'Theses on the Philosophy of History' ('Über den Begriff der Geschichte'). For Benjamin, the conventional linearities of historiography, narrative, and progress (*Fortschritt*) need to be blown apart — his analogy is with the Austrian nineteenth-century explosive ecrasite — in order that the splinters and fragments can be rearranged in new, non-conventional ways. As Susan Buck-Morss has convincingly set out in her comprehensive study of Benjamin, this idea of locating and combining splinters of diverse historical and geographical origin is rooted in Benjamin's understanding of the Kabbalah and discussions on the subject with Gershom Scholem.[22] It is also the structuring principle behind his unfinished magnum opus, the *Arcades Project* (*Das Passagen-Werk*). The German term has an ambiguity entirely lost in translation: the 'passages' are not simply the shopping arcades of nineteenth-century Paris, but passages through and of documents literary, scholarly, and theological. It is here that the analogy with Huillet and Straub becomes apparent: their films, in their dependence on literary, musical, and artistic documents, are passages through cultural and political history. They are, invariably, 'history lessons', and it is unsurprising that the term appears in the titles of two films, first the 1972 adaptation of Brecht's Julius Caesar novel and, second, Straub's 2013 Maurice Barrès adaptation *Concerning Venice (History Lessons)* mentioned above. Moreover, as noted in Chapters 3 (on the early films) and 9 (on the Dante adaptation *O somma luce*), theology and mysticism are always present.

We know from interviews, Straub's and Huillet's *Writings*, and from Pedro Costa's short cinematic studies of Huillet and Straub at work and at home, *6 Bagatelles* (*6 Bagatelas*, 2001), that Straub is fond of quoting from the famous passage on temporal tiger-leaps from Thesis XIV of Benjamin's history essay:

> History is the subject of a structure whose site is not homogenous, empty time, but time filled by the presence of the now [*Jetztzeit*]. Thus, to Robespierre ancient Rome was a past charged with the time of the now which he blasted out of the continuum of history. The French Revolution viewed itself as Rome reincarnate. It evoked ancient Rome the way fashion evokes costumes of the past. Fashion has a flair for the topical, no matter where it stirs in the thickets of long ago; it is a tiger's leap into the past. This jump, however, takes place in an arena where the ruling class give the commands. The same leap in the open air of history is the dialectical one, which is how Marx understood the revolution.[23]

The horizontal juxtaposition or vertical layering of fragmentary documents is discussed in many of the essays in this collection, often in the context of a related concept popularized by Gilles Deleuze: *stratification*. It has become almost a mantra to state that the filmmaking of Huillet and Straub is geological, telluric, or archaeological. In interview in 1999 Huillet described this characteristic of their work in the following lucid and polemical terms:

> Strata, as in geology. [...] [C]inema *isn't* a language; [it's] an apparatus for radiography, a mirror that helps to see and... hear, to discover, under the accumulation of habit and clichés, reality — the truth? [...]
> That you want to call 'our' cinema — our films — tragic is a compliment, especially as today's society tries hard to eliminate, to erase the feeling of the tragic, even if the earth, and life, remains tragic. But of course, as in Corneille, the tragic and the comic reinforce each other... Happiness, by flashes, horror, all around. No appeasement.[24]

Collisions, encounters, fragments, quotations, juxtapositions. This is the stuff out of which Huillet's and Straub's films are constructed: material that is separated and recombined, defamiliarized and reframed. However, as Straub himself noted in a much earlier interview in the context of their Kafka adaptation *Class Relations* (1984), the prerequisite for these processes of appropriation and adaptation is in fact quite simple — careful, attentive reading:

> First, you have to know what interests you or not. Most people in our world don't even know that anymore. And you have to know what has to do with your own experiences, i.e., what really relates to you or doesn't. Because you don't 'film' a book, you engage with a book, you want to make a film out of a book, because the book has to do with your own experiences, with your own questions, with your own outbursts of hate or your own declarations of love. The first thing I do is to start transcribing.[25]

Transcription is, of course, a kind of 'adaptation', even if that term has become a controversial or adulterated one, with all its spurious connotations of fidelity to an 'original' text, when we have known for decades — or at least since Roland Barthes and others wrote about these matters in the 1960s — that an 'original' text never existed in the first place. Interestingly and controversially, however, and as noted on a number of occasions in this volume (see for example Chapters 1, 9, and 10), Huillet and Straub do approach different authors in different ways and with differing degrees of reverence.

In an interview with Andi Engel, reproduced in the aforementioned journal *Enthusiasm*, Straub quite straightforwardly admitted to adopting a different approach to different authors, and to being willing to chop up some, but not others. There is almost a kind of literary hierarchy, a quirky and idiosyncratic canon, to be read out of his pronouncements on this matter. Asked why in certain films, notably *Othon* (1970) and *Moses and Aaron* (1975), the source is taken word-for-word (Pierre Corneille) or note-for-note (Arnold Schoenberg), Straub replied:

> Yes, I think that the approach is so different in that the works are stronger. They are works where I as a small 'Straub' wouldn't assume the right to take something out — neither in Corneille nor in 'Moses und Aron'. Therefore I take the things completely and show them in a way where the people can judge them or reject them and though the film is partly in contradiction the work is introduced in its entirety to the people. On the contrary, in 'Billiards at half past nine' I took the things which I really thought the best texts, the most beautiful. What we did cut were things that we didn't like and which we thought were of little value, and texts and details which I thought wouldn't survive the screen.[26]

Later in the same interview Straub returns to the question of variations in their 'editorial' approach, noting even more baldly, regarding their abridgment of Böll: 'I chopped the text about a lot [...] I have more respect for Corneille than for Böll'.[27] As discussed in Chapter 3, one of the most extreme cases of condensation (of a text Straub professed to disliking intensely) is the 1968 micro-digest of Ferdinand Bruckner's play *Sickness of Youth* (*Krankheit der Jugend*) in *The Bridegroom, the Actress and the Pimp*; it is followed in 1970 by *Othon* in which the text survives unscathed. Adaptation for Straub-Huillet is not a method or programme, but an array of situation and text-dependent strategies which can mean taking a *document-fiction* — the term is Straub's — as is, cutting it, abridging it, fragmenting it, or citing it.[28] In this, their work is very much of our times: it constitutes a kind of critical, at times even deconstructive 'archiveology'.[29]

★   ★   ★   ★   ★

In an essay entitled simply 'Adaptation', Dudley Andrew discusses the various ways in which films borrow from and intersect with their source material, identifying a specifically modernist strand to the transformation of literary texts into cinema, or perhaps more accurately the interplay of literature and cinema. In his remarks, which at times echo André Bazin's reflections on cinema as an impure medium, he places (Huillet and) Straub alongside Robert Bresson and Pier Paolo Pasolini:

> Bresson, naturally, has given us his Joan of Arc from court records and his *Mouchette* once again from Bernanos. Straub has filmed Corneille's *Othon* and *The Chronicle of Anna Magdalena Bach*. Pasolini audaciously confronted Matthew's gospel, with many later texts (musical, pictorial, and cinematic) that it inspired. His later *Medea*, *Canterbury Tales*, and *Decameron* are also adaptational events in the intersecting mode. All such works fear or refuse to adapt. Instead they present the otherness and distinctiveness of the original text, initiating a dialectical interplay between the aesthetic forms of one period and the

cinematic forms of our own period. In direct contrast to the manner in which scholars have treated the mode of 'borrowing,' such intersecting insists that the analyst attend to the specificity of the original within the specificity of cinema. An original is allowed its life, its own life, in the cinema.[30]

Straub's remarks on adaptation-as-transcription quoted above chime with Andrew's sketch of modernist adaptation in proclaiming a refusal to adapt in the sense commonly associated with discourses of fidelity. Instead, Straub claims that for him (and Huillet) adaptation is akin to reading.[31] The German verb *lesen*, as famously pointed out by Martin Heidegger amongst others, has a suggestive double meaning which is relevant in this context: it denotes both reading and collecting.

In his introduction to the volume in which Andrew's essay appeared, *Film Adaptation* (2000), James Naremore — with a nod to Benjamin's essay on mechanical reproduction — takes the idea of adaptation-as-aggregation, as collecting and reading, one step further and proposes that film adaptation should be understood as a subset of a much broader and less readily definable practice: 'The study of adaptation needs to be joined with the study of recycling, remaking, and every other form of retelling in the age of mechanical reproduction and electronic communication'.[32] These remarks helpfully pinpoint the contemporary relevance of adaptational or, perhaps more precisely, transcriptive processes of the kind engaged in by Huillet and Straub.

By chance rather than design most of the essays in the present volume engage with films based on, or at least extensively quoting, literary sources. Moreover, all of the authors address questions of what Philippe Dubois, in an essay on Jean-Luc Godard, terms 'the complex and dialectical interplay between the order of the visible and that of the readerly'.[33] None, however, engage with the 'discourse of fidelity' and it is perhaps worth noting, as an aside, that not one of the torrent of volumes published on film adaptation in the last two decades includes discussion of the work of Huillet and Straub. Although Colin MacCabe, for example, refers to 'vertical meanings', 'productivity that preserves identity at the same moments that it multiples it', and 'division and multiplication' in the introduction to his co-edited collection *True to the Spirit* (2011), there is, symptomatically, no mention of Huillet and Straub, even in passing, in his essay or those of Naremore, Andrew, Frederic Jameson or, indeed, any of the volume's other nine authors.[34] If Rick Warner, writing about Godard's *Contempt* (*Le Mépris*, 1963) in the same collection, is right that there are three 'transcriptive' modes — adaptation, translation, and quotation — then it could be argued that the films of Huillet and Straub *should* be at the centre of the debates thrashed out in these volumes on adaptation.[35] The fact that they are not even peripherally present, despite their centrality to the writing of Deleuze and Rancière for example, suggests that the films of Straub-Huillet are not generally understood as adaptations, presumably because they do not stage or perform the works appropriated in a conventional way. On this matter, perhaps uniquely, Huillet and Straub and film scholars appear to be in complete agreement.

If, as film scholarship and the present volume suggest, the films of Huillet and Straub that use literary source material are not strictly speaking adaptations at all, then they also manage to side-step the 'cannibalistic' relationship between film and literature compellingly sketched out by Frederic Jameson in his afterword to *True to the Spirit*.[36] In 1996 Brian McFarlane had already noted in the introduction to his seminal theory of adaptation, *Novel to Film*, that the process of adaptation can encompass anything from near-reverential fidelity to 'a *commentary* on or, in more extreme cases, a *deconstruction* ("bring[ing] to light the internal contradictions in seemingly perfectly coherent systems of thought") of the original'.[37] Jameson goes one step further in arguing that 'difference is also opposition, antagonism, struggle' and proposes that in the entanglements of cinematic adaptation, both film and literature desire nothing less than 'the death of the other'.[38] He concludes that for adaptation studies this means that a 'philosophical emphasis on antagonism and incompatibility' is the only productive course to follow. By default, rather than intention, the authors of the current volume follow Jameson in identifying the essential indissolubility of the 'literary and linguistic hypotext' within individual films. However, rather than viewing the encounter of literature and film as what he terms 'generic cannibalism or anthropophagy',[39] they engage with the illumination generated by 'intersemiotic transposition' (the term is Robert Stam's) and the disjunctive intersections of historically, politically, generically, and aesthetically diverse material that remains 'not reconciled' within the hypertext.[40] Here difference is productive rather than cannibalistic. As Straub put it in response to a question about the use of literary source material as an appropriation of the cultural heritage:

> We want to show something already formed by the past that has affected us and give it to people to deal with, just as we did when we made the film. Because when we encounter such material, we have no clarity about it at all. Only at the end, when the film was edited, did we really digest the Brecht texts, for example. We then share the results. Moreover, I think it's important for the collective memory to bring things to the table that speak knowledgably of history and are ready-made. So that they don't get lost.[41]

At the risk of oversimplification it could be claimed that a key strategy in the films of Straub-Huillet, evident not least in the selectivity noted above, is, on the one hand, to take Marxist texts and challenge them critically — for example Franco Fortini in *Fortini/Cani* (see Chapter 4), Friedrich Engels and Mahmoud Hussein in *Too Early, Too Late* (Chapter 5), Cesare Pavese and Elio Vittorini repeatedly (Chapters 6 and 7), even Brecht in *History Lessons* — and, on the other, to take ostensibly non-communist texts (Bach, Schoenberg, Kafka, Hölderlin most obviously) and read them as or through Marxism. As Straub said of *Moses and Aaron*, 'in writing an anti-Marxist work [Schoenberg] was in no way writing a non-Marxist one'.[42] This brings us back to the notion of passages *through* texts as well as passages *of* texts. It was after all Benjamin who, in a redolent image, suggested in 'Theses on the Philosophy of History' that the task of materialist historiography is to 'brush history up against the grain'. Such (counter-)brushing is what Straub and Huillet practice in their art of appropriation and citation. As Benjamin put it in Thesis VII of his essay:

> They are called cultural treasures, and a historical materialist views them with cautious detachment. For without exception the cultural treasures he surveys

have an origin which he cannot contemplate without horror. They owe their existence not only to the efforts of the great minds and talents who have created them, but also to the anonymous toil of their contemporaries. There is no document of civilization which is not at the same time a document of barbarism. And just as such a document is not free of barbarism, barbarism taints also the manner in which it was transmitted from one owner to another. A historical materialist therefore dissociates himself from it as far as possible. He regards it as his task to brush history against the grain.[43]

Nothing is exempt from this task in the cinema of Huillet and Straub, and it is worth noting that their antipathy to established and received readings also underpins, for example, a healthy scepticism in relation to dogmatic 'Brechtianism'. As early as 1968, in an essay on Carl Theodor Dreyer, appropriately entitled 'Ferocious', Straub lamented the slavish 'paint-by-numbers' adherence of certain young 'auteurs' (the disparaging quotation marks are present in the original) to the principles of Brechtian theatre.[44]

★   ★   ★   ★   ★

In a brief résumé of the upcoming *Moses and Aaron* project, included as an 'Afterword' in Richard Roud's 1971 volume, Straub described approaching Schoenberg's opera 'in the simplest way possible, naïvely if you like'; it will be 'almost naturalistic' but in a way that will 'change that naturalism into realism'; in summary he intends 'to do the opera in the most materialist way possible'.[45] As the essays in this volume demonstrate, the common denominator of simplicity, realism, and materialism is attentiveness: attentiveness to place, to documents textual, visual and acoustic, and to bodies.

The authors in this volume do not attempt to impose a particular theoretical line or reading of the work, although all engage, in one way or another, with its communism. This is perhaps why the notion of a political rupture, as suggested by Rancière and proposed as a starting-point for our face-to-face discussions at the first post-retrospective workshop, was not adopted in any of the readings that follow. The volume parts ways with Rancière's position precisely at the point where 'post-Brechtian', as explained at the outset of this Introduction, is equated with post-communist.[46] It can be argued, and this is the position expressed across the essays in this volume, that Straub-Huillet's work was always to some extent 'post-communist' if by that term we understand a utopian Marxism that is neither fanatical nor Stalinist. There is, for example, no equivalent of Godard and Jean-Pierre Gorin's Dziga Vertov Group films in Huillet and Straub. As is noted in Chapter 3, in 1968 Huillet and Straub's emancipatory gesture consists of a woman reciting the poems of John of the Cross by a window which frames a sun-lit tree swaying in the wind.

In his writing on the cinema of the Portuguese director Pedro Costa, Rancière presents Huillet and Straub as remaining faithful to a communist utopia, but considers that from the late 1970s onwards they 'take the camera "off the world's suffering" and place before us, in some grassy amphitheatre evocative of ancient grandeurs and modern revolutions, [...] ordinary men and women who face up to history'.[47] Moreover, he reads *From the Cloud to the Resistance*, and then also *Humiliated* (2003), as taking them towards the melancholy and the dwelling on domestic detail that can be found in filmmakers like Costa, whom Rancière celebrates as the successor to the school of political modernism.

In our view, a survey of the whole of the work of Huillet and Straub makes it clear that Rancière confuses the texts chosen with the filmmakers who choose them. He reads the texts as a reflection of the position of the filmmakers when this is, as the discussion on adaptation above demonstrates, not the case. This doesn't work for Böll, Bruckner, Kafka, Duras, or Mallarmé, or later for Barrès and Malraux. Similarly, it would be possible to misconstrue the use of music as affirmation, leaving us with a strange concatenation of Bernd-Alois Zimmermann, Mahler, Kurtág, and Eisler alongside Bach, Schoenberg, and Beethoven. As discussed above, Huillet and Straub, as modernist transcribers in the intersecting mode, do not speak directly through the texts but rather, as Andrew puts it, 'attend to the specificity of the original within the specificity of cinema'.[48] Paraphrasing Andrew's idea that an original is allowed its own life in the cinema, we might say that Huillet and Straub bring the cultural heritage to the screen to confront it with their consistently dialectical, Marxist revolutionary, but also, as Straub puts it, theological and mystical standpoint. The attempt to create a historical development based on this choice of texts equates the material with the appropriator of it, and then extrapolates an ideological shift. This was never the case with Huillet and Straub. The shift(s) identified by Rancière are a projection onto the films rather than simply an analysis of or commentary on them.

In one of the light-hearted asides in the interview of 1990 (Chapter 11) Straub jokingly scolds a questioner for being 'more fanatical than we are'. For example, despite a preference for amateur performers, their approach to casting is non-dogmatic. Professional actors Libgart Schwarz, Mario Adorf, Howard Vernon, Werner Rehm, and others appear in their films, as do professional musicians Gustav Leonhardt, Günter Reich, Louis Devos, Christine Whittlesey, Richard Salter, and others. The discussion of sound in Chapter 5 demonstrates how direct sound, elevated to the status of a quasi-religious dogma by some commentators, is selective, directional, mixed, layered, and edited. Many of the films use music, inevitably to emotional effect, even if generally banished to the opening or end credits: the dramatic closing organ chords of *Machorka-Muff*, Johann Sebastian Bach's *Ascension Oratorio* in *The Bridegroom, the Actress and the Pimp*, Beethoven in *The Death of Empedocles* and *Black Sin* (1989), Bernd Alois Zimmermann in *The Antigone of Sophocles* (1992), Mahler in *Artemide's Knee* (2008), Varèse in *O somma luce*, Kurtág in *Jackals and Arabs*, Eisler in *Communists*, to name but a few. As Straub says to the rigorous questioner in London, 'it's a mixture'.

Of course, this does not mean that the mix in any given film is in some way arbitrary or capricious. On the contrary, it is invariably meticulously researched and rigorously constructed. However, as the four different versions of *The Death of Empedocles* programmatically demonstrate, there is always space for contingency

— unforeseen effects of light, of wind, of animal life (butterflies, insects, lizards). Much is also left 'as found', plastic tubing in Tuscan woodland, for example (see Chapter 7). As Straub once noted, 'Films, like life, are *made* from fortuitous or provoked experiences and encounters'.[49]

It can, indeed almost invariably is, a matter of contingency when a film is shot: Straub points out in the interview in this volume, for example, that *Chronicle* can hardly be a product of the New German Cinema, heralded in 1962 with the Oberhausen Manifesto, given that it was conceived and worked out in detail in the 1950s in France, a decade before the money was available to realize it. As Huillet notes, financing a film generally takes 'two, three, four years'. It is only short, cheaply made interventions — *Europa 2005, 27 October* (2006) following the deaths of two youths outside Paris in 2005 or *Jackals and Arabs* during the Arab Spring of 2011 — that can react more-or-less simultaneously.

The waves of critical interest in the films of Huillet and Straub are also the result of contingencies such as the enthusiasm or otherwise of critics and journals to engage with their films. Straub expresses his frustration with the British press for ignoring the 1990 retrospective at the Goethe-Institut and the interviewer (Julian Petley) names and shames the London listings magazine *Time Out*, and the *Guardian* and *Independent* newspapers. Conversely it was the enthusiasm amongst film critics and historians which fuelled a surge of articles on their work in France in the 1960s and early 1970s (in *Cahiers du cinéma*, *Positif* etc.) and in the UK in the 1970s (*Screen*, *Afterimage*, *Enthusiasm*, *Jump Cut*). In turn, the forensic engagement with *History Lessons* in *Screen* — the subject of a workshop at the 2019 London retrospective with Laura Mulvey, Ian Christie, Martin Brady, and Nicolas Helm-Grovas — would not have been possible without the work of distributors including Politkino, The Other Cinema, and Artificial Eye set up by Andi Engel and Pamela Balfry in 1976. Engel's company, for example, framed the way, or rather the ways, in which Straub-Huillet's films were seen and interpreted, in this case at the intersection of art-house and experimental film. An Artificial Eye poster circulated in Cannes in May 1976, for example, lists the breadth of films being distributed in a single hand-drawn and written diagram with Huillet and Straub, represented by all the films up to and including *Introduction to Arnold Schoenberg's Accompaniment to a Cinematographic Scene* (seven in total) alongside ten films of Stephen (Steve) Dwoskin and one each of Jonas Mekas, Godard, Kenji Mizoguchi, and Theo(doros) Angelopolos.[50] A decade later it would be the failure of UK distributors to take on the films after *Class Relations* — in which, incidentally, Engel himself appeared — which would to all intents and purposes eliminate the visibility and availability of the later work of Straub-Huillet, roughly from the Hölderlin films onwards, and of Straub's solo work.

In summary, what we find across the work of Huillet and Straub is a consistent or rooted *Einstellung* (that redolent German term that encompasses 'attitude', 'outlook', 'preference', and the cinematic 'shot' or 'take') manifest across an array of different situations. These situations are determined in part by measurable and quotidian geographical, linguistic, and economic considerations — where the filmmakers are based at a given time, who is funding the film and to what extent, the availability and cost of rights clearance, the intended audience (see Chapter 5, for example, on *Fortini/Cani* as a film for Italian audiences) — and partly by the less-easily quantifiable 'outbursts of hate' and 'declarations of love' referred to by Straub. As Huillet put it in the remark cited as an epigraph to this Introduction, there needs to be a spark to ignite interest.[51] The opening workshop of the London retrospective, at KCL, aimed to capture some of this spontaneity in its title: 'Incendiary Fictions'.

★   ★   ★   ★   ★

The essays in this volume chart the sources and trajectories of the sparks. The first three address multiple films from a single perspective: the intellectual, landscape, and the embodiment of text in quotation and provide what might be termed a wide-angle view of the filmmakers' *œuvre*. The seven that follow offer close-ups on individual films in a chronological sweep: *Fortini/Cani*; *Too Early, Too Late*; *Sicilia!* (1999); *Workers, Peasants* (2001) and *Return of the Prodigal Son – Humiliated* (2003); *Itinerary of Jean Bricard* (2008); *O somma luce*; *Jackals and Arabs*. The collection concludes with the hitherto unpublished interview with the filmmakers in London in 1990, chiefly apropos *The Death of Empedocles* and *Black Sin* screened on the same evening, but which repeatedly broadens out spontaneously to encompass discussion of other films.

The volume opens with Nicolas Helm-Grovas's essay on a central aspect of Straub-Huillet's films, but one which has received surprisingly little attention over the years: the role of the intellectual. This character is a recurring point of analysis in their work: from the composer in eighteenth-century Germany in *Chronicle of Anna Magdalena Bach*; to the investigations of the Young Man (writer of a historical narrative) in *History Lessons*; to the statements of Brecht and Schoenberg voiced by Günter Peter Straschek, Peter Nestler, Huillet, and Straub in *Introduction to Arnold Schoenberg's Accompaniment to a Cinematographic Scene*; to the dialectic of idea versus word for rousing 'the people' in *Moses and Aaron*; to Franco Fortini in *Fortini/Cani*; to the philosopher Empedocles in *The Death of Empedocles* and *Black Sin*; and to the remodulation of this figure into the 'organic intellectual', or perhaps the disappearance of the intellectual altogether, in the Buti films. As this list indicates, the intellectual may be embodied or inflected in different ways: as teacher (Empedocles), student, sage (Tiresias, Empedocles), prophet (Moses, Empedocles), researcher (the Young Man in *History Lessons*), artist (Bach, Cézanne, Schoenberg, Brecht), as the filmmaker(s), and numerous readers, and writers. Helm-Grovas suggests that the figure allows an investigation, in displaced form, of political questions. He investigates these questions through discussion of, for instance, the spatial disposition of bodies and speech in the films, hypothesizing that for Huillet and Straub, the intellectual is constituted through a linguistic act. His conclusion, focusing on the proscribed nature of Vittorini's commune, relates his own account of the intellectual to current concerns by noting the lack of diversity in Huillet and Straub's source material in terms of ethnicity and gender.

While Helm-Grovas engages with the history of debate within critical theory regarding the status and role of the intellectual in a revolutionary society, Sam

McAuliffe draws on Georg Simmel and the concept of *Abgrenzung*, or delineation, to articulate the complex vision that constitutes Huillet and Straub's engagement with space and landscape. Landscape for Simmel is an intrinsically paradoxical form of representation, inasmuch as it remains locked in tension with the order of nature out of which it is composed. 'By nature,' he writes in 'The Philosophy of Landscape', 'we mean the infinite interconnectedness of objects, the uninterrupted creation and destruction of forms. [...] Nature is not composed of pieces. It is the unity of a whole'.[52] It is in this sense that the particular ensemble of elements to which a landscape gives expression institutes a break in this open-ended continuum. It detaches itself from the whole by tracing a line of demarcation where there would otherwise be none: 'to conceive of a piece of ground and what is on it as a landscape, this means that one now conceives of a segment of nature itself as a separate unity, which estranges it from the concept of nature'.[53] In the films of Huillet and Straub something of this schema appears in more than one iteration, to more than one end, but always tied to a certain conception of politics. McAuliffe considers the cinematic protocols and textual mediations through which such an appeal to nature takes place, as well as the specific constructions of landscape to which it gives rise, running through a span of work that includes *Too Early, Too Late, Proposition in Four Parts* (1985), and *Moses and Aaron*.

Chapter 3 turns to Brecht, Theodor W. Adorno, and Benjamin with Martin Brady's account of Huillet and Straub's adaptations of works by the German-language authors Heinrich Böll and Ferdinand Bruckner. Brady's focus on Huillet and Straub's drilling of the actors in *Not Reconciled* to deliver text semi-automatically serves as a focus for understanding the filmmakers' translation of Brechtian estrangement techniques in their early films into a new method of materialist filmmaking. Drawing a parallel with Susan Buck-Morss's analysis of the Kabbalistic structure of Benjamin's *Arcades Project*, Brady argues that the montage and vocal delivery of *The Bridegroom, the Actress and the Pimp* calls for a new kind of theological reading, in which the actors embody, dissect, and become redeemed or emancipated by the fragments they are quoting. According to Brecht it 'is precisely the innovators who will expropriate' (*BFA* XXI: 404). This essay demonstrates how Huillet and Straub's citational practice gives voice to the actors, the texts, and the directors themselves.

Rather than bringing several works together to trace a theme, the following chapters focus on individual films. Chapter 4 homes in on a single segment of the film *Fortini/Cani* in a further analysis of the stratified landscape discussed by McAuliffe in Chapter 2. What is important for this chapter is Huillet and Straub's relevance to contemporary, twenty-first-century filmmakers engaged with *lieux de mémoire* (sites or places of memory) and memory work, particularly as the generations pass. Chris Groenveld (Chapter 4) points to the immediate recognition by commentators of the Apuan Alps sequence in the film as an historically significant moment for materialist filmmaking. She argues that the apparent calm of this episode supports the viewer in their recognition of landscapes as visible sites of memory, commemorating the trauma of Mussolini's fascist Italy and contextualizing Italian support for the state of Israel through the commentary of Franco Fortini reading from his book *The Dogs of the Sinai* (*I cani del Sinai*). In the final section of her essay, on 'attention and resistance', she argues that the film provides a model for how to make a dialectical approach to history visible through cinema.

Sound is the focus for Chapter 5 in which Laura Lux returns to the much-discussed 'dogma' of direct sound in the work of Huillet and Straub. Lux gives an overview of the impact of the filmmakers' work on debates about sound in cinema from the 1970s, mentioning Serge Daney, Michel Chion, Deleuze, Gilberto Perez, Burlin Barr, and Turquety, before demonstrating how extensive and complex the sound-image relationships are in the film *Too Early, Too Late*. She draws out moments of signification which emerge from acoustic foregrounding, using sound to accompany black film, or inserting moments of silence. Lux goes on to discuss a rare case of the direct influence of Huillet and Straub's approach to direct sound, arguing that their friend and protégé Harun Farocki took from them the lesson of working with sound in a non-dogmatic way. She chooses two lesser-known short films of Farocki — *The Taste of Life* (*Der Geschmack des Lebens*, 1979) and *The People are Standing Forwards in the Streets* (*Die Menschen stehen vorwärts in den Straßen*, 1987) — and demonstrates how they engage with direct sound, recitation, and music in different ways from his canonical films.

Chapters 6 and 7 develop contrasting interpretations of adaptations of the works of the Italian writer Vittorini. The theological substratum mentioned in Chapter 3 returns in the analysis of *Sicilia!* developed by Brendan Prendeville in Chapter 6, who offers the tranquil thought that there can be 'no political film without grace'. The imperative 'look at me!' ('guardami!') spoken from mother to son in *Sicilia!* has an abruptness and emphasis lacking in the text, because the subsequent phrase in Vittorini's novel, 'but finish eating', has been omitted, and also because the performative injunction has a double force for the audience: as the son, off-screen, looks at her, she is framed in a prolonged three-quarter standing pose. Prendeville argues in his report on watching *Sicilia!* that the pictorialism of the film, while singular in its exploitation of tonal modelling, is broadly typical of Straub-Huillet in presenting people as having the stillness of things, rather in the manner of a still life. Straub-Huillet often deny their subjects the animation expected of cinema and thereby enjoin in us a deepening of attention. This idea is given momentum through reference to Simone Weil, along with the idea that paying attention is the act of a humble rather than a proud person. More than most of their films, *Sicilia!* dwells on individuals, in a sequence of face-to-face encounters with the son returning to his homeland. Prendeville takes his cue from the idea of cinema as portraiture and cites Cézanne as a direct inspiration for Huillet and Straub.

Jane Madsen, in Chapter 7, notices a change in the use of location in Huillet and Straub's subsequent collaborations with the Italian theatre group Teatro Francesco di Bartolo in Buti. The films *Workers, Peasants* and *The Return of the Prodigal Son – Humiliated* depart in significant ways in their engagement with space and landscape from Huillet and Straub's previous films. The woods at Buti cannot easily be read as 'stratigraphic' sites, despite the fact that the actors in Buti are working in a tradition which derives from *maggio epico* folk theatre and approach their texts through acts of recitation (from memory) and reading (from a script). The turn from landscape to nature, which can be traced back to the Hölderlin films, is intensified by the compression of space in these Vittorini adaptations. Madsen argues that a political space of *near*-ness between workers and peasants is constructed within the displaced green edgeland spaces of undifferentiated woodland. The task of bringing the workers and peasants together visually, socially, and politically is at the heart of these films and echoes the political aspirations represented by Huillet and Straub's vision of 'eco-communism'.

Chapter 8 is given over to three translations by Ricardo Matos Cabo of texts relating to the film *Itinerary of Jean Bricard*: the photo essay of the same name by sociologist Jean-Yves Petiteau published in the literary journal *Interlope la Curieuse*; an essay by Petiteau and Isabelle Rolland that accompanied the *Itinerary*; and a further text by Petiteau about his meeting and collaboration with Huillet and Straub. This material makes the documentation of an important collaboration, and the final film of Huillet and Straub together, accessible to an English-speaking audience for the first time.

In Chapter 9 Rastko Novaković examines Straub's solo film *O somma luce* as a de-Christianized, estranged staging of verses from Dante's *Paradiso*. He claims that while relying on the various strata of Dantean thinking, the film also treats the text as a springboard for thinking about a '*longue durée* communism' that has often taken inspiration from nature in all its plenitude. Straub's specific, political reading of Dante — here Novaković picks up on Straub's assertion that there can be no political film without theology, mysticism, and memory, discussed in Chapter 3 — is framed through the cinematographic apparatus and specific use of music and voice. Starting from a detailed reading of the text and film, he examines the annotated scripts of Straub and the actor Giorgio Passerone to investigate how a precise vocal and gestural treatment of Dante's verses produces new meanings. Novaković notes the place that Edgard Varèse's *Déserts* (1950–54) holds in the film, with specific analysis of the recording of the piece's premiere used by Straub. Thesis IV of Benjamin's essay 'Theses on the Philosophy of History' and his concept of 'heliotropism', together with passages from Sergei Eisenstein's *Nonindifferent Nature*, contribute to an account of what Novaković terms 'communist photosynthesis', the primary political and artistic gesture of Straub's *O somma luce*.

Another shift in spatial practice, this time in a film planned by both Huillet and Straub (in 1987), but in the end made by Straub alone, is registered by Helen Hughes in Chapter 10. In *Jackals and Arabs*, a short and controversial story by Franz Kafka of 1917 is relocated to a flat in Paris in 2011, the year of the Arab Spring. Drawing on recent scholarly work on the reception of Kafka's text in the Arabic-speaking world, Hughes reads Straub's short digital film as a pithy contribution to the debate about Kafka and Zionism. Just as the woodland of Buti becomes the bland European edgeland (see Chapter 7), the parquet floor of Straub's Paris flat becomes the desert site for a twenty-first-century iteration of the encounter between the Jewish diaspora, European neo-colonialism, and Arab revolt. Although some recent scholars have insisted that Kafka was referring to Palestine, Straub's film locates the text to the European city. Discussing the film's quotation of György Kurtág's *Kafka Fragments* and referring to Deleuze and Félix Guattari's *Kafka: Toward a Minor Literature* (*Kafka: Pour une littérature mineure*), Hughes demonstrates that Kafka's multiple heritage — as Czech, German, and Jew — means not only that the text's relevance remains undiminished, but also that it is politically and intertextually reanimated in Straub's taut adaptation.

Following this final essay is an edited and in part translated script of the post- or rather inter-screening interview with Huillet and Straub held in London during the 1990 retrospective of their work. The interview, perhaps because it took place on 'neutral ground', was a friendly occasion in which Huillet and Straub promoted the value of creating space for alternative ideas and approaches to filmmaking, responding to the interviewer's and the audience's questions with characteristically helpful explanations of their methods. In order to capture the spirit of the occasion, the edited translation retains aspects of their overlapping responses, mutual linguistic corrections, and the frequent laughter that accompanied their consistently forthright yet undogmatic conversation.

★   ★   ★   ★   ★

In appropriating the cultural heritage to discover and/or to generate the sparks referred to in the epigraphs at the top of this Introduction, Huillet and Straub turn to their advantage what Adorno in 1968 termed the 'self-weight of the apparatus', deploying it as a kind of cine-technological dynamite — the explosive invoked at the end of both *Not Reconciled* and *Sicilia!*.[54] This is made manifest in their work together in the use of the recording studio locations chosen for the reading of the Schoenberg and Brecht texts in *Introduction to Arnold Schoenberg's Accompaniment to a Cinematographic Scene* and also for the staging of Schoenberg's comic twelve-tone opera in *Von heute auf morgen*. Reference has already been made in this Introduction to the enduring tendency to foreground the apparatus in the later films of Straub alone — *Homage to Italian Art!*, *Concerning Venice (History Lessons)*, *The Aquarium and the Nation* (2015). Another aspect of the reflexivity of these later films is the revisiting and quoting of earlier work. As well as returning to unrealized projects with Huillet — *Jackals and Arabs* (see Chapter 10) and the writings of Georges Bernanos (*Dialogue of Shadows* (2014), *France Against Robots*) — Straub also incorporated substantial quotations of previous works into his later films. As already noted, an episode from *Chronicle of Anna Magdalena Bach* concludes *Concerning Venice (History Lessons)*.

More substantially, Straub's only feature-length solo film, *Communists*, includes five episodes drawn from films made between 1976 and 2001. In the order they appear these are: *Workers, Peasants, Too Early, Too Late, Fortini/Cani, The Death of Empedocles*, and *Black Sin*. Only the film's first three brief episodes are new: the GDR national anthem (music by Hanns Eisler, text by Johannes R. Becher) over black film and two sequences drawn from Malraux's novel *Le Temps du mépris* (*Days of Contempt* or *Days of Wrath*) of 1935. Malraux's text tells the story of a communist imprisoned by the Gestapo and of underground resistance against the Nazis. It was his only book to be published in the Soviet Union. Patently, the title of Straub's film is programmatic, and it can be read as a digest of his and Huillet's political perspective: the opening sequence sets the scene, so-to-speak, the anthem of the GDR was written by a composer and author who came to communism in the 1920s, were driven into exile by National Socialism, and returned to Germany to join in the physical, intellectual, and ideological building of real-existing socialism only to see these hopes dashed. This disappointment is famously palpable in the late works of both men: Eisler's melancholy song cycle *Serious Songs* (*Ernste Gesänge*) of 1962 and Becher's essay 'The Poetic Principle' ('Das poetische Prinzip'), written in 1956 but only published in the GDR in 1988, in which he refers to his belief in socialism as the 'basic mistake of my life'.[55] In what follows in *Communists* we are presented with both the ideological vigour and the practical failures of communism in Europe and North Africa in the pre-war (Malraux) and post-war years (Vittorini, Hussein, Pavese) in a broad historical sweep that embraces Nazism, post-war Italian fascism, European colonialism, and the Arab-Israeli conflict. The films quoted are addressed in detail in Chapters 4, 5, and 6 of this volume.

Communists ends with two shorter extracts from the Hölderlin films: Empodocles's speech before Etna, quoted above, and the first shot of the last sequence of *Black Sin* (Figure I.2) in which Huillet, as the Chorus, speaks just two words ('New world') from the fragmentary final scene of Hölderlin's third draft of his drama, accompanied by Beethoven's String Quartet No. 16, Op. 135, his final completed work. We hear the opening of the last movement headed 'The Difficult Decision' with its famous refrain 'Must it be? ... It must be!'. The message could scarcely be simpler in *Black Sin* and it is even clearer in *Communists*: despite all the failures of real-existing socialism, the revolutionary goal of a new world — what Huillet and Straub repeatedly refer to as 'Hölderlin's communist utopia' — remains and the films are there to sustain it.[56]

FIG. I.2. Danièle Huillet and Jean-Marie Straub, *Black Sin* (1989, courtesy of BELVA Film).

Notes to the Introduction

1. Karsten Witte, 'Interview' [interview with Danièle Huillet and Jean-Marie Straub], in *Herzog/ Kluge/ Straub*, ed. by Peter W. Jansen and Wolfram Schütte (Munich & Vienna: Carl Hanser, 1976), pp. 205–18 (p. 210). All translations are the contributors' own, unless stated otherwise.

2. See Daniel Fairfax's summary of the response to the film in *Cahiers du cinéma*, in *The Red Years of Cahiers du Cinéma (1968–1973)*, 2 vols (Amsterdam: Amsterdam University Press, 2021), i, 127.

3. Peter Wollen, 'The Two Avant-Gardes', in *Readings and Writings: Semiotic Counter-Strategies* (London: Verso/NLB, 1982), pp. 92–104. The shorthand 'Godard-Straub' has been used by A. J. Rees and many others.

4. Jean-André Fieschi, 'Jean-Marie Straub and Danièle Huillet', trans. by Michael Graham <https:// kinoslang.blogspot.com/2019/07/jean-marie-straub-daniele-huillet-by-j.html> [accessed 22 May 2022]. Originally published in English by Richard Roud in his 1980 book *Cinema: A Critical Dictionary*, a substantial extract from Fieschi's essay was also included in the 64-page programme of the 2019 retrospective of Huillet and Straub in London <https://www.goethe.de/ resources/files/pdf182/straub-huillet-retrospective-july20191.pdf> [accessed 4 January 2022].

5. In this context Barton Byg quotes Sylvia Harvey's claim that the 'Brechtianisms' of 1970s film theory include 'distanciation, anti-illusionism, deconstruction, the critique of identification processes and the dismantling of "classical" narrative': Barton Byg, *Landscapes of Resistance: The German Films of Danièle Huillet and Jean-Marie Straub* (Berkeley, Los Angeles & London: University of California Press, 1995), p. 118. Fairfax discusses Jean Narboni's recourse to Derridean deconstruction in the latter's 1970 article on Huillet and Straub's *Othon*: Fairfax, *The Red Years of Cahiers du Cinéma*, pp. 128–36.

6. Quoted in the programme to the 2019 London retrospective (see note 4), the passage can also be found here: <https://kinoslang.blogspot.com/2017/02/blog-post_20.html> [accessed 22 May 2022].

7. A number of contributors to this volume are also active as filmmakers: Chris Groenveld (Chapter 4); Jane Madsen (Chapter 7); Rastko Novaković (Chapter 9).

8. Jacques Rancière, *The Intervals of Cinema*, trans. by John Howe (London & New York: Verso, 2014).

9. Ibid., p. 104.

10. Ibid., p. 103.

11. Ibid., p. 105.

12. *Jean-Marie Straub & Danièle Huillet*, ed. by Ted Fendt (Vienna: SYNEMA, 2016). Jean-Marie Straub and Danièle Huillet, *Writings*, ed. and trans. by Sally Shafto (New York: Sequence Press, 2016); Benoît Turquety, *Danièle Huillet, Jean-Marie Straub: 'Objectivists' in Cinema*, trans. by Ted Fendt (Amsterdam: Amsterdam University Press, 2020); *Tell It to The Stones: Encounters with the Films of Danièle Huillet and Jean-Marie Straub*, ed. by Annett Busch and Tobias Hering (London: Sternberg Press, 2021).

13. Richard Roud, *Jean-Marie Straub* (London: Secker & Warburg/BFI, 1971); Byg, *Landscapes of Resistance*. Ursula Böser's 2004 book *The Art of Seeing, the Art of Listening* extends the focus beyond the literary — her principal focus here is Franz Kafka — to examine how the composers Arnold Schoenberg and Johann Sebastian Bach, and the painter Paul Cézanne engender alternative modes of filmic representation in the works of Huillet and Straub: Böser, *The Art of Seeing, the Art of Listening: The Politics of Representation in the Work of Jean-Marie Straub and Danièle Huillet* (Frankfurt am Main: Peter Lang, 2004).

14. See <https://www.goethe.de/resources/files/pdf182/straub-huillet-retrospective-july20191. pdf> [accessed 4 January 2022].

15. Jacques Rancière and Philippe Lafosse, 'Politics and Aesthetics in the Straubs' Films', trans. by Ted Fendt <https://mubi.com/notebook/posts/politics-and-aesthetics-in-the-straubs-films> [accessed 29 December 2021]. Daniel Fairfax, a speaker at the London retrospective, has addressed these questions in an essay for *Senses of Cinema*: Fairfax, 'Straub/Huillet's Ecological Communism', *Senses of Cinema*, 19 (2019) <https://www.sensesofcinema.com/2019/jean-marie-straub-daniele-huillet/straub-huillets-ecological-communism/> [accessed 29 December 2021].

16. A number of Huillet and Straub films, including *En rachâchant* (1983), *Lothringen!* (1994), *Sicilia!*, *Von heute auf morgen*, and *O somma luce*, tend to be referred to by their original language titles. This practice has generally been followed in this volume. Other titles are given in English, with their original titles supplied in the Filmography.

17. For documentation of this project see <https://www.atelierimpopulaire.com/jean-marie-straub-homage-to-italian-art!.html> [accessed 4 January 2022].

18. This question is addressed in *Recycling Brecht*, ed. by David Barnett and Tom Kuhn, Brecht Yearbook, 42 (Rochester, NY: Camden House, 2017).

19. Bertolt Brecht, 'Anweisungen an die Schauspieler', in *Werke: Große kommentierte Berliner und Frankfurter Ausgabe*, ed. by Werner Hecht and others, 30 vols (Berlin, Weimar & Frankfurt am Main: Aufbau, Suhrkamp, 1988–2000), XXII.2, 667–68 (p. 668). Edition referred to hereafter as *BFA* followed by volume and page numbers. For the English translation see Misha Donat's translation of the film in Roud, *Jean-Marie Straub*, pp. 124–71 (p. 124).

20. For a slightly different translation see also Bertolt Brecht, 'Theatre for Pleasure or Theatre for Instruction', in *Brecht on Theatre*, ed. by Marc Silberman, Steve Giles, and Tom Kuhn, 3rd edn (London: Bloomsbury, 2015), pp. 109–17 (p. 110).

21. This translation is taken from an earlier collection of Brecht's dramatic writings: Bertolt Brecht, 'The Modern Theatre is the Epic Theatre', in *Brecht on Theatre: The Development of an Aesthetic*, ed. and trans. by John Willett (London: Eyre Methuen, 1964), pp. 33–42 (p. 37).

22. See Susan Buck-Morss, *The Dialectics of Seeing: Walter Benjamin and the Arcades Project* (Cambridge, MA, & London: MIT, 1989).

23. Walter Benjamin, 'Theses on the Philosophy of History', in *Illuminations*, ed. by Hannah Arendt, trans. by Harry Zohn (London: Bodley Head, 2015), pp. 245–55 (pp. 252–53).

24. Bernard Mezzadri, 'Interview: No Appeasement' [interview with Danièle Huillet], in Straub and Huillet, *Writings*, pp. 252–53.

25. Wolfram Schütte, 'Gespräch mit Danièle Huillet und Jean-Marie Straub', in *Klassenverhältnisse: Von Danièle Huillet und Jean-Marie Straub nach dem Amerika-Roman 'Der Verschollene' von Franz Kafka*, ed. by Wolfram Schütte (Frankfurt am Main: Fischer, 1984), pp. 37–58 (p. 46).

26. Andi Engel, 'Andi Engel Talks to Jean-Marie Straub, and Danièle Huillet is There Too', *Enthusiasm*, 1 (1975), 1–25 (p. 20).

27. Geoffrey Nowell-Smith, 'After "Othon", Before "History Lessons": Geoffrey Nowell-Smith Talks to Jean-Marie Straub and Danièle Huillet', *Enthusiasm*, 1 (1975), 26–31 (p. 26).

28. Michel Delahaye, 'Entretien avec J.-M. Straub', *Cahiers du cinéma*, 180 (1966), 52–57 (p. 54).

29. Catherine Russell, *Archiveology: Walter Benjamin and Archival Film Practices* (Durham, NC, & London: Duke University Press, 2018).

30. Dudley Andrew, 'Adaptation', in *Film Adaptation*, ed. by James Naremore (New Brunswick, NJ: Rutgers University Press, 2000), pp. 28–37 (p. 31).

31. Writing on cinematic adaptation Robert Stam concludes that adaptation is 'a form of criticism or "reading"': Robert Stam, 'Beyond Fidelity: The Dialogics of Adaptation', in *Film Adaptation*, ed. by Naremore, pp. 54–76 (p. 58).

32. James Naremore, 'Introduction: Film and the Reign of Adaptation', in *Film Adaptation*, ed. by Naremore, pp. 1–16 (p. 15).

33. Philippe Dubois, 'The Written Screen: JLG and Writing as the Accursed Share', in *For Ever Godard*, ed. by Michael Temple, James S. Williams, and Michael Witt (London: Black Dog Publishing), pp. 232–49 (p. 232).

34. Colin MacCabe, 'Introduction: Bazinian Adaptation: *The Butcher Boy* as Example', in *True to the Spirit: Film Adaptation and the Question of Fidelity*, ed. by Colin MacCabe, Kathleen Murray, and Rick Warner (Oxford & New York: Oxford University Press, 2011), pp. 3–26 (pp. 7, 22).

35. Rick Warner, '*Contempt* Revisited: Godard at the Margins of Adaptation', in *True to the Spirit*, ed. by MacCabe, Murray and Warner, pp. 195–213 (p. 196).

36. Frederic Jameson, 'Adaptation as a Philosophical Problem', in *True to the Spirit*, ed. by MacCabe, Murray and Warner, pp. 215–33.

37. Brian McFarlane, *Novel to Film: An Introduction to the Theory of Adaptation* (Oxford: Clarendon Press, 1996), p. 22.

38. Jameson, 'Adaptation as a Philosophical Problem', p. 230.

39. Ibid., p. 232.
40. Stam, 'Beyond Fidelity', p. 62.
41. Witte, 'Interview', p. 211.
42. Roud, *Jean-Marie Straub*, p. 123.
43. Benjamin, 'Theses on the Philosophy of History', in *Illuminations*, p. 248.
44. Jean-Marie Straub, 'Ferocious', in Straub and Huillet, *Writings*, pp. 102–04 (p. 102).
45. Roud, *Jean-Marie Straub*, p. 123.
46. Rancière, *The Intervals of Cinema*, p. 104.
47. Ibid., p. 128.
48. Andrew, 'Adaptation', p. 31.
49. Jean-Marie Straub, 'Autofilmography', in Straub and Huillet, *Writings*, pp. 254–55 (p. 255).
50. For a reproduction of the poster see <https://lux.org.uk/dwoskin-project-blog-6-somewhat-reconciled> [accessed 5 January 2022].
51. Huillet's observation about the encounter of fiction and documentary echoes a remark made by Godard in interview as early as 1962: 'fiction is interesting only if it is validated by a documentary context' (quoted in Warner, '*Contempt* Revisited', p. 207).
52. Georg Simmel, 'The Philosophy of Landscape', trans. by Josef Bleicher, *Theory, Culture and Society*, 24.7–8 (2007), 20–29 (p. 21).
53. Ibid., p. 22.
54. Theodor W. Adorno, 'Musik im Fernsehen ist Brimborium', in *Gesammelte Schriften*, ed. by Rolf Tiedemann and Klaus Schulz, 20 vols (Frankfurt am Main: Suhrkamp, 1970-86), XIX, 559–69 (p. 564).
55. Johannes R. Becher, 'Selbstzensur', *Sinn und Form*, 40 (1988), 543–51 (p. 550).
56. Danièle Huillet and Jean-Marie Straub, 'Questionnaire on May 1968', in Straub and Huillet, *Writings*, pp. 266–67 (p. 267).

❖

CHAPTER 1

'Nor do I seek out difficult postures': Huillet's and Straub's Intellectuals

Nicolas Helm-Grovas

> Bad intellectuals have never yet become good proletarians.
> — GÜNTER PETER STRASCHEK[1]

The composer in eighteenth-century Germany in *Chronicle of Anna Magdalena Bach* (1968); Arnold Schoenberg and Bertolt Brecht, whose words are read by Günter Peter Straschek and Peter Nestler in *Introduction to Arnold Schoenberg's Accompaniment to a Cinematographic Scene* (1973); the titular characters, bearers of idea and word, in *Moses and Aaron* (1975); critic and poet Franco Fortini in *Fortini/Cani* (1976); the philosopher on the slopes of Etna in *The Death of Empedocles* (1987) and *Black Sin* (1989); the villagers who recall and reflect on their lives and labour in *Workers, Peasants* (2001) — across Huillet and Straub's films, there is a fascination with a cast of characters who could be grouped under the rubric of 'intellectuals'. As this list suggests, the category of the intellectual is inflected in their work in different ways: as teacher, sage, prophet, researcher, artist, worker, or peasant, for instance. Moreover (despite Huillet and Straub's stated distaste for biographical interpretations of artworks), even when intellectual labour is not the explicit subject matter of their films, they show a recurring interest in the *producers* of the writings, music, and paintings that their films reinscribe cinematically.[2] At the end of *Every Revolution is a Throw of the Dice* (1977) there is a photograph of Stéphane Mallarmé at his desk; a photograph of Elio Vittorini, author of *Conversations in Sicily* (*Conversazioni in Sicilia*), source-text for *Sicilia!*, appears after the credits of that film (Figure 1.1). For a text to accompany a 1973 festival screening of *History Lessons* (1972), meanwhile, Straub selected extracts from Klaus Völker's *Brecht Chronicle* (*Brecht-Chronik*), detailing Brecht's writing process of *The Business Affairs of Mr Julius Caesar* (*Die Geschäfte des Herrn Julius Caesar*), the unfinished novel on which the film is based.[3] In other words, despite anti-humanist critiques of authorship from the 1960s onwards, Huillet and Straub demonstrate a stubborn interest in the working lives of the figures behind their films' source materials, and persistently model such figures — thinkers, artists, and writers — within their films.

FIG. 1.1. Danièle Huillet and Jean-Marie Straub, *Sicilia!*
(1999, courtesy of BELVA Film).

This chapter investigates this recurring motif in the work of Huillet and Straub. Yet to group all these figures under the heading of 'intellectuals' might seem incongruous or problematic. After all, the category of the 'intellectual' is often thought to crystallize in the nineteenth century, as a result of 'a dramatic extension of the opportunities for intellectual labour' in Europe, and 'a progressive extension over a period of at least three centuries', i.e. Western modernity, of this intellectual labour's 'independence from such established institutions as the Church and State'.[4] This is the century of the emergence of the term as a noun in English, the coalescence of a group known as 'the intelligentsia' in Russia, and the shaping of the long-lasting stereotype of the intellectual as universal mouthpiece of morality and reason, 'speaking truth to power' in the public sphere, in the Dreyfus Affair in France.[5] One could track this history further into the transformations in intellectual labour in the twentieth and twenty-first centuries, its increasing subsumption into the culture industry and knowledge economy. It might be argued, then, that while this term is appropriate for twentieth-century writers like Brecht and Fortini, it is anachronistic when applied to the ancient Greek Empedocles or the biblical Moses. However, my claim is that Huillet and Straub's films themselves already recode such figures under the modern category of the intellectual. Their sources are always later reinterpretations (Friedrich Hölderlin's version of Empedocles from the end of the eighteenth century, Schoenberg's Moses from the 1920s and 1930s), which are then recast a second time by the films in the 1970s and 1980s. The untimeliness generated by this process opens up unexpected questions about the politics of intellectual labour.

In emphasizing this politics, I take my cue from statements by the filmmakers, such as Huillet's remark that 'if we take a utopia, the greatest utopia there is — that suddenly all intellectuals, men and women, would strike, and this shit-society would collapse'.[6] This statement indicates both a strong investment in the category of the intellectual, and a conception of the intellectual as a particular kind of worker, whose refusal of work can be a disruptive act. This is a conviction they share with Brecht. In *Turandot or The Whitewashers' Congress* (*Turandot oder Der Kongreß der Weißwäscher*), Brecht's satire of how intellectuals are trained and make their living, the elderly peasant Sha Sen watches with increasing distaste the activities of the 'Tuis', those intellectuals (the majority) whose mental labours are dictated by and serve the state. Angrily, he exclaims, 'I'm done thinking. [...] The thoughts you can buy here stink. The whole country is governed by injustice, and in the Tui Academy all you get to learn is why it has to be that way'.[7] Engineering know-how builds bridges, Sen remarks, but 'the powerful are carried over them into indolent luxury, while the poor are herded into slavery'. Medical knowledge cures, but 'the few are restored to health so they can commit injustice, while the rest are made fit in order to sweat on their behalf'. Thinking, Sen laments, is debased to a commodity on the market, as 'opinions are bartered like fish, and thought itself has fallen into disrepute'. Thinking becomes scheming and apology for the present state of things. But 'thinking,' Sen remains convinced, 'is the most useful and pleasurable of activities'. Indeed, Sen has a book in his hands by one Kai Ho, someone foreign to the officially sanctioned Tui Academy. And:

> Wherever [Kai Ho] has been and done the thinking, there are wide fields with rice and cotton, and the people seem to be happy. And if the people are happy when someone has been thinking, then, [...] he must surely have done some good thinking, that's the proof.

For Brecht, ever the materialist, the proof of good thinking is in its effects. Yet thinking is not a mere tool to be discarded after the crops are grown. It is a capacity worth developing for its intrinsic value. After the land is shared out, Sen promises his grandson, 'we'll all get wide fields to plough and even wider fields to study'.[8]

If an analysis of the intellectual in their films is not problematically to reaffirm various clichés of bourgeois, patriarchal Western thought — the Man of Letters, the 'great individual thinker', the solitary genius — then it must emphasize the difficult status of intellectuals in the context of the emancipatory politics that underpins Huillet and Straub's cinematic project. One must directly address the contradiction that, as Theodor W. Adorno puts it, intellectuals 'are at once the last enemies of the bourgeois and the last bourgeois'.[9] Or as Alberto Toscano states: 'A communist cannot be an intellectual. A communist can only be an intellectual'.[10] On the one hand, Toscano notes, the intellectual's role is dependent on 'baseline premises of capital's domination' such as the 'separation between mind and hand, design and execution, reflection and compulsion', and exhibits a deceptive 'universalism whose condition of enunciation is that only some have access to it'. On the other, Toscano points to 'the programmatic conviction that intellectual life is both a generic condition of human beings in society *and* something that will only flourish after capitalism's demise, through revolutions in pedagogy and the pedagogy of revolution'.[11] The intellectual is the embodiment, the personification, of intellectual labour, and as such always signals the division of this labour from manual labour. In their representations of the intellectual, Huillet and Straub's films underscore this, but rather than celebrating it, they confront it and maintain fidelity to the possibility of its overcoming.[12] After all, the privilege of intellectual labour is not abolished by pretending it doesn't exist. Bad intellectuals are not necessarily good proletarians. Yet Huillet and Straub's allegiance to this figure must be measured against the pitfall that Adorno describes, that the intellectual 'runs the risk of believing himself better than the others and misusing his critique of society as an ideology for his private interest'.[13] To represent 'intellectuals' without romanticizing the present division of labour must therefore involve depicting the traps they fall into, and modelling alternative or future modes of intellectual work. This, I argue, is what the films of Huillet and Straub do.

The division of labour is closely related to the other important thread of my analysis, the distribution of speech. Huillet's and Straub's intellectuals are, frequently, constituted through speech acts.[14] In films such as *The Death of Empedocles*, *Fortini/Cani*, and *Workers, Peasants*, figures are almost always sitting or standing still, rooted to the spot — all the force of action is condensed into the words that come out of immobile bodies. Modes of speech can differ: exhortation, criticism, prophecy, analysis, testimony. But words issue from somewhere, and are addressed to others, even if only speculatively. This does not mean that words in their films always have an unambiguous origin or endpoint, that they are the unproblematic expression or property of the speaker. But what is at stake is, to use Roland Barthes's distinction, primarily 'speech' as opposed to 'writing' (*écriture*). Writing, for Barthes, is 'atopical', unsituated, attempting to displace the position of enunciation and escape 'the traps of "dialogue"'.[15] Speech, in contrast, opens up a social circuit with a listener, who may interrupt, influence, or reply. Barthes's distinction is conceptual rather than literal: the intellectual, significantly, is a 'person who prints and publishes their *speech*', and therefore a speaker, even when their words circulate written down.[16] Without accepting the evaluative dimension of Barthes's model, which elevates writing at the expense of speech, my attention to the networks of speaking and listening positions in Huillet and Straub's films is underpinned by a similar notion of speech. This allows the films to be seen as diagrams of the social relations into which intellectual labour is placed; even, or especially, when they trace the blockages and difficulties of speech.

In this chapter I lay out a partial and provisional typology of the intellectual in Huillet and Straub's films. As a way of drawing out various distinct threads, I deploy three categories: programmes (emphasizing a visionary, utopian conception of intellectual work), negations (emphasizing its critical aspect), and abolitions (exemplifying a desire to overcome the intellectual as a distinct social type opposed to the manual worker). These three categories are not exhaustive. However, through this process, I hope, the films can act as materials for thinking about the social relations into which intellectual work is inscribed, and the political possibilities that arise from these.

Programmes

The etymology of 'programme' is Greek: 'to write before'. In the films in which the intellectual's function involves a programme — notably *Moses and Aaron* and *The Death of Empedocles* — the intellectual describes an ideal or scheme in words, one that is anticipatory, referring to the future. To provide a programme, *to write before*, is to lay out in words an image of a possible future, in both of these films a liberated one.[17] The programme is directed towards others, a community or people who must carry it out, usually represented on screen in the drama. *Moses and Aaron* and *The Death of Empedocles* use, respectively, the figure of the Jewish prophet and the ancient Greek philosopher, who have a special knowledge and understanding inspired or directed by God or nature, to interrogate the difficulties in this conception of the intellectual.

Moses and Aaron, a staging of an unfinished opera by Arnold Schoenberg, begins, in its very first line, with the idea.[18] Moses in the desert declares it aloud: 'Unique, eternal, omnipresent, invisible and unrepresentable God!'. It is only after this that the voice in the burning bush gives him God's command to set the Jewish people free from slavery in Egypt. The Jewish people are 'chosen before all peoples, to be the people of the unique God, that it may know him and devote itself to him alone', but they are also, importantly, a people chosen to 'endure all the trials to which in millennia *the idea [der Gedanke]* is exposed'. Moses must take the divine idea to the people. But the problem is that Moses cannot communicate well. As Schoenberg's libretto says, 'My tongue is not flexible: I can think, but not speak'. So God assigns Aaron to be Moses's 'mouth', to put his idea into words. The motor of the narrative is two troublesome relationships: first, between the intellectual and the people, and second, between two aspects of the intellectual function itself, thought (Moses) and representation (Aaron).

In the opera and film, speech is not simply the vessel of thought but its antagonist. In their first interaction, Moses and Aaron face each other adversarially. Aaron sings 'Image of the highest fantasy'. Moses sternly corrects, 'No image can give thee an image of the Unrepresentable'. God's attributes are unthinkable, infinite abstractions ('Unique, eternal, omnipresent') or the negations of attributes, only to be given indirectly in language by saying what they are not ('*un*representable, *in*visible'). Aaron is constantly trying to provide conceptions for the inconceivable, which, for Moses, can only be false. For Moses, thought is primary, both logically (the signifier is inevitably insufficient to the infinitude of the signified) and chronologically (he had his idea before Aaron was assigned as his mouthpiece). Moses represents an absolutism of the signified. He is the opposite, in fact, of Barthes's description of the writer. For Barthes, one of the characteristics of 'writing' is that it is irreducible to summary: writing's work on the signifier means it cannot be put into other words, reduced to a content whose linguistic articulation is inconsequential.[19] Writing, for Barthes, resists the move from language to ideational content. Moses has the opposite problem: his idea cannot be translated into representation without being travestied. No language or image is ever commensurate to his idea — language always fails radically. Aaron, according to Moses, seduces and misleads thought through the machinations of language.

Yet, for Aaron, Moses is in denial about the fact that thought always requires a medium, whether voice or image or demonstration — even the stone tablets with the commandments and the burning bush are representations. Words are not mere instruments for pre-existing thoughts. They have a tendency to assert their autonomy, to introduce thoughts of their own, which is precisely what happens with Aaron (after the incident of the Golden Calf he is chastised by Moses, 'I did not instruct you', to which he responds, 'Nevertheless, I still comprehended'). Schoenberg's opera, as almost all commentators point out, is a philosophical reflection on the *Bilderverbot* or 'ban on images' in the Old Testament. In the score the clash is also embodied in the fact that Moses is a speaking part for which pitch is given only approximately, while Aaron is a sung tenor role. This antinomy is not resolved in a satisfying, i.e. dialectical, way. Instead, thought asserts itself over language: Moses smashes the stone tablets, and the film ends with language (Aaron) bound up on the floor, thought (Moses) standing above him along with two soldiers, castigating him.

A parallel structure plays itself out between the intellectual and the people. One might understand the film as turning the conflict in Schoenberg's opera into an allegory of the classical revolutionary party: Moses, the most 'advanced' in his knowledge, obtains the programme for an emancipated future, and together with Aaron (a skilled communicator and propagandist) tries to lead the people, through a mixture of exhortation and teaching, to enact it. Moses and Aaron together function as a kind of 'collective intellectual', bearers of special knowledge, a mind giving understanding and guidance to the body of the people (Figure 1.2).[20] At these moments, they stand side-by-side, addressing the chorus. However, this liberation reproduces a division of labour where some think and direct, and others act and follow. Emancipation entails, paradoxically, a new kind of servitude: '*to serve* the idea of God, *is the freedom* for which this folk has been chosen', Moses claims. Vanguard leadership is difficult to extricate from rule over the people. The programme to be enacted is also a law to be obeyed. This is emphasized in the way the film introduces verses from Exodus not adapted in Schoenberg's opera, read aloud by Huillet before the opening credits. These describe Moses ordering the Levites to slay three thousand men as a punishment for the debacle of the Golden Calf. When the people fail to live up to the idea, the people are sacrificed.

In *The Death of Empedocles*, based on the first version of Hölderlin's play, Empedocles is a wise and holy man who, like Moses, has a vision of the future, in this case for the 'children of the earth' rather than the Jewish people. Like Aaron, Empedocles, with his 'golden words', is a master of speech.[21] The film is a sequence of dialogues shot in static takes, the camera position never moving within a scene. Speakers' movements rarely exceed a few motions of the hand and head, and leaving and entering the frame at the beginning and end of scenes. All the energy of action is boiled down to the arrangement of bodies in space and their framing by the camera, a few charged gestures (kneeling, picking up a knife, collecting water), and the spoken words.

What is at stake is the power of speech itself, and speech's resistance to and complicity with other forms of power. Empedocles's loss of his powers manifests

FIG. 1.2. Danièle Huillet and Jean-Marie Straub, *Moses and Aaron*
(1975, courtesy of BELVA Film).

itself as silence: 'his spirit taciturn', he wishes to avoid 'pestilential talk'.[22] Empedocles's interactions — with his pupil Pausanias, and with the different layers of Agrigentian society: leaders, citizens, peasants, slaves — lay out the institutional and interpersonal power relations in which the intellectual is enmeshed (Figure 1.3). On the one hand, Empedocles's speech is dangerous to religious and state institutions. The priest Hermocrates and archon Critias, fearing the way that under the influence of Empedocles's words the people 'know nothing of the law' and 'respect no judge', conspire to turn the citizens against him.[23] Unlike Moses and Aaron, Empedocles refuses the opportunity to lead the people, rejecting the citizens' offer to make him king. On the other hand, Empedocles has not been innocent of power up to this point. His relationship to the citizens has been ambivalent: while they are 'dear friends' to whom he gives counsel, he has also called them 'the vulgar folk', 'the rabble', inferior to him, the philosopher, 'the friend of the gods'.[24] Most conspicuously, there is the glaring contradiction that Empedocles, who preaches the coming kingdom of equals, has had slaves. For the philosopher to devote himself to thinking, he has been content for others to be stripped of political rights and coerced into work, having their being violently reduced to property.[25]

These dialogues between figures in space are punctured by several 'figureless shots'. As Empedocles or Panthea speak, the film cuts to a shot of trees or steps, the speech continuing as voiceover. The longest of these shots is an image of trees with Etna in the background accompanying Empedocles's speech in which, although he refuses to lead the people himself, he gives them an image of a future in which 'the green of earth will glisten once again', and 'no form of servitude | Will cramp and crush the breast — ' (Figure I.1).[26] For Straub, the ideology of this speech is ecological and communist. Publishing this monologue in a German cinema journal in 1988, he added the comment: 'That is the dream of something that humanity

FIG. 1.3. Danièle Huillet and Jean-Marie Straub, *The Death of Empedocles*
(1987, courtesy of BELVA Film).

has dreamed of for so long, the powerful dream of humanity: communism, now the only way to save the earth'.[27] This shot of trees and volcano marks the importance of nature in Empedocles's discourse, but it also, crucially, shifts its recipient. Although Empedocles ostensibly continues, in the fiction, to speak to the citizens of Agrigent, the cut to this 'figureless shot' allows Empedocles's repeated second person pronoun 'You' — the very first word spoken after this 'figureless shot' appears — to effectively interpellate the spectator. Addressed by Empedocles's exhortations, it is the task of the film's spectators to enact this dream. Thus, although Empedocles, like Moses, orientates his discourse towards the future and typically speaks to other characters in the diegesis, these moments of quasi-direct address suggest my next category.

Negations

The films in my second category centre on modern historical examples and emphasize the negative, critical role of the intellectual. These films — *Introduction to Arnold Schoenberg's Accompaniment to a Cinematographic Scene* and *Fortini/Cani* — work, I argue, from Brecht's premise that the 'revolutionary intellect' is 'a dynamic, politically speaking, liquidating intellect'.[28] To be properly critical this stance must be self-critical, interrogating the intellectual's own place within the apparatuses of communication and the relations of cultural production, the conditions that allow some people's speech to circulate, and others' not. The shift away from the intellectual's speech addressing other figures in a fictional world signals these works' attention to these problems.

One might imagine that making a film in relation to Arnold Schoenberg's 1930 musical composition 'Accompaniment to a Cinematographic Scene' would entail

FIG. 1.4. Danièle Huillet and Jean-Marie Straub, *Introduction to Arnold Schoenberg's Accompaniment to a Cinematographic Scene* (1973, courtesy of BELVA Film).

producing the cinematographic scene, the images, to go with the music. Instead, in *Introduction to Arnold Schoenberg's Accompaniment to a Cinematographic Scene*, Huillet and Straub find more sounds. Most of the film takes place in a recording studio. A microphone is visible, and the readers — filmmakers Günter Peter Straschek and Peter Nestler, friends of Huillet and Straub — speak directly into it (Figure 1.4). A white screen is visible in the background, but Straschek and Nestler face away from this, backs turned to where images might appear. This screen suggests the studio might be used for dubbing, which we know Huillet and Straub are against.[29] Dubbing (*doubler, doblar*) swaps one soundtrack accompanying an image for another. *Introduction*, though, is a real example of doubling — a second soundtrack of spoken words is produced to go with Schoenberg's instrumental composition. When Nestler reads, the camera begins from the engineer at the mixing desk and then pans to the filmmaker speaking in the booth. In other words, we see the apparatus through which speech is structured, controlled, cut up, and transmitted.

As Serge Daney describes, this setting underscores the power of the media apparatus, 'connoting officiality, the weight of legitimate discourse, heavy, coming from above and destined to provoke no response'. This apparatus, Daney argues, 'dispossesses a priori' the speech that goes into it. Any speaker who wishes to say something oppositional is therefore 'constrained [...] to take charge of the device of enunciation (in order to "mark their distance from it" [*afin de "se démarquer"*]), even before enunciating whatever it is'.[30] The apparatus has its own enunciating power, preceding any utterance. If their speech is not merely to be subordinated to it, speakers must try to confront and work against the apparatus their speech is fed into. (This seems a clear reference to Brecht's 'Notes on the Opera *Rise and Fall of the City of Mahagonny*', in which he criticizes intellectuals who naively believe the apparatus that distributes their productions works at their service, when really the

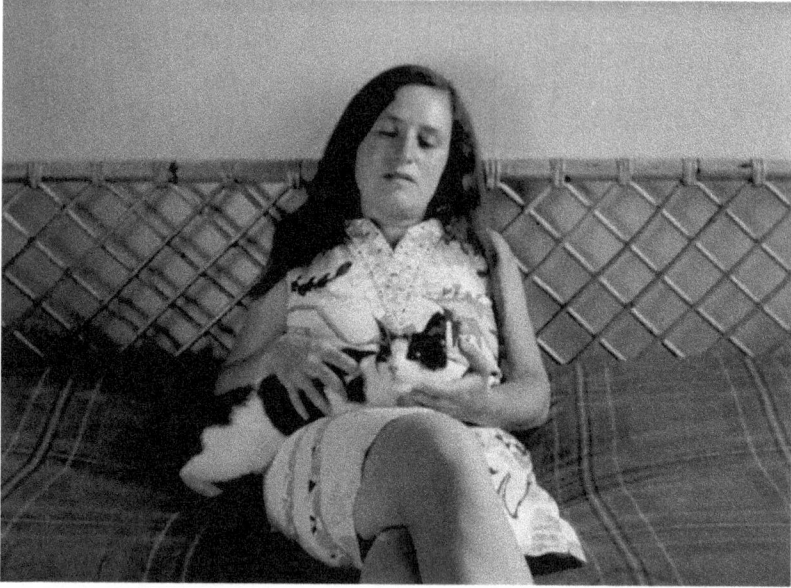

FIG. 1.5. Danièle Huillet and Jean-Marie Straub, *Introduction to Arnold Schoenberg's Accompaniment to a Cinematographic Scene* (1973, courtesy of BELVA Film).

FIG. 1.6. Danièle Huillet and Jean-Marie Straub, *Introduction to Arnold Schoenberg's Accompaniment to a Cinematographic Scene* (1973, courtesy of BELVA Film).

reverse is true.)[31] *Introduction*, according to Daney, paradoxically 'lodge[s] discourses "of resistance" in the dominant devices'.[32]

There are six 'speakers' in the film. There is Schoenberg, images of whom are shown near the beginning and parts of whose 1923 letter to Wassily Kandinsky are spoken in the film, and Brecht, a short extract from whose 1935 text 'Five Diffi- culties in Writing the Truth' ('Fünf Schwierigkeiten beim Schreiben der Wahrheit') is read as well. There is Straschek, who reads Schoenberg's words, and Nestler, who reads those of Brecht. Two cultural workers in 1972 read the words of two cultural workers from nearly half a century before. Straschek and Nestler are shot in black and white in the recording studio, always looking down at papers on the desk, reading these documents of social devastation in neutral tones. They don't 'embody' their roles. And there is Straub, who introduces the background of Schoenberg's composition, and Huillet, who links from Schoenberg to Brecht. They are shot in colour, on a balcony overlooking Rome (where they lived at this time) or at home on a sofa or bed, hinting at their lives outside the film, casual or even aloof: Huillet is stroking a cat (Figure 1.5), Straub takes his time to light a cigarette before speaking (Figure 1.6) and looking in the direction of the camera. They quote and paraphrase the words of Schoenberg and Brecht, framing those words in historical context and in relation to other texts.

Schoenberg's letter, the reading of which occupies more than half of the film, addresses the rising anti-Semitism in Europe in the 1920s. It attacks the participation of Kandinsky, who sustains an anti-Semitic stance despite his friendship with Schoenberg by telling the latter that he doesn't see him as Jewish. Schoenberg, in his letter, starts from his own identity, which is both socially imposed and defiantly embraced ('I have been forced to learn', he writes, 'that I am a Jew', adding, 'I am satisfied with it!'). He follows this understanding into its wider political consequences, since 'it is not an individual case, not an accident', asking 'where should anti-Semitism lead, if not to violent deeds?'. By linking the 1930 musical piece by Schoenberg to this 1923 letter, the 'threatening danger, fear, catastrophe' described in Schoenberg's notes to the composition is given a political referent, one that Schoenberg had recognized the danger of several years before, and which is (as Straub says in his description of the composition) 'otherwise unrepresentable': fascism.

The film connects Schoenberg's letter to Brecht's text, written after Hitler's rise to power, which stresses that in order to 'say the truth about fascism' and to make this truth 'practicable', writers must also spell out its intrinsic relation to capitalism.[33] As Ming Tsao points out, the film does this through Huillet, who begins by saying 'But, asks Brecht...'. This 'But', as Tsao convincingly argues, 'forces a relation' between the two discourses in order to ask a final question that Schoenberg doesn't raise, regarding 'the often hidden connections between racism and capitalism'.[34] The film allows six different speakers to participate in a dialogue about the ties between intellectual work, individual existence, and historical forces by bringing them into the same cinematic space and time ('Everything is in the present', Daney says), yet it simultaneously refuses, as Daney puts it, 'the forces of *homogenization*' that would make everything the same, clearly marking out the disparate places (in the open air, at home, in the recording studio) and historical moments (the 1920s and 1930s, the 1970s), accentuating the gap or interval between speaker (Straschek, Nestler) and spoken (Schoenberg, Brecht).[35] Intellectual work here is a collective endeavour of comradely critique.

Fortini/Cani, meanwhile, centred around Franco Fortini reading from his own 1967 book *The Dogs of the Sinai*, would seem to be the paradigmatic example of the intellectual in Huillet and Straub's films. We see a pair of glasses, stereotypical signifier of the intellectual, resting on the pages of a copy of the book, open at its preface (Figure 1.7). We see a pair of hands holding the book, and the rise and fall of the speaker's chest as he reads aloud. And about a third of the way in, we see the face and upper body of Fortini as he reads (Figure 1.8). But this set-up presents a problem, not found in *Introduction*. Fortini might become an authoritative figure and his speech pass unproblematized. *Here is an intellectual, in all his powerful self-presence.* The film therefore constantly strives to mark the distance between Fortini the reader and his own thought objectified in the book in his hands. As Fortini wrote to Straub, 'the text estranged itself under my gaze'; the 'I' who wrote *The Dogs of the Sinai* is not 'that gentlemen who in Straub-Huillet's footage [...] reads, almost unbelieving, what another himself has written'.[36] As Mark Nash and Steve Neale describe, 'the time of the enunciation of Fortini reading from his book is the present, yet in reading passages from the book, he is quoting from the past', and the film continually underscores this difference between past and present, text and reading, by emphasizing 'the fact and time of enunciation' through 'hesitations of the reading voice' (deliberately exacerbated by the fact that Fortini was not allowed to rehearse) and 'the rigidity of the body of the reader, duplicated in the "rigidity" of the camera framing'.[37] This process, Neale and Nash write, 'works against any imaginary construction of "Fortini" as coherent identity, as an origin/source of discourse', and is emblematized in a phrase that Fortini reads: 'You are not where your destiny is decided'. As Jean Narboni similarly argues, the pauses and hesitations in Fortini's reading mean that we are not just watching a speaker but a listener, someone listening to themselves, receiving words which seem to come from elsewhere. The film, as Narboni puts it, is always trying to mark out a 'there' distinct from a 'here', which will give us a position to look back at here.[38]

This distance, crystallized in the film's title, *Fortini* and *Cani* divided by a punctuation mark, /, is necessary because in order to analyse something, one must, as Stuart Hall says, 'construct that inevitable difference between the subject that is thinking and the subject that is being thought about'.[39] Fortini himself — poet and critic, intellectual, born in 1917, European, Italian, with a Jewish father — is subjected to a stereoscopic inquiry. This reinscribes the self-inquiry of Fortini's book, which intercuts between a present around the Six-Day War in 1967 and the past of Fortini's youth in Mussolini's fascist Italy, working the political conjuncture of 1967 against the facts of his own biography and vice versa. Fortini's discourse shifts between 'the alleged objectivity of the historical' and 'the subjective tension of the biographical', to use Paolo Caffoni's words.[40]

Fortini's own intellectual production emerges out of this relation. 'I don't yet know and find it rather difficult to know the history of the European and Italian

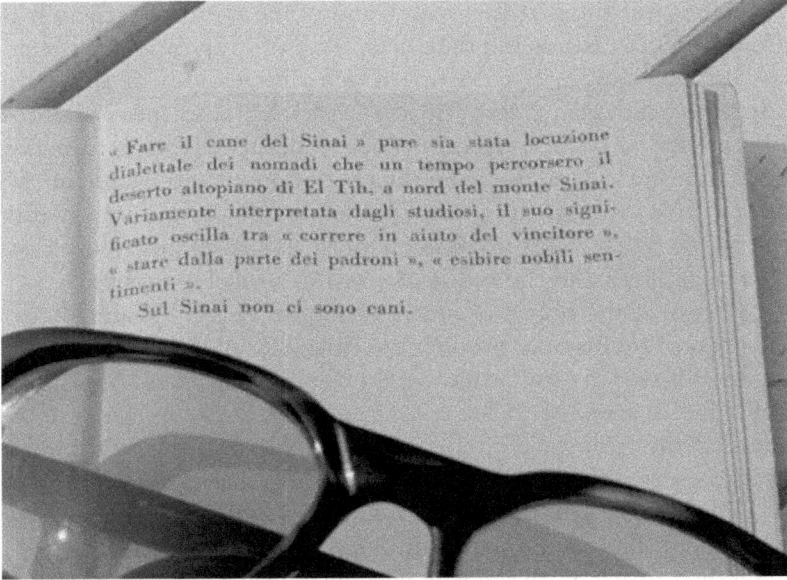

FIG. 1.7. Danièle Huillet and Jean-Marie Straub, *Fortini/Cani*
(1976, courtesy of BELVA Film).

FIG. 1.8. Danièle Huillet and Jean-Marie Straub, *Fortini/Cani*
(1976, courtesy of BELVA Film).

petty bourgeoisie over the past fifty years; and of me within it, if you'll allow me', he reads from his book, admitting the uncertainty of his position in the movements of history. But he is aware that to try to get a better idea of this is important, recognizing, like Schoenberg, that the self is social: 'I also speak about my affairs because I know they're not just mine'. A writer can move from personal experience to a diagnosis of historical forces: 'from the experience of anti-Semitism, it's possible to discern, if you're willing, the ultimate dilemma of the modern world'. The 'I' that Fortini speaks in the film is complex, both a shifting position in language ('a modest rhetorical ploy') and the index of a real historical existence.[41]

To select Fortini as the object of such a cinematic inquiry is already to stress the wider conditions of intellectual production, since, like Brecht, one of his recurring concerns is the historically mutating social position of writers.[42] It is important to state this because, in contrast to the recording studio *mise-en-scène* of *Introduction*, it might seem that the film shelters Fortini from the world. He is filmed alone at a secluded house on the island of Elba, often against a background of green foliage, sky, and a distant house, reading from a book he wrote nearly a decade before. He is not in the places (Florence, the Apuan Alps) or times (1925, 1938, 1967) he talks about. Yet his discourse is always woven into the world. It is intercut with newspaper cuttings, footage filmed in a synagogue, television news, city streets, mountains. His words are a material object, which we see in the very first shot, a book whose spine is worn by reading, which gives a hint of the conditions of its production and distribution (we see the name of the publisher), and which is affected by the world (its pages gently move in the breeze). His voice mingles with birdsong and traffic. This is a dialectic of separation and embeddedness, the former necessary for critical distance, the latter so that one is not removed from history. To take up residence at this site is not to be an isolated prophet, 'the enemy of the century, a sullen preacher in the desert', nor is it to 'seek out difficult postures', to take up antagonistic stances just to be contrary.[43] It is to recognize that present conditions place critical thought in a paradoxical position of solidarity and alienation, a 'there', as well as a 'here'. 'Your nearness to me, my distance from you', as Fortini says.

Abolitions

Finally, by 'abolitions' — a category exemplified by *Workers, Peasants*, based on Elio Vittorini's novel *Women of Messina* (*Le donne di Messina*) — I mean the attempt to overcome the intellectual as a distinct and alienated social category. This attempt is not so much the criticism of present social relations, like in *Introduction* and *Fortini/Cani*, as a *practical* refusal of what Jacques Rancière calls 'the division between those whose lot is production and struggle, and those whose lot is discourse and ideology'.[44] It is 'the eruption of negativity, of *thinking*, into a social category always defined by the positivity of doing'.[45] The protagonists of *Workers, Peasants* may be workers and peasants, but we don't see manual labour in the film, not even its traces (ploughed fields, tools). Instead, standing in a quiet glade, they speak about their world (Figure 1.9). In a series of monologue fragments, we hear about the practicalities and pleasures of making cheese, and critical reflections on how work

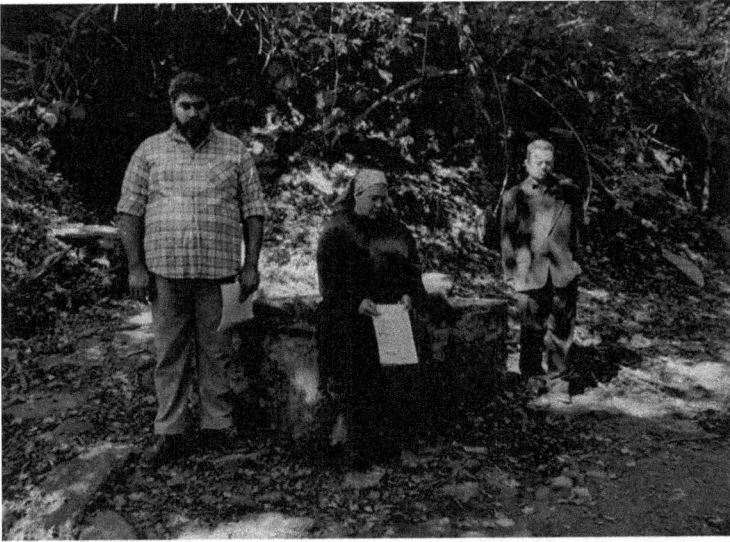

FIG. 1.9. Danièle Huillet and Jean-Marie Straub, *Workers, Peasants*
(2001, courtesy of BELVA Film).

should be organized (when should one rest?). The protagonists transform their
world into discourse.

This 'translation' that occurs 'between words and things', as Rancière describes
the activity of worker-intellectuals, is done by the workers and peasants themselves,
who do not limit themselves to doing and let others take charge of thinking and
speaking.[46] And this is echoed in the performers in the film, non-professional
actors who take speech for themselves as they hold texts in their hands and declaim
a series of what Manuel Ramos-Martínez calls 'exuberant oratories'.[47] Thinking
and speaking is distributed evenly across the characters in *Workers, Peasants*; there is
not one privileged speaker who directs their words to an undifferentiated 'people'
or chorus. There may be groupings (of three workers and three peasants, say), but
each individual has their say. And, unlike the other films I have discussed, women
as much as men appropriate this function. Speech is distributed evenly because of
the communal property relations of the village. However, rather than having a pre-
existing programme or idea to be turned into action, the characters 'do not have
principles' or 'any definite purpose'.[48] The ideas and feelings they verbalize arise
out of their activity.

But these gestures are undermined in *The Return of the Prodigal Son — Humiliated*
(2003), which stages scenes from further on in *Women of Messina*. The villagers are
confronted by a surveyor who represents the normalization of work and property
that the village will undergo (Figure 1.10). Before there was no hierarchy of
speech. The surveyor criticizes this: 'You all talk at once [...] so we're not getting
anywhere'.[49] The equality of expression that arose from collective labour is
reprimanded as an undifferentiated hubbub, characteristic of a disorganized group.
The villagers prefer a straightforward exchange of words ('You have your say, and
we'll have ours').[50] But the surveyor wants to institute a formal meeting and select

FIG. 1.10. Danièle Huillet and Jean-Marie Straub, *Humiliated*
(2003, courtesy of BELVA Film).

a chair, someone who legally ratifies an individual's status as speaker, deciding who has the legitimate right to speak and who does not. The surveyor monopolizes speech to teach the villagers, now primarily a group of listeners, the law and the 'good sense' of capitalist property relations. This structure is repeated later, when some former partisans lecture the villagers on the value of Coca Cola and the need to adjust to the post-1945 order. Confronted with this authoritarian education, the villagers are humiliated and put in their place.

Conclusion

The abolition enacted in *Workers, Peasants* is not a fantasy. But, as *The Return of the Prodigal Son — Humiliated* demonstrates, it is temporally and spatially circumscribed — to a single village, for a year or so, in the exceptional circumstances after World War Two. It needs to be generalized, but this can only happen through the forging of post-capitalist social relations. As such, the category of 'Abolitions' returns us to the orientation towards possible futures I discussed in relation to 'Programmes' and the critical analysis of the present conditions of intellectual work in 'Negations'. *Workers, Peasants* presents an image of those doing intellectual activity encompassing manual labourers and women. This is especially important because although I have argued that Huillet and Straub's devotion to the idea of the intellectual is inextricable from their concern with criticizing and overturning the exploitative social relations that allow only a privileged few to access this position, their presentation of certain noteworthy models (Empedocles, Brecht, Fortini, Schoenberg) tends to reinforce a canon of intellectuals that is almost exclusively white, male, and European.[51] This is aggravated by a problematic engagement, in later films, with conservative writers such as Maurice Barrès and Georges Bernanos.[52] For these reasons, the models provided by Huillet and Straub's films must be treated critically. Despite these caveats, their body of work provides singular material for reflecting on the category of the intellectual. Their films sharpen a perception of the habitual dependence of intellectuals' speech on an exploitative division between manual and intellectual labour. At the same time, they justify the conviction that intellectual activity is necessary in order, as Hall says, to think a world that is 'fundamentally resistant to thought'.[53] In fact, the concerted withdrawal of this labour is for Huillet a 'utopia' that might bring down an oppressive society. Intellectual activity is highlighted as an aspiration — a potential to be generalized and revolutionized — and part of the work of transforming the world.

Notes to Chapter 1

1. Günter Peter Straschek, 'Filmkritik: Straschek 1963–74, West Berlin', in *Günter Peter Straschek: Film — Emigration — Politik*, ed. by Julia Friedrich (Cologne: Museum Ludwig, 2018), pp. 162–81 (p. 162). Thank you to James Clow, Anneke Kampman, and Sebastian Truskolaski for suggestions and/or comments.

2. See, for example, Manfred Blank, 'Wie will ich lustig lachen, wenn alles durcheinandergeht', *Filmkritik*, 28 (1984), 269–82, in which Straub, invoking Schoenberg, dismisses comparisons between his own working experiences and *Chronicle of Anna Magdalena Bach*.

3. Jean-Marie Straub, 'On the Business Affairs of Mr. Julius Caesar', in Straub and Huillet, *Writings*, pp. 140–55.

4. Jeremy Jennings and Tony Kemp-Welch, 'The Century of the Intellectual: From the Dreyfus Affair to Salman Rushdie', in *Intellectuals in Politics: From the Dreyfus Affair to Salman Rushdie*, ed. by Jeremy Jennings and Tony Kemp-Welch (London & New York: Routledge, 1997), pp. 1–21 (p. 7).

5. See David Bates, 'Introduction: Marxism, Intellectuals and Politics', in *Marxism, Intellectuals and Politics*, ed. by David Bates (Basingstoke: Palgrave Macmillan, 2007), pp. 1–18 (pp. 2–4); Peter Osborne, 'Introduction: Philosophy, and the Role of Intellectuals', in *A Critical Sense: Interviews with Intellectuals*, ed. by Peter Osborne (London & New York: Routledge, 1996), pp. ix–xiv; Raymond Williams, *Keywords: A Vocabulary of Culture and Society* (London: Fontana, 1983), pp. 169–71.

6. Helge Heberle and Monika Funke Stern, 'The Fire Inside the Mountain: A Conversation with Danièle Huillet', trans. by John Crutchfield, in *Tell It to the Stones*, ed. by Busch and Hering, pp. 250–64 (p. 260).

7. Bertolt Brecht, *Turandot or The Whitewashers' Congress*, trans. by Tom Kuhn, in *Collected Plays*, ed. by Tom Kuhn and David Constantine, 8 vols (London: Methuen, 1970–2003), VIII, 127–193 (p. 189).

8. Ibid.

9. Theodor Adorno, *Minima Moralia: Reflections from Damaged Life*, trans. by E. F. N. Jephcott (London & New York: Verso, 2020), p. 30.

10. Alberto Toscano, 'The Non-State Intellectual: Franco Fortini and Communist Criticism', in Franco Fortini, *The Dogs of the Sinai*, trans. by Alberto Toscano (London, New York & Calcutta: Seagull Books, 2013), pp. 89–129 (pp. 90–91).

11. Ibid.

12. Esther Leslie has made a similar argument in relation to Fortini's poetry: Esther Leslie, 'Anti-Fascism, Anti-Art, Doubt and Despair', *Third Text*, 33.3 (2019), 293–313 (p. 299).

13. Adorno, *Minima Moralia*, p. 29.

14. The 'artist films', on Bach and Cézanne, are an exception to this worthy of more critical elucidation. It is notable, though, that Cézanne is, in part at least, portrayed through his verbal pronouncements, as in the voicing of his comments on other artists in *A Visit to the Louvre* (2004).

15. Roland Barthes, 'Writers, Intellectuals, Teachers', in *Image Music Text*, ed. and trans. by Stephen Heath (London: Fontana, 1977), pp. 190-215 (p. 213).

16. Ibid., p. 190, my emphasis.

17. My use of the term 'programme' in this section is influenced in part by Théorie Communiste's somewhat different notion of 'programmatism'. See: Théorie Communiste, 'Much Ado about Nothing', *Endnotes*, 1 (2008), 154-206.

18. Schoenberg's work was primarily composed at the end of the 1920s, shortly before he reconverted to Judaism in 1933, the same year that Hitler became chancellor in Germany and the beginning of Schoenberg's exile from Austria. For historical details and interpretation, see Michael A. Rosenthal, 'Art and the Politics of the Desert: German Exiles in California and the Biblical "Bilderverbot"', *New German Critique*, 118 (2013), 46-53.

19. Barthes, 'Writers, Intellectuals, Teachers', p. 193.

20. The most influential articulation of this conception of the vanguard revolutionary party is Vladimir Ilyich Lenin, *What is to Be Done? Burning Questions of Our Movement*, trans. by Joe Fineberg and George Hanna (New York: International Publishers, 1969). The text was originally published in 1902 and has been much disputed since. There is considerable argument about the specifics of the relationship between the party and the working class described, whether or not this maps onto a relationship between intellectuals and the working class, and the relationship between Lenin's ideas and those of Karl Kautsky, whom Lenin cites. For criticisms of Lenin, see Rosa Luxemburg, 'Organizational Questions of Russian Social Democracy', in *The Rosa Luxemburg Reader*, ed. by Peter Hudis and Kevin B. Anderson (New York: Monthly Review Press, 2004), pp. 248-65; and Paul Mattick, *Anti-Bolshevik Communism* (London & New York: Routledge, 2018), pp. 27-53.

21. Friedrich Hölderlin, *The Death of Empedocles: A Mourning-Play*, trans. by David Farrell Krell (Albany: State University of New York Press, 2008), l. 828 (all references are to the first version in the book).

22. Ibid., ll. 566, 551.

23. Ibid., ll. 192-93.

24. Ibid., ll. 1487, 926, 934, 923.

25. Although Empedocles frees his slaves, the scene serves to demonstrate that he has had them up to this point. In any case, Empedocles's action seems primarily motivated by the fact that he is leaving and no longer needs them.

26. Hölderlin, *The Death of Empedocles*, ll. 1519, 1539-40.

27. Jean-Marie Straub, 'Cézanne/Empedocles/Hölderlin/Von Arnim', in Straub and Huillet, *Writings*, pp. 208-12 (p. 212).

28. Bertolt Brecht, 'Intellectuals and Class Struggle', trans. by David Bathrick, *New German Critique*, 1 (1973), 19-21 (p. 21).

29. See Jean-Marie Straub, 'Dubbing is Murder', in Straub and Huillet, *Writings*, pp. 113-16.

30. Serge Daney, 'A Tomb for the Eye (Straubian Pedagogy)', trans. by Stoffel Debuysere and others <http://sergedaney.blogspot.com/2014/09/a-tomb-for-eye-straubian-pedagogy.html> [accessed 7 August 2021]. Translation of the second quotation modified.

31. Bertolt Brecht, 'Notes on the Opera *Rise and Fall of the City of Mahagonny*', in *Brecht on Theatre*, ed. by Silberman, Giles, and Kuhn, pp. 70-71.

32. Daney, 'A Tomb for the Eye (Straubian Pedagogy)'.

33. Bertolt Brecht, 'Five Difficulties in Writing the Truth', trans. by Laura Bradley and Tom Kuhn, in *Brecht on Art and Politics*, ed. by Tom Kuhn and Steve Giles (London & New York: Bloomsbury, 2003), pp. 141-57 (p. 145); Danièle Huillet and Jean-Marie Straub, 'Introduction to Arnold Schoenberg's Accompaniment to a Cinematographic Scene — Scenario', *Screen*, 17.1 (1976), 77-83 (p. 81).

34. Ming Tsao, 'Refuse Collection: Schoenberg/Lachenmann — Straub/Huillet — J. H. Prynne', in *Tell It to the Stones*, ed. by Busch and Hering, pp. 102-25 (p. 108).

35. Daney, 'A Tomb for the Eye (Straubian Pedagogy)'.

36. Franco Fortini, 'A Note for Jean-Marie Straub', in Fortini, *The Dogs of the Sinai*, pp. 74-82 (pp. 80, 77).

37. Mark Nash and Steve Neale, 'Film: "History/ Production/ Memory"', *Screen*, 18.4 (1977), 77-91 (p. 88).
38. Jean Narboni, 'Là', *Cahiers du cinéma*, 275 (1977), 6-14. The French title translates into English as 'There'. Narboni also cites this as a Brechtian emphasis on heightening the distinction between performer and role.
39. Stuart Hall, 'Through the Prism of an Intellectual Life', in *Essential Essays*, ed. by David Morley, 2 vols (Durham, NC: Duke University Press, 2019), II, 303-23 (p. 304).
40. Paolo Caffoni, 'A Revolutionary Copywriter: Franco Fortini and his Relations to Film', in *Tell It to the Stones*, ed. by Busch and Hering, pp. 160-81 (p. 176).
41. Fortini, *The Dogs of the Sinai*, pp. 31, 32, 14.
42. See, for instance, Franco Fortini, 'The Writer's Mandate and the End of Anti-Fascism', in *A Test of Powers: Writings on Criticism and Literary Institutions*, trans. by Alberto Toscano (London, New York & Calcutta: Seagull Books, 2016), pp. 214-69. This essay connects its reflections to Brecht's 1935 speech at the First International Congress of Writers for the Defence of Culture in Paris. See also Alberto Toscano, 'Translator's Introduction: The Labour of Division', in the same volume, pp. 1-55.
43. Fortini, *The Dogs of the Sinai*, pp. 26, 27.
44. Jacques Rancière, 'The Proletarian and his Double, or, the Unknown Philosopher', in *Staging the People: The Proletarian and his Double*, trans. by David Fernbach (London & New York: Verso, 2011), pp. 21-33 (p. 30).
45. Jacques Rancière, quoted in Kristin Ross, 'Introduction', in Jacques Rancière, *The Ignorant Schoolmaster: Five Lessons in Intellectual Emancipation*, trans. by Kristin Ross (Stanford, CA: Stanford University Press, 1991), pp. vii-xxiii (p. xviii).
46. Jacques Rancière, 'Heretical Knowledge and the Emancipation of the Poor', in *Staging the People*, pp. 34-56 (p. 42). Given the closeness between this aesthetic and his project from the 1970s, it is no surprise that Rancière has taken an interest in Huillet and Straub's films, particularly *Workers, Peasants*. Rancière's specific readings of the films, though, which recruit them to his wider critique of any 'Brechtian' art that tries to tutor the audience through distancing and the staging of dialectic, requires more critical interrogation than it has received so far, at least in English. There is not enough space here to undertake this. See, for instance, Rancière and Lafosse, 'Politics and Aesthetics in the Straubs' Films', and Jacques Rancière, 'Fireside Conversation: Straub and Others', in *The Intervals of Cinema*, pp. 103-26.
47. Manuel Ramos-Martínez, ' "Actors Simply Explode": To Act in the Cinema of Jean-Marie Straub and Danièle Huillet', *Camera Obscura*, 31.2 (2016), 93-117 (p. 106).
48. Elio Vittorini, *Women of Messina*, trans. by Frances Frenaye and Frances Keene (New York: New Directions, 1973), pp. 95, 96.
49. Ibid., p. 189.
50. Ibid., p. 190.
51. An exception here is *Too Early, Too Late* (1981) in which the film's second voiceover, based on a text written under the pseudonym 'Mahmoud Hussein' by Egyptian-French writers Bahgat Elnadi and Adel Rifaat, spoken by Elnadi, can be understood as an instance of the intellectual's speech. Huillet and Straub have worked with texts by women writers such as Marguerite Duras and Janine Massard, but these writers do not figure in their films as examples of 'the intellectual'.
52. In *Lothringen!* (1994), *An Heir* (2011), *Concerning Venice (History Lessons)* (2014), based on texts by Barrès, *Dialogue of Shadows* (2014) and *France Against Robots* (2020), based on texts by Bernanos. All except the first of these were directed by Straub alone, after Huillet's death in 2006.
53. Hall, 'Through the Prism of an Intellectual Life', p. 304

CHAPTER 2

Part and Whole:
On Some Uses of Landscape in the
Films of Huillet and Straub

Sam McAuliffe

What makes landscape an intrinsically paradoxical arrangement, Georg Simmel suggests, is that the framework over which it presides is locked in tension with the order of nature out of which it is composed. The conditions under which this form of representation emerges, the ways in which it organizes the field of perception, the modes of sensibility it cultivates, and the worldview to which it gives expression are each in their turn traversed by this tension, which must therefore be understood as constitutive of the form itself. In 'The Philosophy of Landscape', a short study of 1913, Simmel approaches this tension through a stringent categorical opposition: *landscape is to nature as part is to whole.* 'By nature,' he writes:

> We mean the infinite interconnectedness of objects, the uninterrupted creation and destruction of forms, the flowing unity of an event that finds expression in the continuity of temporal and spatial existence. [...] To talk of 'a piece of nature' is in fact a self-contradiction. Nature is not composed of pieces. It is the unity of a whole. The instant anything is parceled out from this wholeness, it is no longer nature pure and simple since this whole can be 'nature' only within that unbounded unity, only as a wave within that total flux.[1]

It is over and against the natural order conceived as such that landscape takes shape. Whereas nature intersects with itself as a totality in each of its particular instantiations, landscape is instead comprised of an ensemble of discrete elements that make manifest a *locality*, in and through its specificity. The prospect this affords is a partial one, circumscribed in principle. Its formation therefore institutes a break in nature's open-ended continuum. It detaches itself from the whole of which it is part, by tracing a perimeter where there would otherwise be none. And yet since this part still belongs to the whole — it is, after all, nowhere else — in the same stroke this process of detachment separates the whole from itself, depriving the whole of itself as something whole. Simmel continues:

> As far as landscape is concerned, however, a boundary [*Abgrenzung*], a way of being encompassed by a momentary or permanent field of vision, is quite

essential. Its material foundation or its individual pieces may simply be regarded as nature. But conceived of as a 'landscape', it demands a status for itself [*Für-sich-Sein*], which may be optical, aesthetic or mood-centred. [...] To conceive of a piece of ground and what is on it as a landscape, this means that one now conceives of a segment of nature itself as a separate unity, which estranges it from the concept of nature.[2]

Abgrenzung, delimitation, the determination of place through the delineation of limits, must therefore be considered one of landscape's predominant structural features: a boundary that renders distinct what it encloses by setting it apart, a 'unique, characterizing detachment' ('eine singuläre, charakterisierende Enthobenheit'), Simmel writes. It is therefore along this borderline that the antagonism between landscape and nature, part and whole, inside and outside, is at its most concentrated. And yet the boundary can be ascribed this set of functions only insofar as it is not itself a visible part of the resulting arrangement. If it makes the field of representation possible — determining what will and will not be made visible, what is given prominence and what is consigned to the periphery, and so on — it is not itself representable therein.

Landscape's relation to what it detaches itself from necessarily involves a certain force. (How else would the work of detachment be possible without an application of force in some form or another?) In an earlier text, a study of the frame as it pertains to the organization and reception of aesthetic materials, Simmel even refers to the *violence* implicit in bringing a limit to bear upon nature. As if any position ascribed to the limit in situ always ran the risk of appearing arbitrary and therefore lacking in legitimacy, considering the constitutive unboundedness of what it, the limit, is being brought into contact with. Simmel writes in this text:

> The frame is suited only to structures with a closed unity, which a piece of nature never possesses. Any excerpt from unmediated nature is connected by a thousand spatial, historical, conceptual and emotional relationships with everything that surrounds it more or less closely, physically or mentally. [...] Around the piece of nature, which we instinctively feel to be a mere part in the context of the greater whole, the frame is therefore contradictory and violent.[3]

It is in this sense that the tension between landscape and nature is irreducible, attested to here by the fact that the line of demarcation separating the former from the latter must itself remain unbreachable: 'the frame, through its configuration, must never offer a gap or a bridge through which, as it were, the world could get in or from which the picture could get out'.[4]

And yet for Simmel it is this same feature — the inviolability of the boundary, the 'inner resoluteness' that comes from 'its self-contained contours' — which grants the segment of terrain enclosed a self-sufficiency it wouldn't otherwise have, allowing landscape to become a ground for itself by giving it a means of subsisting without external support. Here is the moment of dialectical inversion on which Simmel's account ultimately rests, the point at which 'one part of a whole should become a self-contained whole itself, emerging out of it and claiming from it a right to its own existence'.[5] Not only, then, does this particular part cease to derive its cohesion from the whole, it manages to re-inscribe the whole as whole within itself as part. Having ceased to be one part among others, no longer commensurable with any other part, the paradox of landscape is therefore that of a part which is greater than the whole it is part of. 'The specific object thereby created and transposed onto quite a new level then, so to speak, from within itself opens up again towards that total-Life [*All-Leben*] and re-absorbs the infinite into *its still intact boundaries* [*in seine undurchbrochenen Grenzen das Unbegrenzte aufnehmend*]'.[6] To bring forth the limitless within given limits and on the basis of such limits is thus the particular demand made of landscape as a form, and the response to this demand in each case commits the use of this form, implicitly or explicitly, to an interpretation of nature. Where the enclosing boundary is situated, by what means and to what ends it is delineated, how this delineation effectuates the detachment of part from whole, but also how the whole is then recovered through this same part: all this implies a set of operations that are responsible for determining the configuration by which 'nature' is then encountered.

★   ★   ★   ★   ★

Throughout the films of Danièle Huillet and Jean-Marie Straub it is possible to discern an engagement with nature undertaken along these lines, through the medium of landscape conceived as such: a diverse repertory of practices and strategies the aim of which is to bring about the 'unique, characterizing detachment' on which the use of this medium rests, through the capacities and facilities specific to cinema. Above all else the work of *Abgrenzung* is recognized by the filmmakers as a political task, not least because it requires a decision to be made concerning the relation of part and whole. A watchword of Brecht, invoked time and again by Straub, provides a schema for this relation: 'To dig out the truth from the rubble of the self-evident, to make a marked link between the specific and the general, to capture the particular within a general process, that is the art of the realists'.[7] If the contexts in which Huillet and Straub make use of landscape are manifold, this 'marked link between the specific and the general' is what the given arrangement is in each case concerned with, and it is on this account that nature is always approached along an axis that sees it treated not as a mere background, extrinsic to the sphere of politics proper, but as the *res publica* itself, the thing that is constituted through the struggle over what is held to be common, a site of contestation traversed by conflicting forms of political agency and subjectivation. In a 2013 conversation, Straub gives an indication of what it might mean to treat this 'marked link' as a principle of method in the context of landscape when he recalls the location scouting for the scenes of present-day rural France that appear in the first section of *Too Early, Too Late* (1981), those fringes of apparently empty terrain, at first sight unmarked by any explicit sign of human drama, the locations of which are drawn from a text of Engels (a letter to Kautsky of 1889) recalling the conditions of peasant life in the period preceding the French Revolution. The search for the prospect that opens up a terrain to filmic presentation, 'the spot from where one can simply see something', is described by Straub in the following way:

And then one discovers that in a village the search often ends where the water tower stands, for needless to say the water tower's location isn't arbitrary. It is placed exactly on that spot where water can be fed to the entire locality. And the standpoint from where the locality can be supplied with water just also happens to be the filmmaker's standpoint, who is likewise attempting to show an entirety. Hence the take of a village then operates like an irrigation system. And Brecht would say: 'What one films then belongs to the irrigators'.[8]

The point of view through which a landscape comes together is thus explicitly situated within the material relations of production that have shaped the terrain's topography and rendered it habitable, making the field of vision coterminous with land understood as something 'transformed and worked by men', as Huillet writes in another text on the film.[9] Establishing a prospect and its sightlines on this basis is what allows the designated site to be determined in its specificity. Sometimes this gives rise to a stationary shot; other times a curvature that, reaching its designated limit, reverses its direction and retraces its own passage, eventually returning to its point of departure; other times still, a movement that travels full circle, providing a complete panorama. These variations are therefore determined by what in each case is required to establish the locale in its 'entirety'. (The same principle is at work in the film's second part, in an Egypt framed by Mahmoud Hussein's *Class Conflict in Egypt: 1945–1971*, with several of the viewpoints onto locations of peasant rebellion determined in an analogous way: if this principle gives rise to a different type of viewpoint in this context — most notably, a forward moving tracking shot running parallel to the Nile — this difference is always derived from the specific features of the terrain and how this terrain has been 'irrigated'.) But as Straub also suggests here, this shooting method is equally concerned with addressing the circumscribed place as a point of entry onto what lies beyond it. 'One doesn't just irrigate a locality,' he says, 'one irrigates the earth'.[10] What does 'earth' signify in this scenario? Precisely that which is manifest *within* the frame *as* unbounded. Landscape understood as a means of surveying the earth in this sense is therefore organized around a distribution of part and whole, with the former acting as a frame for the latter.

Of course in Huillet and Straub's filmic practice a fundamental means of setting this relation in place is through the use of discourse. Landscape is never treated by the filmmakers as a visual proposition alone. It always appears through the mediation of text, in spoken or written form, and the block of discourse thereby assembled is another way of framing what is being registered on the visual plane. The sequences already mentioned from the first part of *Too Early, Too Late* serve as a case in point. As these rural spaces are surveyed, alongside the living sound of each terrain, we hear a voice — Huillet's own — reading from the Engels text in question and focusing in on the table of statistics he provides there, figures gathered from the *Cahiers de doléances* that in each case makes clear the scale of the local population living in beggary despite the fertility of the land, materially excluded from 'active citizenship'. 'Let the figures speak for themselves', Engels writes in this letter, and indeed they do. As this discursive material is recited each terrain comes to appear as a site of class struggle, an arrangement of interests and dependencies that mark a particular point in the development of capital, and on account of which the tracts of land surveyed are shown to have been at odds with the plebian demand for 'well-being for all on the basis of labour'. The function ascribed to text by Huillet and Straub here is not then simply descriptive. Rather, discourse is understood as something like a means for shifting the ground upon which a given referent is perceived and the distribution of categories through which this perception is understood. In doing so it lays bare the extent to which the apparently objective determination of the referent is always in fact an interpretation, and thus itself a site of contestation. In short, discourse relates to its referent here in the form of 'assessment' or 'evaluation' (*Beurteilung*), a term that should be understood as it is applied by Brecht at a particular moment in 'Five Difficulties in Writing the Truth' (1934), and it is in fact worth recalling the practical demonstration provided by this text of discourse behaving in this way:

> Anyone in our times who says *population instead of 'Volk' and land ownership instead of 'soil'* is already denying his support to many lies. He divests the words of their lazy mysticism. [...] The population of an area of land has different, even opposing interests, and this is a truth which is suppressed. Thus anyone who says 'soil', and describes the fields to nose and eyes by speaking of their earthy scent and their colour, is supporting the lies of the rulers; for what matters is not the fertility of the soil, nor man's love of it, nor his diligence, but instead principally the price of grain and the price of labour. The people who draw the profits from the soil are not those who harvest the grain, and the scent of the clods of earth is unknown on the stock exchanges. They reek of something different. On the contrary, 'landownership' is the right word; it is less deceptive.[11]

This is precisely how discourse is called upon in *Too Early, Too Late*, textual reference shifting the frame by which the piece of reality under assessment is being viewed. Indeed, it is in this sense that the discursive element is not subject to the same limits and thresholds that organize the terrain in its visible aspect. Discourse is capable of delineating conditions and circumstances that are otherwise unmarked at the level of vision alone. Gilles Deleuze's striking insight into the *stratigraphic* nature of landscape in Huillet and Straub's work has its context here. Landscape is stratigraphic inasmuch as it is comprised of so many layers of earth superimposed upon one another, history being nothing more than the successive accumulation of these strata, and in relation to which discourse, 'the speech-act' in the lexicon of *Cinema 2*, should be understood as an instrument of excavation, a means of delineating what from the standpoint of the present has been buried beneath the outer surface of things, beyond vision's reach.[12] Traversing a vertical axis, discourse bores down through these strata to draw out the configuration of relations through which the locale in question has been constituted. When Straub refers to the landscapes of *Too Early, Too Late* as a 'geological theatre of figures', it is precisely in this sense: '*geo*, Greek for the earth. Geology is the study of that which is not visible, or barely so; that which is underneath'.[13] Discourse is what grants access to these subterranean levels.

This, then, must be considered a fundamental feature of Huillet and Straub's use of landscape: in their films the work of *Abgrenzung* is pursued across two distinct registers simultaneously — a boundary demarcated at the level of vision, a boundary demarcated at the level of discourse — and a landscape comes together through the exchange developed between these two registers and their respective ways of framing, the co-implication of which is of course a prerogative of cinematic form.

★   ★   ★   ★   ★

It is instructive to consider another work that addresses the thematic configuration at stake here: *Proposition in Four Parts*, made for Italian television in 1985. The work is an exercise in quotation, a montage of sequences, three of which are drawn from Huillet and Straub's previous body of films, and each of which is reframed so as to make explicit the 'assessment' of nature as *res publica* underway there. First, the concluding stage of the first act of *Moses and Aaron* (1975), in which Aaron implores God's chosen people to free themselves from bondage with the promise of milk and honey, a call to arms that is followed by two elevated tracking shots of the Nile and its environs, the second of which comes to a rest in barren desert, the setting for this promise's fulfilment: 'The Almighty changes sand into fruit, fruit into gold, gold into delight, delight into spirit'. Second, the remembrance landscapes of *Fortini/Cani* (1976), sweeping shots that forge a passage along the Apuan Alps, this movement taking in the locations across the region known for the massacre of partisans carried out under Nazi occupation (see Chapter 4). Finally, the sixth dialogue from the first section of *From the Cloud to the Resistance* (1979), an episode under moonlight in which a father and son, sacrificial pyre burning before them, speak for and against the offerings that must be made to the gods to secure the harvest, the son raising his voice against the injustice of this custom and the fatalism which accepts that what once was must always be, especially since this injustice is compounded by another, the masters' exploitation of the peasants' work. Disparate epochs and diverse contexts, broached through modalities of representation and configurations of reference just as disparate and diverse. But common to each of these scenes is an encounter with nature that seeks to make legible the processes of domination and resistance by which it is traversed, thereby allowing the social structure of which these processes are an expression to be accounted for and evaluated. And the same is true of the first segment of the montage, the single 'part' that comes from outside of Huillet and Straub's own *œuvre*. This is D. W. Griffith's short film *A Corner in Wheat* (1909), which plays in its entirety, and given its position within the series it can be said to act as a frame for the work as a whole. The film provides a demonstration, point for point, of Brecht's analysis of 'landownership' already mentioned and the politics of the 'right word'. Beginning and ending with shots of farmers at work on the land, seed being sown on tilled earth, the film presents the afterlife of this labour once subject to the vicissitudes of financial speculation in an age of monopoly capital by following the repercussions that result from a tycoon's manipulations in the wheat market: the price of flour sent soaring; further accumulation of riches for the speculators, further misery for those on the breadline; the link between land and labour broken as farmers return from market out of pocket; and finally, with 'control of the entire market of the world' achieved, the tycoon meeting an infelicitous end on a tour of a processing plant, 'drowned in a torrent of golden grain' as the title card states. In spite of all this, work on the land continues, as the film's final shot confirms.[14] In other words, the narrative's critical impetus is at one with the Brechtian postulate already mentioned: 'The population of an area of land has different, even opposing interests [...]. The people who draw the profits from the soil are not those who harvest the grain, and the scent of the clods of earth is unknown on the stock exchanges'. This is the antagonism that the film makes manifest, something already announced in the very title of Griffith's work, of particular importance here inasmuch as it concerns a certain way of organizing the relation of part and whole, understood as a fundamental tendency of capitalist economy. *A Corner in Wheat*: this of course refers to a situation of monopoly, the acquisition of a stake or share the size of which leaves an entire market subordinate to the interests of a single party. Part appropriates whole. And the same schema is replicated at the level of discourse. *A Corner of Wheat*: this figure of speech is a synecdoche, the part (the corner) standing in for the whole (the market). Here is Roland Barthes, in an essay on Brecht, making clear the politics implicit within this discursive strategy: 'Synecdoche is totalitarian: it is an act of force'. Why? Because 'the Whole is given, abusively, for the part', this part laying claim to the whole on its own terms alone, over and against any other claim.[15] This categorical arrangement once more reiterates the formal problem with which the representation of nature is compelled to negotiate, and given the prominent place it holds in the sequence, it can be said to provide the framework for understanding the 'proposition' that is then re-stated in each subsequent section of the film.

★　★　★　★　★

There is a further aspect of Simmel's understanding of landscape that requires consideration here. According to him, landscape is a modern phenomenon, a representational form that emerges under the specific set of conditions ushered in by modernity (conversely, the 'feeling for nature [*Naturgefühl*]' characteristic of the pre-modern has 'no awareness [*Gefühl*] of landscape').[16] Foremost amongst these conditions that Simmel calls modern is a tendency towards individualization, which sees human existence increasingly channelled through a model of subjectivity the principal feature of which is interiority or inwardness. For him landscape is the evidential sign of this historical development, a way of seeing that is necessarily tied to the individual understood in this sense. Interiority, never a visible dimension of landscape's field of vision, and only infrequently thematized there, would nevertheless be a constitutive structural feature of its form:

> For the essence of modernity is psychologism, in the sense of a way of experiencing and interpreting the world through inner reactions, indeed as an inner world. Modernity is the dissolution of firm contents in fluid elements of the soul, which itself has been purged of all substance and whose forms are pure forms of movement. [...] And it is why landscape painting, too, is the specifically modern accomplishment of painting as the expression of a particular *état d'âme*,

more evidently dispensing with firm logical structure in its use of color and framing than figure painting.[17]

'Mood', *Stimmung*, is the modality Simmel invokes in order to denote this phenomenon. The term encompasses both a disposition of the perceiving subject *and* an innate property of the physical arrangement being perceived: 'it is possible to refer to mood and the coming into being of landscape, that is, the forming of its individual parts into a whole, as one and the same act'.[18] There is no landscape without mood and yet mood has no general form, its manifestation is always untransferable and unrepeatable, it pertains 'to *just this* particular landscape and never to any other', writes Simmel, and it is on this basis that the subject is singled out individually, addressed in the isolation of self-containment.[19]

Now, it is precisely this distribution of categories that Huillet and Straub's filmic apparatus is constructed with a view to intervening in, their use of landscape laying claim to a fundamentally different model of subjectivation, the prevailing concern of which is not the individual but the collective (of course the latter's composition itself subject to much variation across the filmmakers' work). Crucial, then, is the uncoupling of landscape from the inner world of the individuated subject, since the expansion of this dimension is one way in which the conditions for collective forms of experience have found themselves increasingly nullified over the course of modernity, a tendency also noted by György Lukács in *The Theory of the Novel* (*Die Theorie des Romans*), in a manner that shares several points of convergence with Simmel's analysis: 'The autonomous life of interiority is possible and necessary only when the distinctions between men have made an unbridgeable chasm'.[20] How, then, is this reconfiguration of landscape and its frameworks undertaken by Huillet and Straub? By what means does their understanding of cinematic form lend itself to this task?

A response to these questions can be developed with reference to *Moses and Aaron*, the filmmakers' encounter with Schoenberg's unfinished opera, not least because, thematically and compositionally, the question of the collective is what is at stake in this work, a situation recognized by Theodor W. Adorno when he refers to 'the pathos of the music of *Moses und Aron*', in terms of an 'intensity [that] gives reality to a communal "we" at every moment, a collective consciousness that takes precedence over every individual feeling, something of the order of the togetherness of a congregation'.[21] Of particular interest here is the filmic interpretation of the first act's opening scene, the encounter staged between Moses and God, in which the former receives from the latter his calling (*Berufung*): to bring God's word before the chosen people (to constitute this people through this word).[22] From the outset, then, the *mise-en-scène* is concerned with the representation of a space insofar as this space is *sacred*, as the divine voice that first addresses Moses clearly establishes: 'Do not come any closer. Take off your sandals, for the place where you are standing is holy ground' (a citation of Exodus 3:5). A place is sacred inasmuch as its distinction sets it apart from every other place; said otherwise, it involves a determination of place once more conditioned by the work of the boundary. Huillet says as much in the 'Small Historical Excursus', a research document written in conjunction with the film, concerned with the material conditions and cultural practices of the Hebrew tribes in this period:

> When the people settled at the foot of the mountain of God, Moses received the order to set the limits all around the mountain (Exodus 19:12-13, 21-25). In order to understand the significance of this sacred enclosure for the Semites and the rites that were linked to it, it's not enough to imagine a private seat for God, his garden or his park; this place shouldn't be understood either according to current ideas of property but as a place where the radiance of the magical force of the sacred or of taboos is perceptible.[23]

The terrestrial manifestation of the divine is therefore tied to the work of *Abgrenzung* and the particular form of 'enclosure' with which this work is concerned. Regarding the film's own schematics on this count, of course the choice of shooting location, the amphitheatre of Alba Fucens, makes a contribution to establishing this principle of spatial containment.[24] But in the opening shot of the first act the dimensions of this setting are not yet discernible. The demarcation of limits needed to denote the sacred is therefore initially achieved through other means, namely, by the way in which the dramatic subject is positioned within filmic space. The scene opens from an elevated viewpoint, along a sightline that looks down onto Moses who is thereby shown in oblique profile, from behind, meaning his countenance cannot be seen directly, is inaccessible to the field of vision, even as his physical presence takes up the predominant share of the frame (Figure 2.1). His head initially bowed, it will then be raised with a slow, deliberate movement, coming to rest once his gaze has secured an upward trajectory.[25] Only then does Moses deliver his first words, in speech, not song: 'Unique, eternal, omnipresent, invisible and unrepresentable God'. Technically speaking, these words are imparted in the form of *apostrophe*, that figure of speech which addresses someone in their absence and therefore requires the 'turning away' — the meaning of 'apostrophe' — of the one who speaks. If Moses appears turned away or turned aside here, this is because the mode of address that the encounter demands of him dictates the way in which his comportment must be organized. This unconventional rotation of the axis by which he is situated in space relative to the cinematic frame is how the sacred nature of the terrain is first made legible.

As Moses delivers this address, gaze still fixed upwards and directed off-screen, his words are accompanied by a further gesture, a gradual raising of hands that are then brought down momentarily over the eyes as a shield, a gesture signifying that in the presence of this God, the gaze cannot act as a guide, it is as good as blind (Figure 2.2). With these words and this action the film is thereby placed under the sign of a presence that remains withdrawn from the order of visibility, a kind of absolute out-of-frame (and how to bring this presence before the people — through the naked immediacy of the word or through the mediation of the image — is of course what the dispute between Moses and Aaron consists in). The exchange continues, Moses voicing his resistance to what is being asked of him. And then the camera begins to move, so that for the first time in this scene the field of vision is modified at the level of the frame. Both the orientation and gradient of

FIG. 2.1. Danièle Huillet and Jean-Marie Straub, *Moses and Aaron*
(1975, courtesy of BELVA Film).

this movement follow the trajectory of Moses's line of sight, and because of this from the moment this movement begins it unsettles, insofar as the protention this movement harbours — that which, at any given moment, is not yet present at hand but is on the point of being so — concerns the unrepresentable itself. Once in motion the viewpoint first of all takes in a section of the arena's stonework and the parched vegetation that borders it, next a stratum of timeworn rockface, all the while rising incrementally, until it finds the upper verge of the enclosure, lined sparsely with trees, its movement now settling along this curving perimeter that henceforth forms a ribbon of matter along the frame's lower edge, earth and stone flecked with greenery, above which or behind which blue sky and dense cloud, white, then grey, growing denser as the sweep continues until, a little way short of completing a full rotation, it alights upon a mountain formation in the far distance, two distinct peaks, joined — or separated — by a plateau running between them, an arrangement that stands for Mount Sinai (Monte Velino in reality), and with this viewpoint achieved the opening scene comes to a close.

This extraordinary movement, one of the great acts of *Abgrenzung* in Huillet and Straub's *œuvre*, engenders a landscape the compositional rule of which could be considered 'disorientation'. For Jean-François Lyotard, such *dépaysement* is in fact landscape's constitutive feature. 'This estrangement [*dépaysement*] is absolute', he writes in 'Scapeland', his short study of landscape (*paysage*):

> It is the implosion of forms themselves, and forms are mind. A landscape is a mark, and it (but not the mark it makes and leaves) should be thought of, not as an inscription, but as the erasure of a support.[26]

In the scene in question, this sudden absence of ground, the 'vanishing of a standpoint', is precisely what the upward drift of the camera achieves, all the more

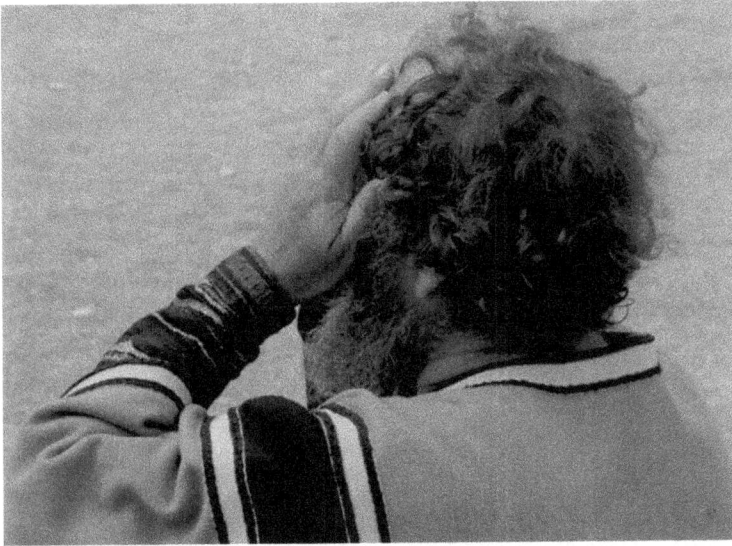

FIG. 2.2. Danièle Huillet and Jean-Marie Straub, *Moses and Aaron*
(1975, courtesy of BELVA Film).

so because the further this movement progresses, the more difficult it is to situate
its course in relation to the little square of earth from which it initially took its
leave and to which it in principle still remains tied, given that the pan has taken
place in a single continuous motion, without the interruption of a cut. This has
a further disorienting effect: delineated through the tracing of this unbroken arc,
the resulting landscape is left to manifest *successively*, across variable depths of field,
making it a composite the parts of which are always contiguous and yet never
present to one another as a totality. In an interview of 1974 Straub explains that
the schema of this structure was the result of a specific reading of the original
opera: whereas Schoenberg envisaged staging the work through a principle of
simultaneity, meaning each scenic arrangement would harbour several courses of
action undertaken at the same time within a single field of vision, the filmmakers
conscientiously supplanted this principle with another, that of succession. An act of
demystification, Straub says, inasmuch as it contests the possibility of representing
divine presence in its immediacy. But in the context under discussion here, this
formal move from simultaneity to succession also has concrete implications for the
determination of landscape: it means, for instance, that the burning bush, the token
of presence from which the divine voice issues in this episode, is not confined to a
single form, but instead appears as though relayed through the metonymic chain of
terms established by the pan. As Straub put it: 'the bush transforms itself. There are
the sky, the rocks, and the mountain'.[27] 'Landscape' here consists in the movement
that passes along the terms of this series, terms that belong to the series only on
account of this movement.

Disorientation, *dépaysement*, has at least one further source in this scene. What
the encounter between God and Moses also brings to the fore is an irreducible gap

between vision and speech, the gaze and the voice, inasmuch as the divine presence must remain withdrawn from the field of visibility — recall that when Moses asks God to appear before him, he is met with the following response, 'Thou canst not see my face: for there shall no man see me, and live' (Exodus 33:20). The encounter with God therefore casts the gaze and the voice in a relation of mutual exclusion, so that their respective spheres, whilst always co-present to one another, are at the same time fundamentally dissociated, without a common frame or a possible point of intersection. Huillet and Straub organize the cinematic frame in recognition of this situation. For instance, when the divine voice addresses Moses in frame, the space from which this voice issues is not an out-of-frame contiguous with the field of vision; it is, with respect to this field, on screen or off, always elsewhere. In 'Speaking is Not Seeing', a canonical treatment of this thesis, Maurice Blanchot writes the following:

> This is sight's wisdom, though we never see only one thing, even two or several, but a whole: every view is a general view. It is still true that sight holds us within the limits of a horizon. Perception is a wisdom rooted in the ground [sol] and standing fixed in the direction of the opening; it is of the land [paysanne], in the proper sense of the term: planted in the earth and forming a link between the immobile boundary and the apparently boundless horizon — a firm pact from which comes peace. For sight, speech is war and madness. The terrifying word passes over every limit and even the limitlessness of the whole: it seizes the thing from a direction from which it is not taken, not seen, and will never be seen; it transgresses laws, breaks away from orientation, it disorients.[28]

The 'wisdom of sight', derived through a stance or a standing that makes of the earth a foundation or a ground: this is the wisdom that Moses finds himself suddenly deprived of by the calling. His ordeal is the giving way of ground in this sense, an uprooting. After the camera begins its upward drift, quickly leaving Moses out of frame, what makes the movement so vertiginous is that its passage across the field of vision no longer appears connected to or conditioned by the co-ordinates that organize the field; instead the gaze is carried by a voice that reaches it from an absolute outside, having traversed an untraversable interval: 'The terrifying word passes over every limit and even the limitlessness of the whole', in Blanchot's provocative phrase. This is how the divine voice must be heard when it sings these words in the initial passage of the pan — 'As from this thorn bush, dark, ere the light of truth fell upon it, so wilt thou perceive my voice from every thing' — and that this voice is arranged as a chorus heightens the disorientation still, scattering its source across manifold points.

If the gaze is indeed drawn along by the voice here, leaving it to pass along sightlines unaligned with the recognized channels of the visual order, this perhaps accounts for a further disconcerting effect produced by this shot: always in clear and determinate focus, at the same time what is picked out by the pan can appear as if momentarily unbound by the strictures of its given form, manifesting instead as a concentrate of material in open flux. This is what Lyotard means when he insists that the disorientation of landscape is tied to 'the implosion of forms'. On the other side of this implosion lie the 'many untameable states of matter': 'It is a question of

MATTER. Matter is that element in the datum which has no destiny... Landscape as a place without a DESTINY'.[29]

But to reiterate, the point of departure for all this is Moses, Moses insofar as his calling has compelled him *to turn away*. The camera's subsequent movement and the landscape engendered through this movement are one with this turning. No doubt, then, this is a landscape that maintains a relation to the individual as a constitutive point of reference. And yet the individual is treated here in highly specific terms. The moment Moses appears in frame, countenance turned aside, his bearing is organized so as to preclude the possibility of interiority. There is no sense of 'absorption' here, his outer bearing is not a means of expressing an internal state.[30] The one who turns away is first and foremost turned away from himself. 'One of the characteristic traits of this experience,' Blanchot writes, 'is that it cannot be assumed by the one to whom it happens, by a subject in the first person'.[31] This is what the idiomatic arrangement of Moses's physical presence testifies to, and its achievement, formally speaking, is the nullification of the individual's inner space. Interiority is not the correlate of the landscape brought into view here, one sign of which is the uncanny absence of 'mood' that persists throughout the scene. Instead, turning away is what opens up the passage along which Moses will approach the people to be constituted through God's word. As Straub insists repeatedly, the pan *is* this people. This people are what the pan announces.[32] On this account, landscape and the collective find themselves drawn together in one and the same configuration, nature once more staged as *res publica*, 'geology mixed with human history'.[33] And the means by which this association is forged here in the opening scene of *Moses and Aaron* is precisely through this figure of turning away: a manner of speaking, a mode of embodiment, a principle of movement. Huillet and Straub's use of landscape is always tied to a figure in this sense, a figure that, given every landscape implies a 'unique, characterizing detachment', is itself always singular. To reconstruct the workings of each figure in its context is to ascertain the ways in which nature variously appears in their films, traversed by the dominations and resistances of political struggle.

Notes to Chapter 2

1. Simmel, 'The Philosophy of Landscape', p. 21.
2. Ibid., pp. 21-22. In this essay, terms have been added in the original language for clarification as needed.
3. Georg Simmel, 'The Picture Frame: An Aesthetic Study', trans. by Mark Ritter, *Theory, Culture and Society*, 11.1 (1994), 11-17 (p. 14).
4. Ibid., p. 12.
5. Simmel, 'The Philosophy of Landscape', p. 22.
6. Ibid., p. 23. My emphasis.
7. See, for example, Jean-Marie Straub, 'Introduction to Nestler', in Straub and Huillet, *Writings*, pp. 99-101 (p. 100).
8. Mikhail Lylov and Elke Marhöfer, 'A Thousand Cliffs' [interview with Jean-Marie Straub], in *Tell It to the Stones*, ed. by Busch and Hering, pp. 364-90 (pp. 368-69).
9. Danièle Huillet, 'How to "Correct" Nostalgia', in Straub and Huillet, *Writings*, pp. 188-90 (p. 188).

10. Lylov and Marhöfer, 'A Thousand Cliffs', p. 369.

11. Bertolt Brecht, 'Five Difficulties in Writing the Truth', in *Brecht on Art and Politics*, pp. 141-57 (p. 149).

12. Gilles Deleuze, *Cinema 2: The Time Image*, trans. by Hugh Tomlinson and Robert Galeta (London: Athlone Press, 1989), pp. 254-56.

13. Lylov and Marhöfer, 'A Thousand Cliffs', pp. 367, 385. Serge Daney's review of the film also foregrounds this idea: 'If there is an actor in *Too Early, Too Late*, it's the landscape. This actor has a text to recite: History (the peasants who resist, the land which remains), of which it is the living witness': 'Cinemeteorology', in *The Cinema of Jean-Marie Straub and Daniele [sic] Huillet* (Film at the Public brochure, 1982), p. 19 <https://www.straub-huillet.com/wp-content/uploads/2016/05/brochure-cinema1.pdf> [accessed 20 December 2021].

14. For an informative reading of this film, including Huillet and Straub's interest in Griffith's work (albeit without any mention of their direct engagement with it in *Proposition in Four Parts*), see Erik Ulman, '*A Corner in Wheat*: An Analysis', *Senses of Cinema*, 14 (2001) <https://www.sensesofcinema.com/2001/feature-articles/cornerwheat/#11> [accessed 20 December 2021].

15. Roland Barthes, 'Brecht and Discourse: A Contribution to the Study of Discursivity', in *The Rustle of Language*, trans. by Richard Howard (Berkeley: University of California Press, 1989), pp. 212-22 (p. 218).

16. Simmel, 'The Philosophy of Landscape', p. 22.

17. Georg Simmel, 'Auguste Rodin: Part II', in *Essays on Art and Aesthetics*, ed. and trans. by Austin Harrington (Chicago & London: University of Chicago Press, 2020), pp. 309-18 (pp. 317-18). Josef Bleicher, in his translator's introduction to Simmel's essay on landscape, foregrounds this same passage (Simmel, 'The Philosophy of Landscape', p. 20).

18. Simmel, 'The Philosophy of Landscape', p. 29.

19. Ibid. p. 28. This relational structure is also central to Denis E. Cosgrove's account of landscape's development: Denis E. Cosgrove, *Social Formation and Symbolic Landscape* (Madison: University of Wisconsin Press, 1998), p. 27.

20. György Lukács, *The Theory of the Novel: A Historico-philosophical Essay on the Forms of Great Epic Literature*, trans. by Anna Bostock (London: Merlin Press, 1978), p. 66.

21. Theodor W. Adorno, 'Sacred Fragment: Schoenberg's *Moses und Aron*', in *Quasi una Fantasia: Essays on Modern Music*, trans. by Rodney Livingstone (London & New York: Verso, 1998), pp. 225-48 (p. 228).

22. This scene has of course attracted significant critical attention: essential points of reference here are Benoît Turquety, 'Power of Speech (or the Voice), of Seeing and the Path: *Moses And Aaron*', in *Danièle Huillet, Jean-Marie Straub*, trans. by Fendt, pp. 71-125; and Ute Holl, 'Caesuras: Cinematic Procedures', in *The Moses Complex: Freud, Schoenberg, Straub/Huillet*, trans. by Michael Turnbull (Zurich & Berlin: *Diaphanes*, 2017), pp. 179-278.

23. Danièle Huillet, 'Small Historical Excursus', in Straub and Huillet, *Writings*, pp. 161-76 (pp. 168-69).

24. An overview of the historical contexts that shape this setting can be found in Jacques Aumont, 'The Invention of Place: Danièle Huillet and Jean-Marie Straub's *Moses and Aaron*', trans. by Kevin Shelton and Martin Lefebvre, in *Landscape and Film*, ed. by Martin Lefebvre (London & New York: Routledge, 2006), pp. 1-18 (pp. 3-4).

25. The gesture appears in keeping with Kant's understanding of 'the idea of God's sublimity': 'It seems that in religion in general,' he writes, 'the only fitting behavior in the presence of the deity is prostration, worship with bowed head'; the adoption of this posture in supplication gives the body its proper form, as an indication of God's might. But at the same time this submission should never give way to fear of any kind; instead it must form the basis of an attunement (*Stimmung*) that prepares the stance by which God may be met on his own terms, as it were: that is, the worshipper must 'recognize in his own attitude a sublimity that conforms to God's will'. See Immanuel Kant, *Critique of Judgment*, trans. by Werner S. Pluhar (Indianapolis & Cambridge: Hackett, 1987), pp. 122-23. These are the two dispositions that the transition from head bowed to head raised encompasses.

26. Jean-François Lyotard, 'Scapeland', in *The Inhuman: Reflections on Time*, trans. by Geoffrey

Bennington and Rachel Bowlby (Stanford, CA: Stanford University Press, 1991), pp. 182-90 (p. 189).

27. Joel Rogers, 'Jean-Marie Straub and Danièle Huillet Interviewed: *Moses and Aaron* as an object of Marxist reflection', *Jump Cut*, 12-13 (1976), 61-64 <https://www.ejumpcut.org/archive/onlinessays/jc12–13folder/moses.int.html> [accessed 20 December 2021].

28. Maurice Blanchot, 'Speaking is Not Seeing', in *The Infinite Conversation*, trans. by Susan Hanson (Minneapolis & London: University of Minnesota Press, 1993), pp. 25-32 (p. 28).

29. Lyotard, 'Scapeland', in *The Inhuman*, pp. 185-86, 183.

30. Of course, this is Michael Fried's term, a mode of pictorial representation the function of which is tied to a 'capacity for inwardness': Michael Fried, *Absorption and Theatricality: Painting and Beholder in the Age of Diderot* (Chicago: University of Chicago Press, 1976), p. 41.

31. Blanchot, 'The Most Profound Question', in *The Infinite Conversation*, p. 24.

32. See Rogers, 'Jean-Marie Straub and Danièle Huillet Interviewed', for example.

33. Huillet, 'How to "Correct" Nostalgia', in Straub and Huillet, *Writings*, pp. 188-90 (p. 189).

❖

CHAPTER 3

The Incarnation of Language in Quotation: The Böll and Bruckner Films of Huillet and Straub

Martin Brady

> Not a so-called 'adaptation' of the novel. And we didn't ask the
> actors to 'perform' their text in any particular way, but 'to recite it',
> like a very precise score.
> — JEAN-MARIE STRAUB[1]

Words Incarnate

Near the beginning of his 1966 essay 'Transparencies on Film', Theodor W. Adorno claims that 'to the extent that a film is realistic, the semblance of immediacy cannot be avoided' and notes the way in which 'phrases justified by the diction of narrative which distinguishes them from the false everydayness of mere reportage, sound pompous and inauthentic in film'. As an example he cites the dialogue in Volker Schlöndorff's recently premiered Robert Musil adaptation *Young Törless* (*Der junge Törless*, 1966) and goes on to suggest that immediacy, in the form of 'improvisation which systematically surrenders itself to unguided chance', might offer a solution to the problem of literary adaptation.[2] With reference to three early German-language films of Danièle Huillet and Jean-Marie Straub — *Machorka-Muff* (1963), *Not Reconciled, or Only Violence Helps Where Violence Rules* (1965), and *The Bridegroom, the Actress and the Pimp* (1968) — this essay will argue that the very artificiality castigated by Adorno is not only translated into a theory and practice of quotation and textual embodiment in the cinema of Straub-Huillet, but also thereby elevated to the status of an aesthetic and political programme. As will also become apparent, 'unguided chance' plays a part in this process, but not in the way envisaged by Adorno.

Discussing how actors function in their Böll adaptations, Straub, in interview with Michel Delahaye for *Cahiers du cinéma* in 1966, used the metaphor of a tight-rope walker on the verge of falling, with the text as the rope, adding that this tightrope walker is also a somnambulist.[3] According to Straub, actors in their films become living embodiments of the text, which they deliver as an unconscious reflex action: pure incarnate or embodied word ('pur verbe incarné'), not as part of a greater fictional narrative, but as pure text and lived experience.[4] Text delivery is thus an existential and political encounter between actor and text. Describing the conspicuously mechanical performance of Heinrich Hargesheimer playing Heinrich Fähmel at eighty in *Not Reconciled*, Straub concluded that the actor 'attains a certain automatism, a certain mechanical quality [*mécanisme*]. It is inside this mechanism [...] that the old man comes to be simply human and reveals himself. [...] At this moment, he is nothing less than an incarnation of language'.[5] Straub's terminology seems to echo quite strikingly Jean-Paul Sartre's description in *Being and Nothingness* (*L'Être et le néant*) of the bad faith ('mauvaise foi') of the waiter with his mechanical movements and voice: 'He applies himself to chaining his movements as if they were mechanisms, the one regulating the other; his gestures and even his voice seem to be mechanisms'.[6] As we shall see, however, for Huillet and Straub the mechanical quality of the actor's performance is, unlike the automatism of the waiter, an instance of *bonne foi*, liberating both existentially and politically.

This essay will also consider how the early films of Straub-Huillet occupy a position that is, in its embrace of theology and mysticism alongside Marxism, in many ways closer to Walter Benjamin than Bertolt Brecht, despite the conspicuous and readily acknowledged debt to the latter. It will also consider how Huillet and Straub's early adaptations are constructed as constellations — 'through the way in which individual shots are joined up, just like words', as Straub put it at the time — and relate their practice to the history of modernist, specifically Brechtian and Benjaminian, citation.[7] 'It is precisely the innovators who will expropriate', Brecht claimed in around 1940.[8] This essay will demonstrate some of the ways in which Straub-Huillet's citational practice, already fully developed in their first films, gives voice not only to the actors and the texts they recite, but also to the directors themselves.

Not Reconciled

It is not only the protagonist of Straub-Huillet's second Heinrich Böll adaptation who is, in his own words, 'not reconciled'.[9] The same can be said of the film's relationship with its source material. Whilst Böll's 1959 novel *Billiards at Half-Past Nine* (*Billard um halbzehn*) is a meticulously constructed and straightforwardly decipherable historical narrative, the film is, as noted by its first, frequently hostile, reviewers, closer to a deconstruction of both its source text and the history it addresses. The film's programme, which I would argue remained consistent through to the last films of Straub alone, is introduced at the opening of *Not Reconciled* first as theory and second as practice.

First, the protracted opening credits, which roll over memorial sculptures for five victims of the Gestapo and the Cologne dead of World War Two, end with a quotation from Brecht's short essay of around 1940, 'Instructions to Actors': 'Instead of wanting to create the impression that he is improvising, the actor should rather show what the truth is: he is quoting' (Figure 3.1).[10] Before we hear a word from Böll we read Brecht, accompanied by the opening of the first movement of Béla

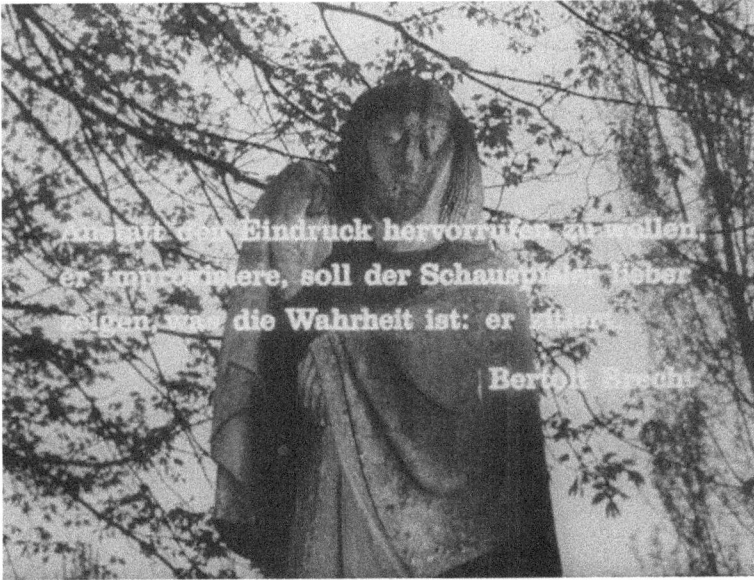

FIG. 3.1. Danièle Huillet and Jean-Marie Straub, *Not Reconciled*
(1965, courtesy of BELVA Film).

Bartók's 1937 Sonata for Two Pianos and Percussion, composed during the decade
in which the film's central narrative events unfold and thus itself an historical
document. Brecht's injunction on citational performance serves as a programme
for *Not Reconciled* with its Brechtian estrangement, not only in the casting, acting,
and delivery of the text, but also in the *mise-en-scène*, cinematography, editing,
music, and use of documentary archive footage and back projection. The principle
underpinning all of these estrangement devices is, as Walter Benjamin notes in
his essays on Brecht's epic theatre, the 'interruption of processes' which, in turn,
is itself inextricably bound up with the principle of cinematic montage: 'Epic
Theatre proceeds by fits and starts, in a manner comparable to the images on a
film strip. Its basic form is that of the forceful impact [*des Choks*] on one another of
separate, sharply distinct situations in the play'.[11] It is in this context that Benjamin
underscores the relationship between interruption and quotation: 'One can expand
here on this point and reflect that the interruption is a fundamental principle
common to all processes of formation. It is to be found in contexts beyond art itself.
To take just one example, it is fundamental to quotation'.[12]

Second, immediately following the theoretical statement of Brechtian intent at
the end of the credits, the narrative proper begins abruptly in the year 1958, although
this is not signalled to the audience, with just three words extracted from the third
chapter of the novel: 'Tell what, boy?'.[13] This opening scene of the story (shot 2) in
which, as it later transpires, the protagonist Robert Fähmel is playing billiards in a
Cologne hotel watched by a fourteen-year-old hotel boy (Hugo), begins *in medias
res* and lasts a bewilderingly brief four seconds. It is followed by the first shot of the
second scene (shot 3), set on the banks of the Rhine almost a quarter of a century

earlier in Summer 1934, although the flashback is not signalled in the way it is in the novel, where there is a transitional passage in which the narrator reflects on the workings of memory and the passage of time.

This single example from the opening of the film demonstrates the method employed by Huillet and Straub throughout *Not Reconciled*: small fragments are extracted from the various historical threads of the novel — late Imperial Germany before and during the First World War, the Third Reich, the Federal Republic of the late 1950s — and montaged together with flashbacks across a single day in Autumn 1958. However, these elliptical flashbacks are not generally announced by changes in location, costume, or even actors; the boy playing the hotel boy Hugo in 1958, for example, is also the schoolboy Ferdi in 1934. Adopting a term frequently used by Straub himself to describe the film at the time of its release, Richard Roud summarized *Not Reconciled* as follows: 'Straub has constructed his "lacunary body" where time has been, as it were, flattened out, and distant past, recent time, present, and even future all co-exist'.[14] It might be more accurate to state that the chronology of the story has, in the terminology used by Benjamin in his essay 'Theses on the Philosophy of History', been exploded into a constellation (or configuration) of fragments. In effect *Not Reconciled* is a series of arrests:

> Materialist historiography [...] is based on a constructive principle. Thinking involves not only the flow of thoughts, but their arrest as well. Where thinking suddenly stops in a configuration pregnant with tensions, it gives that configuration a shock, by which it crystallizes into a monad. A historical materialist approaches a historical subject only where he encounters it as a monad. In this structure he recognizes the sign of a messianic cessation of happening, or, put differently, a revolutionary chance in the fight for the oppressed past.[15]

According to Benjamin, positive potentialities of the past that were not realized at the time can only become productive in the present and for the future when they become 'citable'.[16] This is the spirit in which Huillet and Straub approached Böll's novel when they came to film it in 1965 — as a source of material to be quoted. In its politics and methodology, their filmmaking is strikingly close to Benjamin's materialist historiographical practice.[17]

It is the implied 'progress principle' of Böll's novel which Huillet and Straub attempt to overthrow in their adaptation. Although the prismatic narrative of Böll's novel exhibits on the surface the influence of the modernist French *nouveau roman* of the 1950s (Robbe-Grillet is generally cited as a source), *Billiards at Half-Past Nine* is in fact a relatively straightforward historical novel in which the author is, as Roud put it, 'careful to prepare the reader for the time-shifts' with all the leaps back and forth carefully 'explained'.[18] It unravels into what Benjamin, in his history essay, rather scornfully refers to as the 'rosary' of conventional historiography.[19] The reader-friendly construction and signalling of Böll's novel and the narrative thread of the conventional historian are absent from *Not Reconciled*.

In summary, *Not Reconciled* is a prototypical exercise in Brechtian filmmaking and is militantly realist in the sense of being both concrete and abidingly epic. As Brecht put it in a passage first quoted by Straub in a 1965 typescript entitled 'On

Not Reconciled' and subsequently cited by him in numerous interviews: 'To dig out the truth from the rubble of the self-evident, to make a marked link between the specific and the general, to capture the particular within a general process, that is the art of the realists'.[20] It was to define realist filmmaking — specifically their own Böll adaptations — that Straub, in the interview with Delahaye already quoted, coined the term 'document-fiction', film as a documentation of fictional material.[21] Whilst Roud goes so far as to claim in his seminal study that Straub-Huillet treat literature purely as 'documentary raw material',[22] Straub himself later asserted, rather more soberly, that Böll's texts were, amongst other things, principally valuable as 'sociological documents'.[23]

Before turning to the apotheosis of the 'document-fiction' method, *The Bridegroom, the Actress and the Pimp*, it is important to consider Straub's notion of text as 'language incarnate' in *Not Reconciled*.

Excursus: Incarnation

Benjamin's 'rosary' analogy in the history essay and Straub's discussion of 'incarnation' with Delahaye demonstrate, I would suggest, not simply a chance terminological correspondence, but a common interest in matters both theological and mystical, one that has frequently been highlighted in commentaries on Benjamin, but largely ignored in discussions of Huillet and Straub, although it is pertinent, for example, to Straub's solo films *O somma luce* (2010) and *Jackals and Arabs* (2011). There is a striking resemblance between the messianic rhetoric of Benjamin's essay — what Brecht in a journal entry termed its 'Judaisms' — and Straub's discussion of the actors as 'words incarnate' in the interview with Delahaye and elsewhere.[24] As will become clear in the commentary on *The Bridegroom* that follows, this mysticism is not restricted to Straub's rhetoric, but is also to be found in their choice of text and music and even the cinematography of their early films.

In her study of Benjamin's unfinished *Arcades Project* Susan Buck-Morss dedicates a chapter to the question of theology. The *Arcades Project*, she contends, has to be understood within the framework of its 'theological armature', not least in its basic premise that truth is to be found in things, which she construes as typical of Kabbalistic thought.[25] In discussing the importance of the Kabbalah for Benjamin's philosophy, Buck-Morss notes that 'for the Kabbalists words have a mystical significance', not least in the context of a prelapsarian 'Adamic language of names' in which there is 'no gap between word and referent'.[26] In elucidating the Kabbalistic paradoxes that underpin Benjamin's engagement with existing texts, his extensive deployment of quotation that is, she notes:

> The paradox: one cannot interpret the truth of present reality without past texts, but this reality transforms radically the way these texts are read. The result is that 'old combinations will be interpreted in an entirely new way,' as traditional symbols demonstrate 'their explosive power in shattering tradition'. In short, the Kabbalah reveres the past in order to break from it.[27]

These ideas are strikingly close to the terms in which Straub frames the relationship between text and actor in the 1966 interview with Delahaye. According to Straub, as already noted, the actors become one with the words they (re)cite in a quasi-somnambulant synergy of performer and text, an encounter that seems, on the face of it, to be diametrically opposed to Brechtian estrangement with its injunction that the drama be delivered, in accordance with the principles of epic theatre, 'in the third person'. However, the synergy described by Straub is one which, paradoxically, also involves detachment in the sense that the performer becomes oblivious to the text they are delivering. This is the *bonne foi* I referred to at the beginning of this essay.

In the Delahaye interview Straub describes the synergy of Heinrich Hargesheimer and the text he recites at Denklingen railway station (in shot 118) — his favourite scene in the film he claims — in the following terms:

> It is obvious that this is only possible because the text is an integral part of himself. At that moment, he is nothing other than a kind of embodied word, and, although the text is initially something foreign to him, in spite of this and also precisely because of it, he coincides with this word at the point of arrival.[28]

In the process the old man, the non-professional actor Hargesheimer rather than the character he is playing, 'reveals his secret' according to Straub.[29] It is hard to imagine Brecht making a claim of this kind or using such terminology. In a contemporary interview for the German journal *Filmstudio*, in which he discusses the same scene in almost identical terms, Straub claims that it is as if Hargesheimer:

> might die in front of the camera. [...] Text and framing are really just obstructions on the way to freedom and immediacy. For me the text — I want to emphasize this — is a rope on which the somnambulists were expected to walk; that's why we get the impression that the actors could break their necks at any moment.[30]

The text delivered by the actor is thus essentially a means to an end. As Straub says in the same interview, fending off the frequent objection that the spoken text is at times inaudible in *Not Reconciled* (most notably on the steps descending from the railway bridge in shot 8), 'It isn't a matter of understanding every word. The atmosphere is more important than the meaning of the words', before supporting his claim with a quotation he credits to Bresson: 'When you speak in life, you don't think about the meaning of each word. You string words together like you string beads together to make a necklace'.[31]

It is telling that Straub should cite Bresson in this context, as there is an unmistakable parallel between Straub's remarks on somnambulism and Bresson's notes 'On Automatism' in *Notes on the Cinematographer* (*Notes sur le cinématographe*). Bresson's thoughts are dated 1950-58 in the published collection, and include the following observation which resonates particularly closely with Straub's comments on shot 18 of *Not Reconciled*:

> Models who have become automatic (everything weighed, measured, timed, repeated ten, twenty times) and are then dropped in the medium of the events of your film — their relations with the objects and persons around them will be *right*, because they will not be *thought*.[32]

In *The Intervals of Cinema* Jacques Rancière discusses how the individual actor in Bresson's *Mouchette*, premiered two years after *Not Reconciled*, expresses 'his inner truth, as opposed to his conscious thought' and the way in which the film:

> Fabricates through repetition of words and movements a material automatism intended to awaken another: the unfabricated automaton, the inner automaton whose movements no one can programme and which, if deprived of all outlets, must behave in sole accordance with the truth of its being.[33]

This is very close to Straub's notion, articulated in the 1966 interview with Delahaye, that the text functions as a straitjacket out of which, or perhaps better through which, the actor 'gives himself away' ('se trahit').[34] For Rancière, this technique affords 'a special vibration to the very dullness of "expressionless" speech', i.e. to the artificiality that was lamented by Adorno in 'Transparencies on Film' and is consistently exploited by Huillet and Straub within what is, as Rancière readily acknowledges, a fundamentally 'Brechtian paradigm'.[35]

Atmosphere, secrets, somnambulism, automatism, incarnation, beads — to which one could add the almost ecstatic, enraptured pan and fade from treetops to white screen, held for twenty-six seconds and accompanied by the music of Johann Sebastian Bach in the final moments of the film (shot 164). It should really come as no surprise that Straub claimed that *Not Reconciled*, for all its Brechtian realism, was 'a kind of mystery' ('Mysterium').[36] In a substantial interview four decades later with François Albera at the Centre Pompidou, Straub was to make very much the same claim: whilst 'political films start with realism' there is 'no political film without theology, there is no political film without mysticism' (see also Chapter 9).[37] Theology he adds, when pressed on the matter by Albera, 'has to do with God or the gods' and 'helping people to shun phoney feelings, the practice of sentimentality and piety' before going on to reiterate that 'what interests us is how the text is embodied in human beings'.[38] The consistency of thinking from 1965 to 2001 (and beyond) is remarkable and demonstrates that Huillet and Straub's programme, for all the obvious similarities, connections, and correspondences, is very different from that of Brecht. In a discussion in 1934 with Benjamin about Kafka, Brecht expressed his frustration with any discussion of depth — describing much of Kafka's writing as 'pure mystification', 'nonsense', 'rubbish and waste'[39] — a frustration that resurfaces in his 1941 journal entry already cited, where he speaks disparagingly of Benjamin's theological inclinations, his Judaisms, and 'use of metaphor' ('Metaphorik').[40] Benjamin, for his part, notes in his journal that he rounded off the 1934 discussion on Kafka by asserting that it was his custom to 'delve into the depths'. The same, surely, can be said of Straub-Huillet and it is here that one can identify the limits of their Brechtianism. It is, therefore, hardly surprising that Huillet, in the same interview with Albera already quoted, voices her frustration at being labelled Brechtian: 'quite frankly all the stuff about the alienation effect and so on is pretty silly! There can be no film in which the text is more a part of the people than our films!'.[41] As Straub explains in his 2013 interview published in *Tell It to the Stones*, the Anglo-American notion of 'alienation' is misleading, what Brechtian *Verfremdung* is about is 'making strange' (see also the interview with Huillet and Straub in this volume, Chapter II). What is particularly striking about the notion of 'making strange' in the work of Huillet and Straub, and what distinguishes it from Brecht's own more instrumental deployment of *Verfremdung*, is that their estrangement is not merely a stepping-stone to clarification and enlightenment: a residue of strangeness — mystery, mysticism, or rapture — remains.

Profane Illumination: *The Bridegroom, the Actress and the Pimp*

Benjamin's term *'profane illumination'*, as used in his essay on surrealism, goes some way to clarifying the position of Straub-Huillet between Marx and mysticism.[42] It also sheds light on Straub's claim that it is precisely their most 'mystical' or 'theological' film, *The Bridegroom, the Actress and the Pimp* — which brings together St John of the Cross, Bach's *Ascension Oratorio*, a Jesuit mass, and what Martin Walsh in his book on Brechtian cinema termed 'near-mystical' landscape imagery[43] — that is one of their 'most political films', alongside *Chronicle of Anna Magdalena Bach* (1968) and *Moses and Aaron* (1975).[44]

Straub-Huillet's short black and white thriller is, in the words of Gilberto Perez, a 'document of documents', an assemblage of quotations, allusions, translations, and caesuras.[45] For Richard Roud it is their 'most lyrical, most moving' and 'most mysterious' film.[46] It consists of a mere twelve shots divided into six episodes — Straub compared them to the Six Bagatelles, Op. 9 of Anton Webern — of unequal length.[47] The first is a static shot of hand-written or scratched graffiti, in English, including the lines 'stupid | old Germany | I hate it over here | I hope I can go soon | Patricia | 1.3.68' (Figure 3.2); the second is a slow drive along the Munich

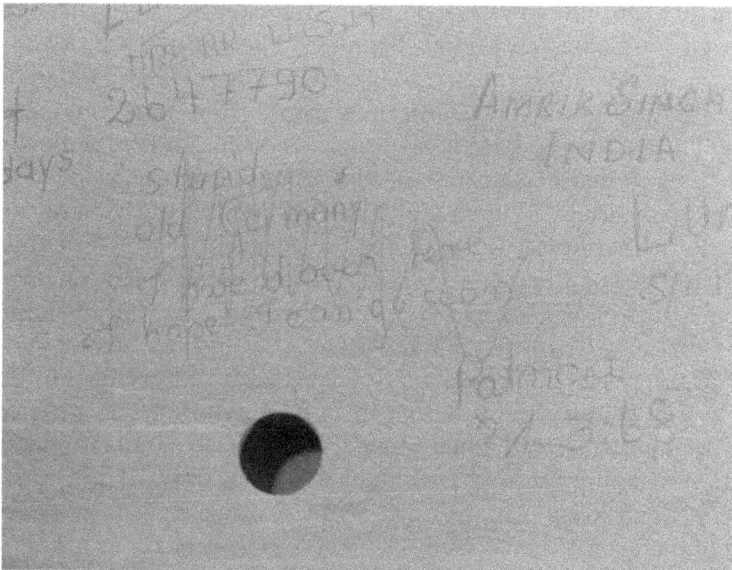

FIG. 3.2. Danièle Huillet and Jean-Marie Straub, *The Bridegroom, the Actress and the Pimp* (1968, courtesy of BELVA Film).

FIG. 3.3. Danièle Huillet and Jean-Marie Straub, *The Bridegroom, the Actress and the Pimp* (1968, courtesy of BELVA Film).

Landsbergerstraße at night with prostitutes waiting in the rain for customers accompanied, following two minutes of silence, by an extract from Johann Sebastian Bach's *Ascension Oratorio* ('Laud to God in all his Kingdoms', BWV 11); the third is a ten-minute, fixed, single-take recording of Straub's production of his own digest of Ferdinand Bruckner's 1926 play *Sickness of Youth* in the Munich action-theater; the fourth is a five-shot car chase sequence; the fifth a Catholic wedding ceremony between the black man (James) and the white woman (Lilith) seen in the opening shot of the car chase; the sixth sees the married couple arrive by car at a suburban semi-detached house and, after reciting to each other extracts of poems by St John of the Cross (Figure 3.3), enter to find the pimp from the play (played by Rainer Werner Fassbinder) waiting for them with a gun. The wife shoots the pimp and moves to the window and the final image of the film shows trees in a garden swaying in the wind and rain, accompanied by the last lines of the wife's recitation and the final bars of the *Ascension Oratorio*.

Despite the film's heterogeneity it is possible, even on a single viewing, to discern a number of simple, over-arching formal and narrative structures which challenge the dissociation implied by the term 'bagatelle': there is, for example, a gradual but inexorable progression from dark to light and from prostitution to emancipation. The film is also structured dialectically: initially unrelated material and ideas of diverse origin — too numerous and complex to untangle in detail here — are drawn together by explicit or implicit connections to the film's nucleus, Bruckner's *Sickness of Youth*.[48] The construction of the film as a whole is similar to Straub's characterization of his digest of Bruckner's drama as a series of 'constellations, people who have certain relations with each other which dissolve and reappear.

FIG. 3.4. Danièle Huillet and Jean-Marie Straub, *The Bridegroom, the Actress and the Pimp* (1968, courtesy of BELVA Film).

Nothing more'.[49] The process of compressing the play, reducing it to a sequence of quotations from the original, may have provided Straub-Huillet with their method for assembling the film itself. *The Bridegroom* sets out in an exemplary, even didactic way the components of their 'document-fiction' methodology; the fictional source material (*Sickness of Youth* and the filmmakers' own prostitution-marriage-and-murder scenario) serves as a pretext and context for the documentary material: the graffiti, the prostitutes, a Mao Zedong quote painted on the back wall of the action-theater stage (probably lifted from the journal *Der Spiegel*, Figure 3.4), the ritual and wording of the Catholic wedding, and so forth.[50]

Quotation is the key to the political dimension of *The Bridegroom*; as Jean-Claude Biette put it in his brief review of the film for *Cahiers du cinéma*: 'Straub's film is a systematic exploration of the power of quotation and its multiple meanings'.[51] Benjamin describes the violence involved in citation: 'To write history thus means to *cite* history. It belongs to the concept of citation, however, that the historical object in each case is torn from its context'.[52] Shot 1 quotes Patricia's graffiti, shot 2 documents four minutes and twenty-three seconds in the life of Munich's red-light district, shot 3 consists of 150 brief quotations from Bruckner's play, none longer than thirty-six words, shots 4–8 quote topoi from the Hollywood thriller, and the denouement not only quotes Straub-Huillet themselves (*Not Reconciled, Chronicle of Anna Magdalena Bach*) and, according to Roud, Bresson's *Les Dames du Bois de Boulogne* (1945), but also shows two people communicating in quotations from (or ascribed to) St John of the Cross, accompanied by a Bach quotation. The resulting film is a lacunary body with five substantial interstitial spaces (between shots 1 and 2, 2 and 3, 3 and 4, 8 and 9, 9 and 10) and seven subsidiary ones (the two blackouts between the acts of Bruckner's play, the four changes of location during the chase, and the move into the house for the final shot).[53] The cinematic text is structured by disjunctures of the kind which, as Benjamin noted, characterize Brechtian epic theatre: 'Quoting a text implies interrupting its context'.[54]

Gilberto Perez argues that each film of Huillet and Straub is essentially 'a document of documents, a juxtaposition of traces from different times in the past, concrete pieces of evidence to be compared with one another in the present' (see also Chapter 5).[55] In the case of *Not Reconciled*, he terms the result an 'agglomerate of fragments, bits and pieces of the past'.[56] According to Martin Walsh, Huillet and Straub present 'each sequence as a document, a fragment, a piece of celluloid material', a technique which results in the predominance of stasis over movement in their films, as one piece of evidence is followed by another in the manner of still photography or early silent film.[57] This analogy is confirmed in the case of *The Bridegroom* by the stasis (at least of the camera) and the silence in both shots 1 and 2. For Walter Benjamin, the 'shocks' of epic theatre and the interruptions they bring about are the pre-requisite for revolutionary political change. The force needed to disrupt the continuum of history, the 'catastrophe' of the '"status quo"', is compared by Benjamin to high explosive ('Ekrazit', ecrasite) and 'splitting the atom', and is represented by the black American James freeing himself violently from his (white) pursuer, and by his wife, the prostitute Lilith, killing her possessive pimp.[58] In the final moments of the film the structural device, quotation, and its thematic equivalent, a violent physical 'grasp', are united in the image of the emancipated Lilith quoting St John of the Cross, not only as a theological or mystical text, but as a radically political one.

The film suggests that it is the very act of quotation, of textual embodiment which — in what might initially seem to be a contradiction — gives Lilith and James their own voice. Lifted from their original context, and translated into another language (and medium),[59] the poems of St John of the Cross have been subjected to the transformation process Benjamin terms 'actualization'.[60] It is perhaps tempting to speak of the film's literary appropriations as the kind of plagiarism championed (and practised) by Brecht and by Guy Debord, who in *Society of the Spectacle* (*La Société du Spectacle*) borrowed a famous passage of Isidore Ducasse (a.k.a. Lautréamont): 'Plagiarism is necessary. Progress implies it'.[61] However, despite Straub's claim that *Sickness of Youth* had become his own play, the thematic and stylistic heterogeneity of the material used in the film means that it is scarcely possible to speak of plagiarism in the conventional sense, there being no single voice to claim the diverse material as its own. The abrupt shifts in stylistic register between the Bruckner play, thriller, and denouement do, however, signal that the texts in *The Bridegroom* constitute a literary montage without quotation marks of the kind proposed by Benjamin: 'This work has to develop to the highest degree the art of citing without quotation marks. Its theory is intimately related to that of montage'.[62]

As an anthology of appropriations, *The Bridegroom* demonstrates how pre-existing texts can be emancipated, juxtaposed, and actualized. As Klaus Harro Hilzinger has pointed out, quotations used in this way function as documents, as facts from the past to challenge the present:

> A quotation [marks] clearly the boundary between fiction and reality and at the same time abolishes it by being signalled as an appropriation from another realm: the referential character is integral to this procedure. [...]
> The montage of quotations captures unresolved contradictions, it presents social structures and behaviours whose necessary substitution is still pending.[63]

According to Hans-Jost Frey, citation is invariably a violent process: 'Quotation tears open texts, or at least makes them porous, so that they flow into or interfere with one another'.[64] In *The Bridegroom* documents from the past are certainly meant to be explosive weapons in the here and now, Benjamin's famous 'now-time' ('Jetztzeit') perhaps (see the Introduction to this volume): the film quotes dissonant instances of insurrection and resurrection, in what Benjamin termed 'an enormous abridgement', to agitate for emancipatory action in the present of the kind undertaken by James and Lilith.[65] In the case of the latter Straub refers to this liberation as 'a rebellious and utopian *amour-fou*'.[66]

Conclusion — Figurative, Abstract Dreams: Machorka-Muff

Returning, in conclusion, to the notion of profane illumination, it is clear that *The Bridegroom* — like *Not Reconciled* and *Chronicle of Anna Magdalena Bach* — unites materialism and mysticism in the service of emancipatory politics. Although space does not permit analysis of Straub-Huillet's first film, it is striking that *Machorka-Muff* opens with a hand-written title-card, signed 'Jean-Marie Straub', which reads, 'A pictorially abstract dream, not a story' (Figure 3.5). The epigraph is in fact a modified quotation from *Billiards at Half-Past Nine*, thus itself a small act of plagiarism given Straub's signature.[67] The idea of the film as a dream takes us back not only to the somnambulism of performance in *Not Reconciled*, but also to Adorno's 'Transparencies on Film'. In his essay Adorno notes not only that film resembles 'the phenomenon of writing', but also compares it to the images of the *laterna magica* that appear in the mind spontaneously as 'in dreams or daydreams'.[68] According to Benjamin, in his *Arcades Project*: 'The realization of dream elements in the course of waking up is the canon of dialectics. It is paradigmatic for the thinker and binding for the historian'.[69] For Huillet and Straub, like Brecht and Benjamin, 'one cannot interpret the truth of present reality without past texts'.[70] Unlike Brecht's epic theatre, the films of Huillet and Straub do not imply that estrangement is just a passage to an unequivocal political truth, but — as incarnation, depth, mysticism, and dreams — is part of truth itself.

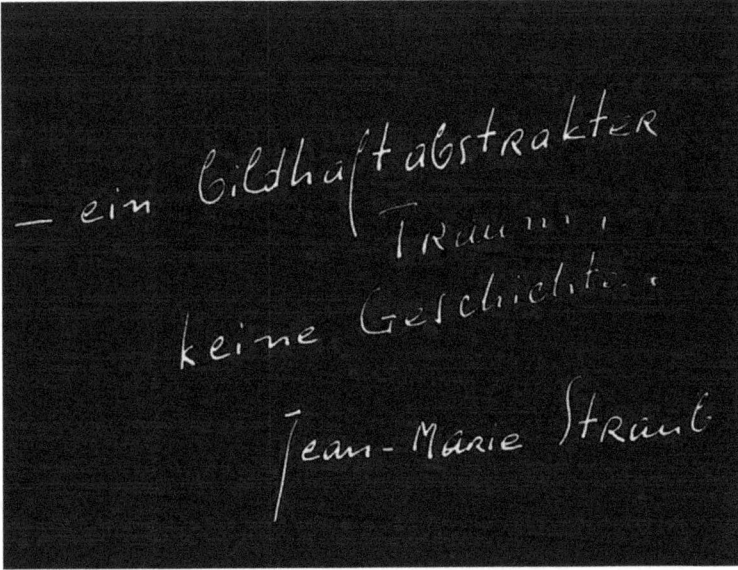

FIG. 3.5. Danièle Huillet and Jean-Marie Straub, *Machorka-Muff* (1963, courtesy of BELVA Film).

Notes to Chapter 3

1. Jean-Marie Straub, 'Not "Performing," Reciting', in Straub and Huillet, *Writings*, p. 65.
2. Theodor W. Adorno, 'Transparencies on Film', trans. by Thomas Y. Levin, *New German Critique*, 24-25 (1981-82), 199-205 (p. 200).
3. Delahaye, 'Entretien avec J.-M. Straub', p. 54. In the early period of their filmmaking (through to the 1970s at least), interviews are almost exclusively with, or at least credited to, Straub alone. No attempt has been made in what follows to conceal this by naming Huillet in the text or references when she is not alluded to. There is usually no evidence as to whether she was present at the interviews. Straub sporadically, but by no means consistently, implies the involvement of Huillet by using the terms 'we' and 'us'. All translations are my own unless otherwise stated.
4. Ibid.
5. Ibid., pp. 55-56.
6. Jean-Paul Sartre, *Being and Nothingness: A Phenomenological Essay on Ontology*, trans. by Hazel E. Barnes (New York, London, Toronto & Sydney: Simon & Schuster, 1992), p. 101.
7. Barbara Bernauer, Wolfram Schütte, and F. W. Vöbel, 'Gespräch mit Jean-Marie Straub', *Filmstudio*, 48 (1966), 2-9 (p. 4).
8. Bertolt Brecht, 'Plagiate' (*BFA* XXI, 404-05 (p. 404)).
9. As Richard Fähmel puts it towards the end of the novel, 'I am not reconciled, not reconciled either to myself or to the spirit of reconciliation': Heinrich Böll, *Billards at Half Past Nine*, trans. by Patrick Bowles (London: Marion Boyars, 1987), p. 208.
10. Bertolt Brecht, 'Anweisungen an die Schauspieler' (*BFA* XXII.2: 668). For the English see Misha Donat's translation of the film in Roud, *Jean-Marie Straub*, pp. 124-71 (p. 124).
11. Walter Benjamin, *Understanding Brecht* (London & New York: Verso, 1998), p. 21.
12. Ibid., p. 26.
13. Roud, *Jean-Marie Straub*, p. 124.
14. Ibid., p. 43.
15. Benjamin, 'Theses on the Philosophy of History', in *Illuminations*, p. 254.
16. Ibid., p. 246.

17. Straub has, on a number of occasions, quoted from Benjamin's essay himself. He cites it on camera in Pedro Costa's *6 Bagatelles* (2001) and also in a text from 1988 entitled 'Cézanne/Empedocles/Hölderlin/von Arnim': 'And poetry should give the children of the earth the courage to turn their backs on so-called progress, so-called science — the courage of the revolution, which according to Benjamin is a tiger's leap, not into the future, but into the past, a tiger's leap *"under the open sky of history"*.' Straub, 'Cézanne/Empedocles/Hölderlin/von Arnim', in Straub and Huillet, *Writings*, p. 209. Parenthetically it is worth noting that Straub once commented, 'I can't stand Adorno at all': Danièle Huillet and Jean-Marie Straub, 'Hölderlin, That is Utopia', in Straub and Huillet, *Writings*, pp. 204-07 (p. 204). This is the only remark on Adorno in the collected writings.

18. Roud, *Jean-Marie Straub*, p. 44.

19. Benjamin, 'Theses on the Philosophy of History', in *Illuminations*, p. 255.

20. Straub, 'Not "Performing," Reciting', in Straub and Huillet, *Writings*, p. 65. The Brecht quotation is from the end of the section entitled 'Discoveries of the Realists' of Brecht's commentary to the twelfth scene of *Mother Courage and Her Children* in *Couragemodell 1949* (*BFA* XXV: 240). See also Straub's reference to this passage in the interview in this volume (Chapter 11) and in the 2001 interview with François Albera at the Centre Pompidou: François Albera, 'Sickle and Hammer, Cannons, Cannons, Dynamite!' [interview with Danièle Huillet and Jean-Marie Straub], in *Jean-Marie Straub & Danièle Huillet*, ed. by Fendt, pp. 109-25 (p. 116).

21. Delahaye, 'Entretien avec J.-M. Straub', p. 54.

22. Roud, *Jean-Marie Straub*, p. 10.

23. Reinhold Rauh, 'Gespräch mit Danièle Huillet und Jean-Marie Straub', in *Machorka-Muff: Jean-Marie Straubs und Danièle Huillets Verfilmung einer Satire von Heinrich Böll*, ed. by Reinhold Rauh (Münster: MAkS Publikationen, 1988), pp. 79-93 (p. 92).

24. Bertolt Brecht, 'Amerika 21.7.41-31.12.41' (*BFA* XXVII: 12). The entry, which records the death of Benjamin as well as Brecht's enthusiasm for the history essay, is dated 9 August 1941.

25. Buck-Morss, *The Dialectics of Seeing*, p. 233.

26. Ibid., p. 235.

27. Ibid., p. 233.

28. Delahaye, 'Entretien avec J.-M. Straub', p. 55.

29. Ibid.

30. Bernauer, Schütte, and Vöbel 'Gespräch mit Jean-Marie Straub', p. 8.

31. Ibid., pp. 2, 3.

32. Robert Bresson, *Notes on the Cinematographer*, trans. by Jonathan Griffin (London: Quartet Books, 1986), p. 22.

33. Rancière, *The Intervals of Cinema*, trans. by Howe, p. 55.

34. Delahaye, 'Entretien avec J.-M. Straub', p. 55.

35. Rancière, *The Intervals of Cinema*, pp. 58, 103.

36. Bernauer, Schütte, and Vöbel 'Gespräch mit Jean-Marie Straub', p. 5.

37. Huillet, Straub, and Albera, 'Sickle and Hammer, Cannons, Cannons, Dynamite!', p. 109.

38. Ibid., pp. 119, 120.

39. Benjamin, *Understanding Brecht*, p. 110.

40. *BFA* XXVII: 12. On the differences between Benjamin and Brecht on matters of depth, see Georges Didi-Huberman, *The Eye of History: When Images Take Positions*, trans. by Shane B. Lillis (Cambridge, MA, & London: MIT, 2018), pp. 244-46. Brecht, Didi-Huberman goes so far as to assert, was keen 'to place the limits on any imaginative position' and reject all 'strangeness' (pp. 244, 246).

41. Huillet, Straub and Albera, 'Sickle and Hammer, Cannons, Cannons, Dynamite!', p. 123.

42. Walter Benjamin, 'Surrealism: The Last Snapshot of European Intelligentsia', in *One Way Street and Other Writings*, trans. by Edmund Jephcott (London & New York: Verso, 1985), pp. 225-39 (p. 227). See Didi-Huberman, *The Eye of History*, p. 231.

43. Martin Walsh, *The Brechtian Aspect of Radical Cinema: Essays* (London: BFI, 1981), p. 58.

44. Huillet, Straub, and Albera, 'Sickle and Hammer, Cannons, Cannons, Dynamite!', p. 110.

45. Gilberto Perez, 'The Modernist Cinema: The History Lessons of Straub and Huillet', in

The Cinema of Jean-Marie Straub and Daniele [*sic*] *Huillet* <https://www.straub-huillet.com/wp-content/uploads/2016/05/brochure-cinema1.pdf> [accessed 20 December 2021].

46. Roud, *Jean-Marie Straub*, pp. 90, 99.
47. Jean-Marie Straub, 'Der Bräutigam, die Komödiantin und der Zuhälter', *Filmkritik*, 10 (1968), 677-87 (p. 681). This issue also contains the full script in German accompanied by stills.
48. See Martin Brady, ' "Du Tag, wann wirst du sein..." ': Quotation, Emancipation and Dissonance in Straub/Huillet's *Der Bräutigam, die Komödiantin und der Zuhälter*', *German Life and Letters*, 53.3 (2000), 281-302.
49. Engel, 'Andi Engel Talks to Jean-Marie Straub, and Danièle Huillet is There Too', p. 14.
50. See [Anon.], 'Die Revolution ist kein Deckensticken: Wang kuang-me, Chinas erste Dame, im Rotgardisten-Verhör', *Spiegel* 14 (1968), 132-35 (p. 135) <https://www.spiegel.de/politik/die-revolution-ist-kein-deckchenstickeni-a-af8a64c6-0002-0001-0000-000046094011> [accessed 26 January 2022]. I am very grateful to Roland-François Lack (1960-2021) for this reference.
51. Jean-Claude Biette, 'Jean Marie Straub: "Le Fiancé, la comédienne et le maquereau" ', *Cahiers du cinéma*, 212 (1969), 9-10 (p. 9).
52. Walter Benjamin, *The Arcades Project*, trans. by Howard Eiland and Kevin McLaughlin (Cambridge, MA & London: Harvard University Press, 1999), p. 476.
53. In describing *Not Reconciled* as a 'lacunary' film, Straub cited Émile Littré's definition of the 'lacunary body': '*body composed of agglomerated crystals that leave intervals between them*'. Jean-Marie Straub, 'Frustration of Violence', in Straub and Huillet, *Writings*, p. 66.
54. Benjamin, *Understanding Brecht*, p. 19.
55. Perez, 'The Modernist Cinema', p. 12.
56. Ibid., p. 13.
57. Walsh, *The Brechtian Aspect of Radical Cinema*, p. 88.
58. Benjamin, *The Arcades Project*, pp. 473, 474, 463. In the published English translation 'Ekrazit' is mis-translated as 'ruins' (p. 474). In *Not Reconciled* Joseph extols dynamite with the cry 'long live dynamite' (shot 160). Dynamite crops up again in *Sicilia!* (1999) and Straub's millennial forecast published in *Cahiers du cinéma*, 542 (2000), p. 28. See also the Introduction to this volume.
59. They were apparently translated word-for-word ('mot à mot') by Straub himself. Jean-Marie Straub, ' "Le Fiancé, la comédienne et le maquereau" de Jean-Marie Straub', *Cahiers du cinéma*, 205 (1968), 15.
60. Benjamin, *The Arcades Project*, p. 460.
61. Guy Debord, *Society of the Spectacle* (London: Rebel Press/ AIM, 1987), section 207 [no page numbers].
62. Benjamin, *The Arcades Project*, p. 458.
63. Klaus Harro Hilzinger, 'Montage des Zitats: zur Struktur der Dokumentarstücke von Peter Weiss', in *Peter Weiss*, ed. by Rainer Gerlach (Frankfurt am Main: Suhrkamp, 1984), pp. 268-82 (pp. 268, 272).
64. Hans-Jost Frey, *Der unendliche Text* (Frankfurt am Main: Suhrkamp, 1990), p. 51.
65. Benjamin, 'Theses on the Philosophy of History', in *Illuminations*, p. 255.
66. Cahiers, 'Questions à Jean-Marie Straub', *Cahiers du cinéma*, 224 (1970), 40-42 (p. 42).
67. Böll, *Billiards at Half Past Nine*, p. 162. Böll's phrase 'ins Bildhaft-Abstrakte', literally 'into a pictorial abstraction', is not rendered word-for-word in the English translation of the novel: Heinrich Böll, *Billard um halbzehn* (Cologne & Berlin: Kiepenheuer & Witsch, 1959), p. 192.
68. Adorno, 'Transparencies on Film', p. 201.
69. Benjamin, *The Arcades Project*, p. 464.
70. Buck-Morss, *The Dialectics of Seeing*, p. 233.

❖

CHAPTER 4

History in the Visible: Memory Through Landscape in *Fortini/Cani*

Chris Groenveld

Introduction

Fortini/Cani (1976) has been the subject of political and philosophical analysis since its release. Early commentators, beginning with Mark Nash and Steve Neale in *Screen* following its UK premiere at the Edinburgh Festival, noted the significance of the remarkable fifteen-minute, ten-shot sequence of panning shots in the Apuan Alps — a 'deafening silence' at the heart of the film, as Fabien Meynier termed it in 2018.[1] Despite the publication of the full script in *Screen,* including detailed shot descriptions and stills, most early commentators did not, however, examine this particular sequence in any great depth.[2] Out of the ten landscape shots, Nash and Neale only comment on one, namely shot 17, which begins with an inscription on a monument to partisans murdered by Nazis in the village of Vinca and then pans skywards (Figures 4.1 and 4.2). However, the questions they pose are a starting-point for understanding the Apuan Alps sequence of *Fortini/Cani* and for this essay:

> What knowledge/memory of Italy does the spectator bring to bear? Do these pans just provide a field for the projection of fantasies of 'holidays in the sun'? Do they enjoin the spectator to recognise scenes of other atrocities? Such questions concern absence — possible amnesia, absence of memory — and difference — difference between the 'real' spectator and the imagined spectator produced in the text.[3]

In what follows I will, as a writer-filmmaker engaged with what Pierre Nora terms 'lieux de mémoire' (sites or places of memory), address questions of documentation, enunciation, mediation, ecology, and the so-called 'post-human' in relation to the Apuan Alps sequence in *Fortini/Cani.* Remarkable for its near complete absence of commentary — Fortini is heard for only fifteen seconds at the start of the first of its ten shots — the sequence has been read as a sub-text or meditation. This essay, however, reads it not only as a complement to Fortini's text, but also as a compelling counterargument to it. Through a close reading of the film's use of openness and what Straub terms its 'density' ('Dichte'), as well as its sites of memory and treatment of attention and resistance, I will uncover how an understanding of history gained from *Fortini/Cani* is dependent on the landscapes, rather than simply its human protagonist.[4]

Unearthing the Apuan Alps

For Meynier, the Apuan Alps sequence is so radically different from the rest of the film that it 'functions as an autonomous whole almost detachable from the rest of the film'.[5] Certainly, it marks the only instance in *Fortini/Cani* in which Straub-Huillet interrupt one of the twenty-seven sections of Fortini's essay. The remainder of the film, before and after the Apuan Alps sequence which begins after around ten minutes, consists of Fortini reading around two-thirds of his controversial 1967 essay in extracts chosen by the filmmakers. *The Dogs of the Sinai* is about the response, or lack of it, among Italian Jewry to Israeli aggression in the Six-Day War. Fortini's recitation, spread over twenty-eight of the film's forty-one shots (including the Alps), is supplemented by Straub-Huillet with a range of documentary material including newspaper reports (from the Italian Communist Party paper *L'Unità* and a feature by Bernard Levin in *The Daily Mail*) and an Italian television news broadcast on the outbreak of the war between Israel and Egypt with the Jewish journalist, essayist, and television anchorman Arrigo Levi. There is also an opening shot of the cover of the original publication of Fortini's text, accompanied by a brief extract from Schoenberg's opera *Moses and Aaron* (1975), two hand-written texts of Fortini, and two shots with actors speaking: the Jewish Holocaust survivor and psychoanalyst Luciana Nissim (Momigliano) in shot 9, referred to in the script as 'she who speaks', and the film critic and friend of Huillet and Straub Adriano Aprà in shot 10 as 'he who speaks'. The final shot of the film, in which Fortini discusses revolution and concludes with a quote from Lenin, pans *c.* 300 degrees away from him to the right, across the terrace and garden on the island of Elba where the film was shot to the sea and hills beyond.

In light of the dominating presence of Fortini himself on screen and the density of spoken, written, and chanted text in the rest of the film — for example in shot 22 a rabbi chants for more than nine minutes from the Book of Numbers — the Apuan Alps sequence with its dense woodland and mountain peaks may initially appear almost devoid of human presence. Closer inspection reveals the traces of habitation: farmsteads, churches, olive groves, a school, houses, and playgrounds. As we are told explicitly by Fortini in shot 13 and the inscription in shot 17, the land is not only a site of natural geology, but also of human geography, containing beneath its surface the remains and environmental consequences of a great number of bodies absorbed and reconstituted by the soil in the decades between the Second World War and the production of the film.

In my filmmaking and research practice on Holocaust memory one of the greatest challenges I address is how to continue representing the truth of this history beyond the lifespans of first-hand witnesses; one solution is the literal and metaphorical unearthing and depiction of sites of memory. *Fortini/Cani* engages in an act of unearthing through the writing and presence of Fortini and associated documentation, as well as an expansive, slow exploration of landscape.

This essay is composed of three closely interlocking parts. First, 'Density' engages with the complexity and layering of textual and acoustic 'enunciation' and images in the film to the point of 'information overload'.[6] Second, 'Sites of Memory' shows that while the text (in 1967) and Fortini's recitation of it (in 1976) draw compelling parallels between Mussolini's fascist Italy and Italian support of the state of Israel, the landscape sequence which interrupts the textual flow serves to contextualize and augment these specific historical moments without denying their significance.

Finally, 'Attention and Resistance' grapples with history on a human and post-human scale, and aims to shed light on the occupation of the landscapes by human beings and how it can challenge and expand the meaning of Fortini's text. It challenges the idea, discussed by Claudia Pummer and others, that this film is an 'adaptation' of *The Dogs of Sinai*.[7] Building on the claim of Meynier that in *Fortini/Cani* 'the passage from one sequence to another [...] proposes a new way of thinking about History', the aim in what follows is to examine how this is accomplished visually and at least partially in defiance of the text on which it is based.[8]

Density

As Straub, and subsequent commentators, have noted, *Fortini/Cani* is a dense film:

> This is a dense text, which is what interested me, a very dense text. The further we progress, the more we look for dense texts and it's clear that these reflections are also ours. We are looking for dense texts, and Fortini's is the densest there is in Italy. That's why it's a thing that's hard to follow if you don't speak Italian.[9]

There are few pauses in Fortini's recitation and the flow of textual information in the film beyond the Apuan Alps sequence: the only two notable exceptions are the conspicuous pause during the short appearance of Adriano Aprà, which seems to leave room for an absentee interlocutor, and in the preceding shot with Luciana Nissim (Momigliano), who breaks off from her text with the words 'when the Jews are threatened' to hear out the chiming of church bells. It has been noted by Meynier amongst others that this density or flow of text and information is interrupted by the silence, deafening or otherwise, of the landscape sequence. It could be argued, however, that this claim relies on a thoroughly anthropocentric notion of what constitutes silence, absence, and indeed information.

The density of the film is, in part, simply a consequence of the sheer quantity of text delivered, despite a number of omissions which become apparent on comparing the film script to Fortini's original text, not least certain references to other writers and thinkers, including a substantial passage from Adorno and Horkheimer's *Dialectic of Enlightenment* (*Dialektik der Aufklärung*) in section 25 of the text. Also omitted are some references to specific events, which enables the film to be understood out of the context in which the text was written in 1967. In their article in *Screen*, Nash and Neale identify at least five levels of enunciation for the audience to grapple with in *Fortini/Cani* and note that the historical reference points, or in Huillet's own

words 'strata, as in geology', are manifold: Fortini's own youth in Fascist Italy, that
of his father before him, his own text of 1967 and various documents relating to it,
the recitation of it in 1977, the time of viewing the film for the audience.[10]

The second order of density is speed. The text was chosen for its complexity,
as noted by Straub, and a questioner at the film's premiere identified a 'kind of
violence' that the rhythm of the film 'imposes on the viewer'.[11] This is a problem,
as Straub also acknowledged, that is exacerbated by the difficulty of reading
subtitles. In the English-language version, this is aggravated by the decision to
mitigate against the sheer weight of the text by only translating certain passages,
a source of controversy at public screenings. Fortini was asked by the filmmakers
to read at a considerable pace, often avoiding pauses, and he himself noted the way
in which this 'estranged' the text for him: 'In the instructions that I received from
Danièle and Jean-Marie, the text estranged itself under my gaze; my defences were
incredibly weak, I allowed unexpected liaisons to alter punctuation and syntax'.[12]
Tight cutting at the beginning and end of shots increases the sense of urgency and
inhalations are eliminated to the point that Fortini speaks almost like a machine
that does not need to breath between sentences. At the beginning of shot 35, for
example, which is separated from its predecessor by a short length of white leader,
we hear his recitation fractionally before he appears on screen.[13]

This brings us to the third order of density and the one that is closest to the
geological analogy: the layering of sound and image. The densest of all is the
opening sequence, which covers sections 1–8 of the essay and directly precedes the
landscapes. In addition to the fast-paced narration of Fortini, it contains newspaper
articles and newsreel. For Meynier, this documentary material has an evidential or
illustrative function:

> In this first sequence, the relationship between Fortini's book and images is of
> the order of illustration. These images aim for an end, they seek to develop a
> thesis, to illustrate words in order to demonstrate the veracity of a speech.[14]

However, the sheer quantity of textual, visual, acoustic, and musical material to be
processed also makes the first ten minutes of the film an assault on the senses. This
is what Fortini had in mind when he commented that there is an 'overpowering of
the narrator' in the film.[15] As Paolo Caffoni neatly puts it in his essay on Fortini
in *Tell It to the Stones*: 'The film is constructed through the struggle of Fortini's
voice with the present time which overwhelms it (the church bells, the traffic jam,
the voice of the rabbi, the television speaker)'.[16] It could be argued, in the light of
this, that the 'assault' on our senses and also on Fortini is a palpable analogy to the
physical, ideological, and theological battles Fortini has faced and continues to face.
It can also be read as a riposte to the simplifications of mainstream mass media. This
is particularly apparent as, in Meynier's words, 'the rhythmic and jerky voice of the
presenter [Arrigo Levi] is replaced by that, rapid and monotonous, of the poet'.[17] As
Geoffrey Nowell-Smith noted in his introduction to the published script in *Screen*,
'the spoken words require to be heard (and the written ones to be read), and this,
in a foreign-language film, is not easily achieved at the time of viewing'.[18] I would
argue that the struggle of contested ideologies, theologies, nationalities, classes,

FIG. 4.1. Danièle Huillet and Jean-Marie Straub,
Fortini/Cani (1976, courtesy of BELVA Film).

FIG. 4.2. Danièle Huillet and Jean-Marie Straub,
Fortini/Cani (1976, courtesy of BELVA Film).

and generations in Fortini's text is translated in the film into a visceral experience, especially for an audience outside Italy.

To each of these three orders of density, the landscape sequence provides a kind of counterpoint. First, it contains very little text: just three lines of Fortini's narration (the opening of section 9 in shot 13) and the inscription on a stone monument to the victims of 'German barbarity' (shot 16, Figure 4.1). Before panning up to the sky, in a gesture that Nash and Neale describe as an expression of the inscription (Figure 4.2), the camera shows the text (subtitled in the English version) for a full six seconds:

> The inscription is itself reinforced by the movement of the pan upward with the denotation of 'reading' and the connotations of the upward movement of the flame, of the soul, and its ending with the cypresses and their connotations of death.[19]

In her 1988 essay on *Fortini/Cani* 'as Marxist reflection', Jane Madsen notes that the refusal of the camera to linger on the inscription of a second monument long enough for it to be read (shot 18), may well be due to its overly 'fervent' tone, although for the viewer the implication will probably be that it is simply interchangeable with the first.[20]

The pacing of the Apuan Alps sequence is notably different from that of the scenes with Fortini's narration. Not only does the slowness of these shots point to a radically different timescale, but it also enables the viewer to scrutinize and ponder not only the landscapes, but also the generally sparse and modest settlements. In a reversal of the way the film has presented Fortini, people caught in the frame in this sequence — a woman working in a field in shot 14, a group of children and adults in shot 19, cars and farm vehicles in shots 19 and 22 — appear incidental and are surveyed with as much or as little interest as an insect or a bird which passes through the camera's field of vision. Longshots of the mountains, for example in shots 13 and 18, carry as much reverence as similarly paced pans across a chapel (Sant'Anna di Stazzema in shot 14) or a church in the middle-distance (Vinca in shot 16). Whereas Fortini is filmed statically with the abrupt cuts between shots already mentioned, the landscape pans are on average 90 seconds in length and each, with the exception of a diagonal sweep down to valley settlements in shot 18 (Figures 4.3 and 4.4), traverses its horizontal or vertical axis unhurriedly. What is more, the pans often double back on themselves or, in the case of shot 22, repeat for a second 360 degrees.

The leisurely landscape pans thus contrast markedly with the urgency of the scenes that precede them with their layering of textual, visual, and acoustic information. Whereas these documents of conflict were layered vertically, the landscapes that follow are surveyed for the most part horizontally with meticulous variations in framing and point-of view and a preponderance of incidental occurrence. In a sense, the lateral pans in shots 14-16 and 18-22 recall the first in shot 13, so that the sequence unfolds in a 'theme and variations' structure. While Fortini's text and Straub-Huillet's documentary framing of it weave together multiple timescales to generate thought-provoking connections between distinct historic events, unlike the landscape shots in the Apuan Alps they do not enact what Michael Rothberg in his influential 2009 study termed 'multidirectional memory'.[21] This term denotes a process whereby formerly disparate memories are linked together in new ways. Multidirectional memory cannot simply be forced into being by external stimuli but is generated within the viewer. The landscapes, in a way almost diametrically

FIG. 4.3. Danièle Huillet and Jean-Marie Straub, *Fortini/Cani*
(1976, courtesy of BELVA Film).

FIG. 4.4. Danièle Huillet and Jean-Marie Straub, *Fortini/Cani*
(1976, courtesy of BELVA Film).

opposed to the polemic of Fortini, offer space — and, above all, time — to filter historical events and to reflect on personal experience. This is the space Nash and Neale allude to in an aside on 'fantasies of "holidays in the sun"' and which Meynier characterizes in the following terms:

> We therefore better understand at what level the following landscape sequence
> can be exotic: the landscapes represented for fifteen minutes and bathed in the
> sound of birdsong do not impose any discourse and do not orient the perceived
> reality in a predetermined direction. These landscape shots thus question, by
> contrast, the relevance of the channels of the meaning of the first sequence and
> question even the capacity of signs to signify something.[22]

The density of *Fortini/Cani* can of course be assessed in strictly human terms
alone. However, as Meynier indicates with his reference to birdsong, much can be
gleaned by applying a less anthropocentric, more ecocentric gaze. This is perhaps
the point at which Marxist (dialectical) materialism overlaps with contemporary,
'new materialist', or ecological modes of interpretation which allow the landscapes
to be read as more-than-human spaces. Straub and Huillet have repeatedly likened
their filmmaking process to geology. Huillet's use of the term 'strata' was noted
above and in 2013 Straub was asked whether the interlinking of 'blocks of film' is
akin to the way tectonic plates fit together, to which he responded, 'with landscape
that need not be the case, that one element has a bearing on another for they can
also be separate. Blocks like granite boulders that collide with each other'.[23] Both
analogies conjure up the mountains, borne of collisions underground millions of
years ago or of volcanic activity, which feature so prominently in the cinema of
Huillet and Straub, not least Mont Sainte-Victoire and Etna in the Cézanne and
Hölderlin films. The transition from Fortini's commentary to the Apuan Alps
sequence, in which the only voices heard are those of children (shot 19) marks a
shift in scale away from a human measurement of physical and acoustic space and
provides an altogether new context in which to reassess the significance of, for
example, human speech.

The second ecocentric aspect of the Apuan Alps sequence is also provided by the
audio track on which we hear those distant voices of children and of cars in shot
19. As Madsen writes:

> Early in the sequence, after the initial voice over, there is a sense of expectation
> that more information will be given, but as the pans continue with only direct
> sound, the spectator adjusts to this and is forced to consider the locations
> themselves.[24]

For Meynier, this shift places the viewer in the position of a 'surveyor', a term
borrowed from the filmmakers themselves, who is encouraged to chart the
'deafening silence'.[25] Of course, following Fortini's recitation, the suggestion that
an absence of language amounts to silence is an anthropocentric position that
underplays the landscapes as active participants in the film. From an ecocentric
perspective, the landscapes furnish us with information of a different magnitude:
for example, contrasts in density between the human and the more-than-human,
between the urban and the rural (not least in the cityscapes of Florence in shots
31, 32, 39, and 40) become apparent through the construction of the film and the
cinematography of Renato Berta.

Sites of Memory

Fortini/Cani is, like *Othon* (1970) and *History Lessons* (1972) before it, a film about sites of history and memory. The locations chosen for the Apuan Alps sequence are prominent examples of such spaces, and include: Sant'Anna di Stazzema (shots 13 and 14), where on 12 August 1944 the German 16th SS Panzergrenadier Division 'Reichsführer-SS' and others murdered 392 villagers and refugees, including more than a hundred children; San Terenzo Monti (shot 15), where the 16th Division and others killed 159 civilians between 17 and 19 August 1944; Vinca (shots 16, 17) where between 24 and 27 August 1944 162 Italians were massacred by the 16th Division and others; San Leonardo al Frigido (shot 20), where the 16th Division murdered 149 prison inmates on 16 September 1944; Bergiola-Foscalina (shot 21) where sixty-one locals including twenty-four children were shot by the 16th Division on the same day; and Monte Sole, Marzabotto (shot 22), cited by Fortini at the beginning of the sequence, where from 29 September to 5 October 1944 the 16th Division murdered 770 civilians.[26] In summary, the sequence charts, chronologically and over fifteen minutes, a murder spree of a single SS division during a six-week period in late summer and autumn of 1944.

For Pummer, the significance of the Apuan Alps is inextricably bound up with its largely invisible history beneath the surface. The film's lack of exposition 'derives precisely from the attempt to confront the viewer with the scene of a past crime that is no longer visible to the eye, that lies buried underground'.[27] In the assertion that what is no longer visible does not exist, one is reminded of Claude Lanzmann's famous observation on his arrival at a former death camp in Poland in preparation for shooting his documentary *Shoah* (1985): 'There was nothing at all, sheer nothingness, and I had to make a film on the basis of this nothingness'.[28]

Whereas Pummer views the landscapes of *Fortini/Cani* as what Lanzmann terms 'non-sites of memory' ('non-lieux de mémoire'), this essay conceives of them as sites of memory of a different magnitude. Non-sites of memory are important in relation to what is absent. However, the sites in *Fortini-Cani*, which in only two cases (shots 17 and 20) include visible memorialization of the massacres committed there, are anything but empty. Some of the sites show little sign of habitation, while others have been redeveloped, such as the school in Bergiola. To focus exclusively on what these spaces conceal is to simplify them as non-sites of memory and to ignore their life in the present. In the context of Fortini's essay and through visible inscriptions in shots 17 and 20, the film links the sites irrevocably to specific moments in time past, but also records their relationship to the living (in 1976) and in the long shots of mountain ranges in particular to the timescales of the sites as geological entities, beyond their relationship with or use by humans. It might be more accurate to call them what Georges Didi-Huberman terms 'sites in spite of everything'.[29]

Seen from this point of view, what is notable for an understanding of these sites of memory is not just what the landscapes hide beneath the surface, as suggested by Pummer and others, but also what they *reveal* about human patterns of habitation and 'progress' in 1976. Although signs of industrialization can only be glimpsed in most of the rural landscapes of *Fortini/Cani*, the camera does capture, alongside the cars and buildings already mentioned, substantial developments along the Ligurian coast in shot 21 and in the middle-ground of shot 22 an industrial complex and what appears to be a large quarry behind it. Moreover, the camera frequently follows or crosses in its horizontal pans the lines of telegraph cables (shots 14, 16, 19) and power cables (shots 13, 14, 19-21), recent additions compared to the hundreds of years of farming on this land and, indeed, the millions of years that the mountains had dominated this space. These lines of power and telecommunication serve, particularly for a contemporary audience, as a reminder of the position of this rural area within a larger, global context. In an interview following the premiere of the film in Pesaro, Straub noted that the Apuan Alps sequence was 'geophysical, geographical, almost geological', adding that it was 'also a "theatre", a place of class struggle'.[30] Of course this struggle was and is inseparable from processes of networking and globalization. Straub's claim that the film in general and the landscapes in particular grew out of project to make 'a kind of documentary about the Peasant Wars', possibly the so-called 'Peasant Agitation' in Italy of 1848-49, not only underscores the political and economic stakes involved in the movement of capital, but also suggests that the power and telecommunications cables in this otherwise rural setting can be read a signifiers of sites of memory and of meaning under construction, both literally and metaphorically.[31]

While Fortini's recollections of a childhood in Italy under fascism are most visually present in the four shots of Florence and the nine-minute-long episode in the synagogue (shot 23), the primary site of conflict alluded to in Fortini's text is the land fought over in the 1967 Arab-Israeli (or Six-Day) War. *Fortini/Cani* offers no images of this space beyond military hardware and maps shown as part of Arrigo Levi's RAI news report. This makes of it an imaginary space at least as far as visible evidence is concerned. Whereas Madsen and Meynier have said that the Apuan Alps sequence is one that viewers are 'forced' to reckon with, it is arguably harder to conjure up a landscape very different from the ones actually seen in the film — the Apuan Alps, Florence, and the Casa Catrin in Cotoncello on Elba where Fortini was recorded — one that is only seen briefly in cartographic form (shot 4).[32] In the twenty-first century, with this conflict still raging and with continued support for Israel in Europe and America, the oppositional stance taken by Fortini remains as radical and relevant as ever.[33] Indeed, this contested space has become even more complex through its connection to subsequent US-led interventions in Afghanistan, Iraq, and Syria. For a contemporary audience, these connections multiply the number of imaginary spaces conjured up by Fortini's text.

In his own response to watching the film, Fortini raises the question of the landscapes and cityscapes in *Fortini/Cani* insofar as they pose the question of 'inhabitability': 'the space of the Apuan Alps,' he notes, 'implies a proposal of inhabitability; inhabitable too is Florence, as long as it is seen from the hill'.[34] The question of inhabitation is underscored in the film by the fact that Fortini is filmed on the terrace of a house which is not actually the one he lives in and whose verdant natural excess he never acknowledges, engrossed in his book, looking 'overcome with tiredness' according to Gilles Deleuze, uncomfortable even.[35] Reading the text as if written by someone else, it might not even be clear to the viewer that these are his recollections. The visible distance or lack of intimacy between Fortini and the natural environment he finds himself in throws into sharper relief the dignity and otherness of this space.

Attention and Resistance

In *Cinema 2: The Time-Image* (*Cinéma 2: L'Image-temps*) Gilles Deleuze discusses the separation of the voice of Fortini and the natural environment that we find in *Fortini/Cani*:

> People talk in an empty space, and, whilst speech rises, the space is sunk into the ground, and does not let us see it, but makes its archaeological buryings, its stratigraphic thicknesses readable; it testifies to the work and the victims slaughtered in order to fertilize a field, the struggles that took place and the corpses thrown out ([...] *Fortini Cani*). History is inseparable from the earth [*terre*], struggle is underground [*sous-terre*], and, if we want to grasp an event, we must not show it, we must not pass along the event, but plunge into it, go through all the geological layers that are its internal history (and not simply a more or less distant past).[36]

If Fortini is cast in the first instance as an authoritative narrator, challenging mainstream media discourses of Levi and others, the landscapes sequence complicates this. Fortini has only just begun the recitation of his past, and already he has had to jostle for legibility with the steadfast voice of a newsreader and the interruptions of 'she who speaks', church bells, and 'he who speaks'. Then, three lines into section 9 of *The Dogs of the Sinai*, he encounters the implacable resistance of the Apuan Alps. As Deleuze puts it, it 'is therefore now the visual image, the stratigraphic landscape, which in turn resists the speech–act and opposes it with a silent piling-up'. Fortini's recitation passes into the landscape with its geological strata, monuments, and inscriptions: 'it is now the earth, the tree, and the rock which resist the speech act'.[37] The filmmakers resist no opportunity to challenge Fortini's recitation of his own essay as 'grand soliloquy'. Having been swept away by the Apuan Alps in full flow, Fortini's relationship to the audience on his return is radically altered by what has happened in the interim, the fifteen minutes in which a different mode of storytelling has taken over from his spoken narrative. As if to underscore this challenge to Fortini's univocal authority, he is immediately interrupted by another ceaseless flow, this time a differently resistant speech–act: the rabbi in the Florentine synagogue.

Considering that Fortini is playing himself in his recitation, the upstaging of his intimate relationship to the text through the film's acts of estrangement and resistance is significant. Fortini himself was initially resistant, hostile even, to the interventions in his text which led to what cinematographer Renato Berta diplomatically describes as 'tensions between Fortini and Jean-Marie'.[38] These tensions persisted during shooting. However, Fortini soon came to appreciate the distance he had gained from himself, the text, and the historical stratifications it addresses. In his own response to the film, he acknowledges that 'the film goes well beyond my text' in 'the relationship between the argumentations (or invectives) of the text and the attention (the word is Simone Weil's) of the camera'.[39]

Acknowledging the 'absence of man' and that the 'the voice too goes quiet' in the Apuan Alps sequence, he readily accepts its significance:[40]

> The pan of the Apuan Alps does not say 'only' what happened there and how much calmness now covers the sites of massacres both ancient and modern. It also 'says' that *this* land is the place inhabitable by human beings, that we *must* inhabit it.[41]

The sequence, he concludes 'affirms *the enormous presence of the dead*; but not only of *those* dead'.[42] The landscapes are thus more than an illustration of his text as suggested by Pummer and others or an absolute rupture within the film as suggested by Meynier, but a transformative power that takes the film and its audience beyond the text.

Recent scholarly work in memory and landscape studies further complicates the contemporary audience's encounter with the landscapes of *Fortini/Cani*. Far from being the exclusive domain of human beings as it was once held, memory is now acknowledged as something that can be stored in the non-human as well. Soil samples, for example, can be analysed for evidence of past conflict to pick up where individual testimony leaves off, allowing new breakthroughs in Holocaust archaeology. These breakthroughs have been described as an ecological turn in Holocaust studies addressing not only the preservation and demarcation of sites of historical import by 'greener' means than stone monuments and signposts, but also introducing a post-human perspective. Less interference and 'restoration' of nature, for example, can mean that more evidence of war crimes will remain underground, to return to Deleuze's terminology, for future generations with more advanced technology. It is now acknowledged that what motivated commentators to claim that the past is 'erased' is that it was no longer visible to the human eye. Today, technology focuses less on visibility or less on that which is visible to humans. To apply this mode of thinking to *Fortini/Cani* is to reconsider not only what is visible within the landscapes captured by the filmmakers and their cinematographer, but also what is invisible.

An ecocentric gaze can highlight the fact that the passage of time has not erased all signs of the ruptures of conflict and resistance. As noted above, soil samples may be analysed to reveal the presence of human remains; similarly, patterns of habitation, populations of insects and birds, may also point to changes in the chemical composition of the soil, or to migration patterns historically disrupted by human interventions in the landscape. Just as Fortini acknowledges that 'in a few years' 'no one will understand what the Vietnam War and the Arab-Israeli conflict were', so he regards the disappearance of his voice as necessary, given that the mountains and the flowering oleander behind his reading seat (Figure 1.8) 'openly allude to a past that could also be a future *if someone will come to want it*'.[43] The task of the viewer after this sequence is to reassess the apparent tranquillity of Fortini, sat reading from his book, as a form of resistance since if 'the present is seen from outside the present, it becomes a place onto which past and future spirits can be projected'.[44]

Conclusion

Fortini/Cani was shot on a modest budget on 16mm and appeared in the wake of *Moses and Aaron*, which was and has remained the subject of much more detailed critical appraisal. In recent years, however, *Fortini/Cani*'s fifteen-minute-long sequence of mountain landscapes has attracted renewed attention. The aim of unpacking the landscape sequence in this essay has been to challenge two prevailing interpretative models: first, that the landscape sequence serves primarily as an illustration of Fortini's essay and, second, that it represents a separate 'film-within-a-film'. Through a close reading of the film, it has been argued that it both evolves from and is resistant to Fortini's narration of *The Dogs of the Sinai*. It has also been demonstrated that *Fortini/Cani* can productively be read alongside the recent turn in the humanities and social sciences towards ecological perspectives on memory and how it is played out in material settings. Finally, this reading has aimed to suggest ways of reconciling social and political conceptions of landscape with more recent ideas about memory and the ecological gaze. I would suggest that a close reading of *Fortini/Cani* focusing on nature and ecology as active participants can also provide a set of tools which enriches our understanding of other films of Straub-Huillet and, moreover, those of other filmmakers past and present.

Notes to Chapter 4

1. Fabien Meynier, 'Dépaysements géographiques, perceptifs et historiques dans le film *Fortini/Cani* de Jean-Marie Straub et Danièle Huillet', *L'Entre-deux*, 4 (2018), 1–11 (p. 3) <https://lentre-deux.com/index.php?b=58> [accessed 5 August 2021]. Page numbers relate to the pdf which can be downloaded from this site. Unless otherwise noted, translations are my own.
2. Jean-Marie Straub and Danièle Huillet, '*Fortini-Cani*: Script', *Screen*, 19.2 (1978), 11-40.
3. Nash and Neale, 'Film', p. 89.
4. Danièle Huillet, Jean-Marie Straub, and Franco Fortini, 'Pressekonferenz in Pesaro', *Filmkritik*, 247 (1977), 4-13 (p. 10).
5. Meynier, 'Dépaysements géographiques, perceptifs et historiques dans le film *Fortini/Cani* de Jean-Marie Straub et Danièle Huillet', p. 4.
6. See Nash and Neale, 'Film'.
7. Claudia Pummer, 'Elective Affinities: The Films of Daniele Huillet and Jean-Marie Straub' (doctoral thesis, University of Iowa, 2011), p. 3 <https://ir.uiowa.edu/etd/2761/> [accessed 27 August 2021].
8. Meynier, 'Dépaysements géographiques, perceptifs et historiques dans le film *Fortini/Cani* de Jean-Marie Straub et Danièle Huillet', p. 4.
9. Huillet, Straub, and Fortini, 'Pressekonferenz in Pesaro', p. 10.
10. Mezzadri, 'Interview', p. 252.
11. Huillet, Straub, and Fortini, 'Pressekonferenz in Pesaro', p. 11.
12. Franco Fortini, 'A Note for Jean-Marie Straub', in Fortini, *The Dogs of the Sinai*, pp. 74-82 (p. 80).
13. In general, this essay follows the script published in *Screen* (see note 2). However, as that publication itself acknowledges, the filmmakers added two further landscape shots to the Apuan Alps sequence after the script was completed. This means that the actual shot numbers following shot 17 do not correspond with the script. In what follows, shot numbers relate to the completed film.
14. Meynier, 'Dépaysements géographiques, perceptifs et historiques dans le film *Fortini/Cani* de Jean-Marie Straub et Danièle Huillet', p. 7.

15. Fortini, 'A Note for Jean-Marie Straub', p. 78.
16. Caffoni, 'A Revolutionary Copywriter', p. 176.
17. Meynier, 'Dépaysements géographiques, perceptifs et historiques dans le film *Fortini/Cani* de Jean-Marie Straub et Danièle Huillet', p. 7.
18. Geoffrey Nowell-Smith, 'Fortini-Cani: Introduction', *Screen*, 19.2 (1978), 9-10 (p. 9).
19. Nash and Neale, 'Film', p. 89
20. Jane Madsen, 'Cutting Through the Seventies to Find the Thirties: A Consideration of "Fortini-Cani" as Marxist Reflection', in *History on/and/in Film*, ed. by T. O'Regan and B. Shoesmith (Perth: History & Film Association of Australia, 1987), pp. 159-65 <https://fremantlestuff.info/readingroom/hfilm/MADSEN.html > [accessed 30 December 2022].
21. Michael Rothberg, *Multidirectional Memory: Remembering the Holocaust in the Age of Decolonization* (Stanford, CA: Stanford University Press, 2009).
22. Meynier, 'Dépaysements géographiques, perceptifs et historiques dans le film *Fortini/Cani* de Jean-Marie Straub et Danièle Huillet', p. 7.
23. Lylov and Marhöfer, 'A Thousand Cliffs', p. 386.
24. Madsen, 'Cutting Through the Seventies to Find the Thirties'.
25. Meynier, 'Dépaysements géographiques, perceptifs et historiques dans le film *Fortini/Cani* de Jean-Marie Straub et Danièle Huillet', p. 5.
26. The statistics given here are taken from the online *Atlante delle stragi naziste e fasciste in Italia* (Atlas of Nazi and Fascist Massacres in Italy), an open-access database set up by a joint historical commission of the Italian and the German governments established in 2009 <http://www.straginazifasciste.it/> [accessed 26 January 2022].
27. Claudia Pummer, '(Not Only) for Children and Cavemen: The Films of Jean-Marie Straub and Danièle Huillet', in *Jean-Marie Straub and Danièle Huillet*, ed. by Fendt, pp. 7-95 (p. 52).
28. Marc Chevrie and Hervé Le Roux, 'Site and Speech: An Interview with Claude Lanzmann about *Shoah*', in *Claude Lanzmann's Shoah: Key Essays*, ed. by Stuart Liebman (New York: Oxford University Press, 2007), pp. 37-50 (p. 39).
29. Georges Didi-Huberman, 'The Site, Despite Everything', in *Claude Lanzmann's Shoah*, ed. by Liebman, pp. 113-23 (p. 115).
30. Huillet, Straub, and Fortini, 'Pressekonferenz in Pesaro', p. 5.
31. Ibid.
32. See, for example, Meynier, 'Dépaysements géographiques, perceptifs et historiques dans le film *Fortini/Cani* de Jean-Marie Straub et Danièle Huillet', p. 5, and Madsen, 'Cutting Through the Seventies to Find the Thirties', for example in the passage quoted above.
33. See, for example, his 'Letter to the Italian Jews' of May 1989, signed off with both his Christian and Jewish surnames and reproduced in translation in Fortini, *The Dogs of the Sinai*, pp. 83-88.
34. Fortini, 'A Note for Jean-Marie Straub', p. 78.
35. Gilles Deleuze, *Cinema 2: The Time-Image*, trans. by Hugh Tomlinson and Robert Galeta (London & New York: Continuum, 2005), p. 243.
36. Ibid., p. 244.
37. Ibid.
38. Renato Berta, 'Portfolio: Photographs and Commentary', in Straub and Huillet, *Writings*, pp. 525-43 (p. 531). He also refers to the need for diplomacy (p. 532).
39. Fortini, 'A Note for Jean-Marie Straub', p. 78.
40. Ibid., p. 77.
41. Ibid., p. 78.
42. Ibid.
43. Ibid., p. 77.
44. Ibid., pp. 77-78.

CHAPTER 5

❖

'The noise, the air, and the wind': Sound and Stratification in the Films of Danièle Huillet, Jean-Marie Straub, and Harun Farocki

Laura Lux

Understanding the significance of direct sound has been a consistent part of the film scholarship engaged with the practice of Danièle Huillet and Jean-Marie Straub ever since their first films in Germany, the Böll adaptations, and their first music film, *Chronicle of Anna Magdalena Bach* in 1968. In an open letter in 1970, published under the title 'Dubbing is Murder', Straub argued forcefully against the dubbing into Italian of their subsequent film *Othon* (1970), writing that the film:

> depends precisely on things that cannot be 'reproduced' — the incarnation of Corneille's language in each character at every moment, the noise, the air, and the wind, and the effort that the actors make and the risks they take, like tightrope walkers, from one end to the other with long texts difficult to record live.[1]

The letter, in part a response to the effort taken to re-record the voiceover for *Chronicle of Anna Magdalena Bach* for Italian television, was a strident contribution to the lively debate about foreign film subtitling versus dubbing. The intervention has, however, provoked a debate about the politics of sound reproduction in cinema that is about much more than dubbing dialogue, as is clear in Huillet's and Straub's highly polemical remarks on mainstream cinema sound in a 1975 interview with Enzo Ungari, where dubbing of dialogue is diagnosed as merely a symptom of a greater sickness of 'bourgeois' filmmaking.[2] Direct sound remains one of the most debated and admired aspects of Huillet and Straub's cinema practice: Serge Daney, Michel Chion, Gilles Deleuze, Gilberto Perez, Burlin Barr, and, more recently, Benoît Turquety have all reflected on it.[3]

In this essay, direct sound in the cinema of Huillet and Straub is explored as a practice that is motivated as much by the materiality of the medium and techniques of estrangement as it is by the idea that original sound itself, particularly ambient sound, is meaningful. Chion has taken Huillet and Straub's staging of Pierre

Corneille's seventeenth-century play *Othon* within the ruins of Roman palaces in twentieth-century Rome, traffic noise penetrating from below, as an example to discuss how their practice relates to the use of ambient sound to define diegetic space. For the voice — which Chion takes as a special case for its capacity to create a sense of internal and external space — ambient sound becomes a 'container', but in *Othon* the location creates an unexpected effect:

> We'd have to agree that the sounds are the actors' voices declaiming their lines, and that the container would be the urban hum of distant traffic in which the voices and lines are heard. Actors in *Othon* often give long monologues offscreen, and yet such voices are not perceived as the traditional offscreen voice entirely determined by the image. Their voices seem to be 'in the same place' as voices of actors we do see, a space defined by the background noise.[4]

The issues for direct sound in the cinema of Huillet and Straub have thus extended beyond the initial arguments about dubbing foreign language films into a debate about sound and cinematic space. By 1975 Straub was expanding further on the significance of sound, asserting that direct sound was in opposition to the 'ideology' of dubbing which 'gives no space to the viewer'. Significantly for what is to be explored in this chapter, Straub states in the same interview: 'the waves that a sound transmits are not just sound waves. Waves of ideas, of movements, and of emotions also travel across sound'.[5]

The debate about sound in the cinema of Huillet and Straub has unfolded gradually. Chion's remarks addressed their conceptualization of direct sound and the effects of what he calls the 'monaural soundtrack' critically, questioning their valorization of on-location sound as against a 'naturalistic', mixed, and rendered soundtrack. Focusing on *Othon* and *Too Early, Too Late* (1981), Chion noticed instead a profound strangeness and unintelligibility for the viewer, but granted the ambient intrusions of noises an 'autonomous' status.[6]

Chion's focus was the unity of image and sound. The direct sound of Huillet and Straub, however, is not simply concerned with synchronization or unity, but with the effects of on-location simultaneous recording which, as Chion pointed out, can vary considerably.[7] Deleuze, analysing Huillet and Straub's sound practice as part of a broader exploration of the sound–image relationship in post-war cinema, has also examined the delivery of speech in their films, placing them in a group with the cinema of Hans Jürgen Syberberg and Marguerite Duras. Deleuze perceives a politics of sound aesthetics in which an emphatic disjuncture — what in Brechtian terminology would be referred to as a 'separation of the elements' (see the Introduction to this volume) — alternates with an equally significant coming together of sound and image. Writing of their film *Every Revolution is a Throw of the Dice* (1977), Deleuze labels speech in the film a phenomenological 'event' in terms that echo and go beyond Straub's words:

> The event is always resistance, between what the speech-act seizes and what the earth buries. It is a cycle of sky and earth, of external light and underground fire, and even more of the sound and the visual, which never re-forms into a whole, but each time constitutes the disjunction of the two images, at the same

time as their new type of relation, a relation of very precise incommensurability, not an absence of relation.[8]

Deleuze's analysis moves back and forth between the idea of disjuncture and the independence of the parts, and the idea of a new connectivity, continuing:

> What constitutes the audio-visual image is a disjunction, a dissociation of the visual and the sound, each heautonomous, but at the same time an incommensurable or 'irrational' relation which connects them to each other, without forming a whole, without offering the least whole.[9]

Deleuze's focus on the voice leads to his labelling of those passages where the image is accompanied by direct ambient sound without a vocal performance as 'silence in cinema'. This act of 'silence', or ambience, allows the direct sound recording to separate into noises that become audible as part of the network of irrational or disjointed relations. The presence of voice before and after the passages of ambience allows the sounds within it to become perceptible and hence differentiated. Moments of this kind throughout *Too Early, Too Late*, for example, enter as conscious choices interspersed with voiceover. For Deleuze, to begin with the image, or with sounds, with speech, or with music is then always to circle back to the others. In his article on *Too Early, Too Late*, film critic Serge Daney made a similar claim which is offered as a starting-point for this essay: 'The cinema, you may persist in thinking, is "images and sounds". But what if it were the reverse? What if it were "sounds and images"?'[10]

The analysis in this essay in part follows Daney, who deemed post-synchronization a 'genocide' against background noise, and who found that Huillet and Straub's direct sound practice offered a re-education of the spectator's ear. It also takes from Deleuze the idea that their exploration of sound plays a role in the development of a philosophical approach to cinema history, and from Barr the suggestion that their filmmaking is anti-ocularcentric and 'cannot be assimilated into a governing vision'.[11]

Recent publications on Huillet and Straub's films, including the volume *Tell It to the Stones*, have begun to examine the impact of their approach to sound on other filmmakers and moving image artists working on the big screen, for television, and in gallery spaces.[12] One filmmaker whose work was directly influenced by friendship and collaboration with them was the essay filmmaker Harun Farocki, who also experimented periodically with sound as documentation. In his film for television *The Taste of Life* (1979), for example, Farocki experimentally blurs the boundary between diegetic and non-diegetic sound, between voices and sounds on and off-screen. In *The People are Standing Forwards in the Streets* (1987) Farocki shot a short, literary adaptation inspired by Straub-Huillet's experiments with text delivery and ambient sound. Farocki's Brechtian 'separation of the elements' in these little-known films joins Huillet and Straub's sound practice in its capacity to produce shocks and surprises and constitutes a unique example of direct engagement by another filmmaker with their theory and practice of sound.

Noise: From the Unreproducible to the Unforeseen

In a conversation about cinema and politics in 2001 at the Centre Pompidou, Straub referred to Bertolt Brecht's practice in *Kuhle Wampe, or Who Owns the World?* (*Kuhle Wampe oder: Wem gehört die Welt?*, 1932) and made the pragmatic point that making films 'politically' means, first and foremost, the freedom and independence of 'using the lenses you need, the amount of film stock you need, shooting in the order you need, with the equipment you need'.[13] To the equipment list could be added the sound recorder, which was, like the editing of their films, mainly the responsibility of Huillet.[14] As Jean-Pierre Duret, who was trained by the pair's long-term sound engineer Louis Hochet, remembers: 'Danièle listened to absolutely every take. With a lot of concentration. [...] Jean-Marie pacing back and forth in front of her, waiting. It was a very religious ritual. When she finished, she'd say, "It's good," and we moved on'.[15]

Hochet and Duret worked mostly with a single microphone, placing the boom at a distance above the actors to capture their voices and incorporate the ambience and sounds of the location. Besides the radical, anti-ocularcentric stance of their attentiveness towards sound in film, this practice also foregrounds the presence of the authors themselves and the moment of recording. For Serge Daney, this constitutes the particular ethics of their practice, and he imagines Huillet and Straub in *Too Early, Too Late* 'in the middle of the field, moistened fingers raised to catch the wind and ears pricked up to hear what it's saying'.[16] The single microphone creates, of course, a singular position from which the sonic world is perceived in tandem with the camera image, placing the sounding world, the actors, musicians as well as the birds or wind in the trees, on the recorded track as a unified whole. The advantage of direct sound is thus, as Duret explains, to let sounds become a 'unique and indissoluble whole, a piece of time. Direct sound is a block of time'.[17]

In *Too Early, Too Late*, these practices become audible, for example, in a slow, protracted (ten-minute) drive through the Egyptian countryside, where the soundtrack is dominated by a mass of birds chirping. Or elsewhere, in *History Lessons* (1972), the microphone, hidden on the back seat of the car, creates the audible experience of the position of a single passenger, or as Gilberto Perez calls it, 'the perspective of the back seat' encountering 'the contingent' through the multiple screens in the image, but also through sound.[18] What stays intact in direct sound is thus the unity of the moment of recording with all its contingency.

The idea of the 'unreproducible' and noise, in Huillet and Straub, is thus not so much an interference in the recording apparatus of cinema which foregrounds the medium in a formalistic way. Rather, it is a practice which permits and attends to surprise, contingency, or the unforeseen. As Straub explained in a more recent interview, their method configures the production and conception of a film so that its internal structures are not deconstructed or broken down by the author, but through 'the air and the light and so on, the sounds and such — the film begins to live in all that isn't foreseen'.[19] Their method of production opens a space for these elements to enter the film by coincidence. Straub distinguishes this from spontaneity, which presumes that the production has no established frame

FIG. 5.1. Danièle Huillet and Jean-Marie Straub, *Fortini/Cani*
(1976, courtesy of BELVA Film).

or method.[20] These elements create the unforeseen in the film and become 'an integral part of the subject matter. If the film exists, then the unforeseen is never an external factor but arises from within'.[21] Less embedded in a discussion of media reproduction then, what cannot be reproduced here is the element of coincidence, the unpredictable. Within this practice, a level of directorial control is relinquished to invite contingency.

Huillet and Straub's direction of sound as noise allows for the unforeseen, but also seeks interruptions and distortions purposefully. For example, in *Fortini/Cani* the monologues of the 'performers' are often inharmoniously integrated into the soundscape: Luciana Nissim (Momigliano) in shot 9, referred to in the script as 'she who speaks', is accompanied by (or perhaps interrupted by) church bells (Figure 5.1); film critic and friend of Huillet and Straub, Adriano Aprà, 'he who speaks', recites against an open window letting in the noise of cars from the street. Similarly, *Othon* unfolds for the most part against the traffic noise of Rome and, in one episode, the splashing water or, in the words of Richard Roud, 'the ceaseless racket' of a fountain.[22]

Too Early, Too Late is divided into two sections of unequal length, both containing twenty-five shots.[23] Part 'A' (entitled 'Friedrich Engels' and lasting twenty-seven minutes) begins with the ambient sound of birdsong and, once again, church bells over a black screen, followed by the credits. The first scene then switches abruptly, and quite unexpectedly given the 'rural' soundtrack that precedes it, to images and the attendant sounds of traffic filmed from a car circling the busy roundabout of the Place de la Bastille in Paris (Figure 5.2). The opening of the film thus programmatically heralds a 'separation of the elements' which can involve

FIG. 5.2. Danièle Huillet and Jean-Marie Straub, *Too Early, Too Late*
(1981, courtesy of BELVA Film).

both disjunction and conjunction. Later, in the second part of the film, part 'B'
(entitled 'Mahmud [sic] Hussein' and lasting one hour and seventeen minutes),
sirens marking the end of a shift at a factory in Cairo noisily introduce Huillet and
Straub's homage to the (silent) *Workers Leaving the Lumière Factory* (*La Sortie de l'usine
Lumière à Lyon*, 1895) of the Lumière brothers. Rather than merely anticipating
the appearance of the space in the image, or as Chion puts it 'inhabiting' it, these
separate ambient sounds intervene in the film beyond the image and demonstrate
that the acoustic space prior to speech — the reading of texts of Friedrich Engels
and 'Mahmoud Hussein' (the pseudonym of Bahgat Elnadi and Adel Rifaat) — is
itself full of sound.[24]

Another way to understand the 'blocks' of sound recording with their often-
unforeseen noises is as 'documents' within Huillet and Straub's practice of layering
quotations. For Perez every Straub-Huillet film is a 'repository of documents, a
juxtaposition of traces' and in the light of this, ambient noise can be understood
as another 'object that comes down to us from the distant or the near past' and
'may be regarded as a document of its own time [...] set in a kind of dialogue with
documents of earlier times'.[25] In the two minutes or so between the credits and the
introduction of the voiceover, the ambient sound is not merely there to construct
the illusion of depth in cinematic space; it does not simply, as Chion puts it,
naturalize the cinematic experience for the sake of realism by creating sonic depth
or spatial immersion. As the voice appears it is still possible to identify the sounds of
passing cars as near or far, but these sounds now serve as a document, a quotation of
place and time within a pluralistic sonic landscape and in a dialectical relationship
to Huillet's recitation of the letter from Engels to Karl Kautsky of 1889.

Ambient sounds are a document of an event of recording. A recording captures the pluralistic nature of sound in a specific place and at a specific time. In Huillet and Straub's films, ambient recordings of specific locations can sometimes even be specifically identified in the script; for example, similarly to *Too Early, Too Late*, the script for *History Lessons* notes 'Noises of the viale dei Fori Imperiali' as accompaniment for the opening black screen and title.[26] Returning to *Too Early, Too Late*, the document of ambient sound is, as noted above, juxtaposed after two minutes with another sonic document, Huillet's reading of Engels on the role of the bourgeoisie during the French Revolution. After a further two minutes, in which the image shot from the car continues accompanied by only ambient sound, the image abruptly cuts to a black screen. Here, for twenty-four seconds, the ambient sound recording of the traffic continues as Huillet recites from Engels on resistance movements among the peasantry. Thus, at this point in the film, the audience is faced with only a stratified soundscape and no images. With the ambient sound seamlessly bridging the cut to black (this occurs repeatedly and in both parts of the film) the separability of the film's visual and acoustic documents is, once again, programmatically signalled. This separation of the elements is, patently, only possible if these documents are 'together' in the first place, as when direct sound is used.

As Engels refers to the French provinces and the struggle for food despite the fertility of the land, the image cuts from black to a pan across a rural French land-scape, and the metropolitan traffic is replaced by the sound of the countryside, which includes almost immediately a loud passing car. In the Parisian episode direct sound recording keeps the ambient sounds rooted to the image of the car on the roundabout, but the noises are not themselves stuck in a singular referentiality. Maintaining the fixed position of the moment of recording, a kind of *Jetztzeit* (now-time) as Walter Benjamin might put it (see the Introduction to this volume), they create a dialectical relationship between the present of the film and the historical momentum of the French Revolution, between Engels's (unseen) text and Huillet's (equally unseen) delivery of it. The presence of the past is thus in a continuum which embraces not only the stasis of the historical text (or document), but also the recorded sonic cacophony of the roundabout, and the speaking voice all brought together through the apparatus of cinema.

Wind: *Umwelt* and Cinema Before Language

The creation of a sonic and historical continuum in *Too Early, Too Late* demonstrates how Huillet and Straub use sound in combination with visual layering. An interesting corollary is the way in which such sound stratification allows the viewer to recognize the particularity of incidental or accidental participants in the film and their *Umwelt* within the whole. The term *Umwelt*, which roughly translates as 'environment', is one associated with the recent revival of the work of the German biologist Jakob Johann von Uexküll in the environmental humanities, but, as Inga Pollmann has demonstrated, it was also taken up by contemporary thinkers such as Walter Benjamin.[27] Here we might follow Pollmann in connecting with Benjamin's claim that cinema is the ideal place to engage with the notion of *Umwelt*, as the cinematic apparatus estranges viewers from their surroundings and complicates the relationships between subject and object. *Umwelten* overlap in ways that are echoed in Huillet and Straub's cinema. In *Too Early, Too Late* nature emerges as things and living beings emerge and disappear from the earth sonically as a plurality of worlds. Daney rightly insists that individual elements become separate actors within the landscapes of the film: 'The fields, roadways, fences and rows of trees are traces of human activity, but the actors are birds, a few vehicles, a faint murmur, the wind'.[28] The disjunctions of image and sound, discussed as a cinematic device above, can also be found in more subtle ways in the natural effects recorded as a consequence of using direct sound. As light travels faster than sound and the camera may be recording an image far away from the microphone, sound and image are not always synchronized. Daney points out that 'at moments, one begins to see (the grass bent by the wind) before hearing (the wind responsible for this bending). At other moments, one hears first (the wind), then one sees (the grass)'.[29] The film, he argues, thus occupies the ambiguous relationship, also described by Deleuze, in which there is an element of synchrony, but also of disjointedness, as in the everyday experience of the human senses. Striking examples of things heard–but–not–seen include, in Part A of the film, water running (in Tréogan), dogs, children, and insistent birdsong and, in Part B in Egypt, children's voices and birdsong again, the aforementioned siren, and airplanes overhead.

The wind in *Too Early, Too Late*, first heard in the sequences in rural France, becomes a recurring sonic motif. The sound of wind from one location sometimes spills over into the next image, most notably as a pan across a flat field, with houses and trees in the distance (Figure 5.3), cuts to a vertical upwards pan of an ancient tree (Figure 5.4) (a camera movement which strikingly echoes shot 16 in *Fortini/Cani*, see Chapter 4) that appears to have the same sound as the previous shot.

How do the elements achieve signification or meaning? With the advent of sound in cinema, ambient sound became an intrusive sonic document beyond the realm of human language systems; unforeseen noises — the repeated off-screen birdsong in the case of *Too Early, Too Late* for example — intrude into the human world of language. As Straub explains, the appeal of coincidence or contingency is that it introduces 'the opposite of mimesis' and 'a way of undermining metaphor'.[30] Huillet and Straub's practice of direct sound posits sound as a cinematic element, an 'acoustic object' in its own right, rather than a symbolic link to the substance of its source.[31] If, as Deleuze maintains, 'the visual image, in Straub, is the rock' and the 'rock is not touched in words', ambient or direct sound can be seen not only as an aspect of Straub-Huillet's Brechtian 'separation of the elements', but also as a challenge to the (pre)dominance of linguistic referentiality.[32] Perhaps this is how to understand Turquety's claim that ambient sound is to be read as 'neither fidelity nor interpretation, but absolute literalness'.[33] In the final shot of *Too Early, Too Late*, following a vertical pan down from a cloudless blue sky and past two tower blocks in construction, the camera comes to rest framing waves as they lap against a river bank, dispersing the reflection of the skyscrapers. The pan down is accompanied by the final lines of commentary:

FIGS. 5.3 & 5.4. Danièle Huillet and Jean-Marie Straub, *Too Early, Too Late* (1981, courtesy of BELVA Film).

[*Blue sky*] And from 1955 to 1967 the mass movement could be dismantled and co-opted by a new ruling caste [*tower blocks*] inheriting all the vices of the old [*river*] and betraying [*grass on the riverbank*] the national dignity which had served its ascension. [*Waves*]

After the commentary ends, the shot of the waves is held for one minute and ten seconds at which point the film ends. The waves, with their repeated, cyclical motion, perhaps suggesting revolution and gradual attrition, are seen and (loudly) heard. The blackness of the film's opening, with its disembodied birdsong and bells,

Fig. 5.5. Danièle Huillet and Jean-Marie Straub, *Too Early, Too Late*
(1981, courtesy of BELVA Film).

is countered at its end by an almost revelatory union of the cinematic elements —
sound and image — to document an unstable meeting of modernity, the tower
blocks, and their natural *Umwelt*, the water, waves, and grass of the riverbank.

Too Early, Too Late thus allows objects, both animate and inanimate, to emerge as
a rich plurality outside of the confines of language — for example in scenes in which
human beings (see Figure 5.5) are immersed in a larger sonic *Umwelt*. The sonic
plurality and stratification in these *Umwelten* allow for an understanding of history
that is not only beyond the linearity associated with established notions of progress,
but which can also embrace unsystematic flow and uncontrollable or contingent
pluralism. Huillet and Straub's fidelity to the quirks in delivery of individual actors,
and their attention to the specificity of different languages, accents, and inflections
as sonic elements in the recitation of literary texts, is consistent with this approach.
In scholarship on their films, ambient or direct sound has often been discussed in
relation to textual recitation and the performance of music — particularly in the
case of *Chronicle of Anna Magdalena Bach*, *Moses and Aaron*, and *Von heute auf morgen*
(1997) — where their direct, mono, location sound recording is in stark opposition
to the standard industry practices of studio recording (multi-tracking, equalization,
Dolby, and so forth). *Too Early, Too Late* not only reminds us momentarily of its
predecessors with a brief snatch of *Moses and Aaron* over the credits for Part B, the
same passage that opens *Fortini/Cani*, but also demonstrates that their theory and
practice of direct sound is consistent across their *œuvre*, also determining the *dispositif*
of their filmmaking at its most essayistic and, as they themselves acknowledged,
most documentary.

Harun Farocki: Stratified Soundscapes

A direct influence of the theory and practice of Straub-Huillet's filmmaking on the *auteurs* of the New German Cinema can be difficult to pinpoint. Aside from direct involvement in the earliest experiments of later feature film directors — they provided Rainer Werner Fassbinder and Rudolf Thome with footage and Huillet edited the latter's black and white gangster short *Jane Shoots John Because He is Cheating on Her With Ann* (*Jane erschießt John, weil er sie mit Ann betrügt*, 1968) — the most tangible and lasting impact of their work can be seen in the films of the documentarist and essay filmmaker Harun Farocki.

Whilst Farocki's debt to Straub-Huillet's political modernism is well-known — the Brechtian aspect of his first feature-length film *Between Two Wars* (*Zwischen zwei Kriegen*, 1978) is axiomatic in this respect — there has been little or no discussion of Farocki's experiments with direct sound. Indeed, the patent differences between their work have often been (over-)emphasized: parallel retrospectives in Berlin in Autumn 2017 were deemed to be a juxtaposition of 'very divergent forms of radical filmmaking'.[34] However, there is evidence, particularly in a number of lesser-known Farocki films, to show that he was keen to experiment with sound and sound-recording — the use of ambient sound, archival recordings of music, and the recitation of text off-screen for example — in ways that would otherwise be more associated with Huillet and Straub themselves. In what follows two examples will be considered briefly: *The Taste of Life* and *The People are Standing Forwards in the Streets*. Each is a unique experiment, demonstrating a less well-known side of Farocki's practice. They engage with direct sound, recitation, and music in very different ways from his more canonical films.

Huillet and Straub were important mentors for Farocki. He met Straub for the first time at the German Film and Television School (DFFB) in Berlin in 1966, where Straub presented *Not Reconciled* to the first generation of film students at the academy. The Brechtian practice of Huillet and Straub was to become exemplary for a number of young filmmakers at the DFFB in their search for a radical, political cinema during and after 1968. Huillet and Straub became 'heroes' in the community of filmmakers and critics around *Filmkritik* in the 1970s and 1980s, the journal of which Farocki was editor until it was wound up in 1984.[35] Farocki met Straub again over the years in Cologne, Munich, and Hamburg and a friendship slowly developed. In October 1977, during the production of *Between Two Wars* (at the time provisionally known as 'The Connecting Tube'), Farocki typed a letter to Huillet and Straub in which he not only writes about the significance of his own film ('with this film we have made something which, i am certain, without being arrogant, is much more important than we are') but also tells them that, following the completion of the shoot, the team all sat down together to watch *Fortini/Cani*:

> yesterday we finished shooting the connecting tube and invited everyone involved to a screening of the rushes and then showed cani [*Fortini/Cani*]. for me it was the first film in three years, i had been isolating.
> your film seemed very lonely to me, what we had shot seemed to me almost popular, like an operetta. i didn't think about it, didn't talk about it and by the end had understood everything.[36]

According to Tilman Baumgärtel, Farocki even went so far as to claim 'perhaps I only made the film in order to be recognised by Straub'.[37] Subsequently, it was through Straub's recommendation that *Between Two Wars* earned Farocki his first mention in *Cahiers du cinéma* in 1981.[38] In 1982/83, Huillet and Straub lived with Farocki in West Berlin and conducted research and location scouting for *Class Relations* (1984) during their stay in the city. Farocki then took on the role of Delamarche in the Kafka adaptation and produced the 'making-of' documentary *Jean-Marie Straub and Danièle Huillet at Work on a Film Based on Franz Kafka's 'Amerika'* (*Jean-Marie Straub und Danièle Huillet bei der Arbeit an einem Film nach Franz Kafkas Romanfragment 'Amerika'*, 1983) for television on a commission from WDR. The film was broadcast on ARD on the 13 November 1983 in the series *Showcase, Images and Reports from the Cinema* (*Schaukasten, Bilder und Berichte vom Kino*). For Farocki, this was a further chance to engage with the methods of his 'heroes'. As he explained in an interview from 2008: 'They have a lot of rules, it is very difficult to talk about it with them [...]. They do not really explain their aesthetic principles and that is why it is much more instructive to observe what they do'.[39]

Aside from the broader, generally acknowledged influence of Huillet and Straub's Brechtianism on Farocki already mentioned — a kinship already evident in his early student films, most notably in *Inextinguishable Fire* (*Nicht löschbares Feuer*, 1968) — and, much more specifically, his integration of the Cairo factory scene from *Too Early, Too Late* into his gallery installation *Workers Leaving the Factory in Eleven Decades* (*Arbeiter verlassen die Fabrik in elf Jahrzehnten*, 2006),[40] he also, from time to time, experimented in quite precise ways with the methods and techniques of Huillet and Straub's films. In the short film *The Taste of Life*, shot in 1979 shortly after *Between Two Wars* and the letter to the 'straubs' about *Fortini/Cani*, Farocki finally realized a long-standing project to capture a more-or-less spontaneous, unscripted impression of city life in Berlin's streets and parks: 'For years I have been trying to get the funds to make it possible to capture everyday life as seen on the street'.[41] Farocki's impressionistic, twenty-nine-minute experimental film was first shown on television (Sender Freies Berlin) on 5 August 1979 and premiered in West Berlin's Cinema Bundesallee on 28 June 1980.

The Taste of Life strings together seemingly unconnected vignettes of Berlin street and park life. There is no camera movement within the individual scenes (beyond hand-held camera shake) although some consist of multiple shots. Vignettes include: a high angle shot, presumably from a window of a flat, onto a minor car accident with attendant police and curious onlookers; a beggar at a street junction; passers-by outside a Karstadt department store; workers repairing the track of Berlin's suburban railway; women standing outside a run-down hotel; children knocking on doors; passers-by outside a prison; what appears to be a drive-in cinema; and people swimming and relaxing by a canal and in a park. Between the different scenes the camera returns, almost obsessively, to a local newsagent where the shopkeeper is seen arranging and rearranging her advertising boards on the pavement as vans deliver the latest edition of the *Berliner Zeitung*. The newsagent and car accident scenes are accompanied by a medley of rock and roll music from the 1960s and 70s, elsewhere there are two brief voiceover commentaries by Farocki relating impressions of daily life in the city (observations on window displays, street vendors, and an overheard conversation). In the opening scene of the traffic accident, comprising a number of takes divided by black, the soundtrack begins with a dull ambient sound of traffic and is then interrupted by background music, distorted as if playing from a record player.

For all its documentary ambitions, *The Taste of Life* also experiments with unexpected disjunctures of image and sound, not least in the mixtape of popular music which accompanies the routines of everyday life in the metropolis, and which includes The Rolling Stones, Ry Cooder and Nicki Hopkins, Tony Conrad and Faust, and Jimi Hendrix. In effect *The Taste of Life* is itself a 'taster', sampling bits and pieces of the Berlin zeitgeist and popular music of the previous decade or so. In many scenes it is difficult to ascertain whether the sound is in fact direct or not. For example, the background rumble in the opening car accident sequence sounds generically metropolitan and does not appear to register passing cars. In the scene with the beggar, the sound of passing vehicles rises and falls, but not only is it out of sync with the vehicles we actually see, it also bridges seamlessly across different shots. Outside Karstadt it is hard to connect the footsteps to actual passers-by, and the traffic is behind the camera. Furthermore, no two scenes are alike in this respect, which suggests that Farocki is experimenting with synchronous sound in a way that is at times reminiscent of the Apuan Alps and Florentine street scenes in *Fortini/Cani* (see above and also Chapter 4) in which sounds off (including children playing and birdsong) are often prominent and in which Fortini's recitation is mixed with ambient sound. This is also the case with Farocki's brief voiceover interjections in *The Taste of Life*.

In one particularly striking scene, shot outside a prison, Farocki appears to be drawing attention to the materiality of sound and image: repeatedly the film appears to 'catch fire' in passages of celluloid flare-out (Figure 5.6), displaying the material substrate of the film in a way we will not encounter so directly in the work of Huillet and Straub prior to the latter's 2015 film Venice Biennale installation *Homage to Italian Art!* (2015, see Introduction). As we see people wandering in and out of the prison and the edges of the celluloid strip appear to ignite, we hear an orchestra of car horn honking which seems to be entirely unrelated to what is seen, and which seamlessly bridges the three different shots that constitute the episode. This self-reflexive gesture is subsequently underscored by a somewhat unexpected passage of voiceover in which Farocki meditates on the film we are watching — noting for example that nowadays life on the street can only be glimpsed — and slips momentarily, for no apparent reason, from his normal speaking voice to a kind of madcap *Sprechgesang*.

Like the shop windows Farocki mentions in his commentary — with their displays covered with posters where, we are told, 'there is more to read than to see' — *The Taste of Life* also puts life on display, for example documenting railway workers on their break fooling around and throwing water at each other. Their activities are not audible, but as the camera retreats to a bridge overlooking the railway line there is — for the first time in the film and a little before its mid-point — an almost revelatory moment of synchronicity as we see and hear a Berlin S-Bahn train pass

FIG. 5.6. Harun Farocki, *The Taste of Life* (1979, © Harun Farocki).

by. This striking moment draws attention to the relationship of sound and image in a way comparable to the shock of sudden quietude at the beginning of the Apuan Alps sequence of *Fortini/Cani* or the traffic noises of Florence that follow it.

With its stratification of diegetic and non-diegetic, synchronous and a-synchronous sound, its abrupt juxtapositions of tripod and hand-held camerawork, and its intermittent use of mood music and commentary, *The Taste of Life* can be read as a mini-essay in stratification à la Straub-Huillet in general and *Fortini/Cani* in particular. Like their films it is, in Perez's previously cited words, a 'repository of documents, a juxtaposition of traces'. Less overtly political than *Fortini/Cani* or, for that matter, *Between Two Wars* — despite passing observations on consumption, commodification, and advertising — the film can be understood as an exercise or experiment in constructing visual and sonic stratification.

Stratification is also the key constructive principle in another unusual Farocki film from a decade later and again one with a direct connection to his on-going engagement with the work of Huillet and Straub. *The People are Standing Forwards in the Streets*, produced by Südwestfunk Baden-Baden and first broadcast by Südwestfunk 3 on 14 November 1987, is an eight-minute short consisting of static shots of access decks to Berlin housing blocks accompanied by direct ambient sound and an off-screen recitation by Adelheid Rogger of Georg Heym's famous expressionist poem which gives the film its title. In his 'making-of' documentary on Straub-Huillet's *Class Relations*, Farocki had already demonstrated an interest in the delivery of text in their films, dedicating a long sequence to the rehearsals with the main actor Christian Heinisch. Just prior to *The People are Standing Forwards in the Streets* Farocki produced a brief television feature entitled *Filmtip: Death of Empedocles* (*Filmtip: Der Tod des Empedokles*, 1987) on Huillet and Straub's then recent

FIG. 5.7. Harun Farocki, *The People are Standing Forwards in the Streets* (1987, © Harun Farocki).

Hölderlin film in which he interviews the lead actor Andreas von Rauch on his working methods and collaboration with Huillet and Straub. It would seem that this experience may have spurred Farocki into experimenting with the recitation of literary texts himself. Space doesn't permit a detailed analysis of the film, which is unusual in Farocki's *œuvre* for its formal rigour and experimentally symmetrical structure. For the first minute or so nine access decks are shown very rapidly one after another (Figure 5.7) framed in deep perspective with ambient sound and sharply contrasting light and weather conditions. Only in the eighth is there a brief glimpse of a passer-by walking towards the camera before turning to descend a stairwell to the right. This rapid sequence is followed by a single shot of a concrete undercroft, held for almost forty-five seconds and which marks, immediately following a prominent peal of church bells, the beginning of Rogger's solemn and increasingly theatrical recitation of Heym's poem. This recitation occupies the remaining six minutes of the film, in which the sequence of nine access decks is repeated in reverse order. This time round the camera lingers on each deck for longer and the ambient sounds, including traffic, birdsong, aircraft, more church bells, and wind, are overlaid with the reading of the poem.

The apocalyptic scenes described in Heym's 1911 poem, generally interpreted as a dystopian vision of early modernity and the dangers of technological progress, estrange the quotidian housing blocks filmed by Farocki's cameraman (Ingo Kratisch) seven decades later. This layering of historical documents — very much in the spirit of Huillet and Straub's 'thoroughly documentary cinema' — is strikingly underscored by the stratification of the imagery, the abrupt cuts from one access deck to the next with an overall trajectory of descent prior to the recitation and rising during it.[42] The uneasiness of the poem is transposed onto contemporary Berlin: we hear Heym's poem over (or perhaps under) the ambient sound of Berlin's *Jetztzeit*, rather as von Rauch had to compete with unexpected gusts of Sicilian wind in *The Death of Empedocles*.

Huillet and Straub employ direct ambient sound — noise, air, wind, and so forth — as a disjunctive, non-immersive experience of ambient listening which highlights the status of direct sound recording as documentation embracing the coincidental, the unforeseen, and the contingent. Their sound practice demonstrates a careful attention to place as a pluralistic, ever-flowing sonic environment (*Umwelt*) in dialogue with text and language. The stratification or dialectics of sound and image examined in this essay, with selected examples from *Too Early, Too Late*, reminds us of the quintessential premise of Huillet and Straub's cinema: that things unfold, transform, and can be otherwise. This is the premise that also underpins the work of Huillet and Straub's 'student', Harun Farocki.

Notes to Chapter 5

1. Jean-Marie Straub, 'Dubbing is Murder', in Straub and Huillet, *Writings*, pp. 113-16 (p. 115).
2. Enzo Ungari, 'Interview on Direct Sound' [interview with Danièle Huillet and Jean-Marie Straub], in Straub and Huillet, *Writings*, pp. 156-60 (p. 159).
3. Selected texts on the subject referred to in this essay are: Michel Chion, *Audio-Vision: Sound on Screen*, ed. and trans. by Claudia Gorbman (New York: Columbia University Press, 1994); Gilles Deleuze, *Cinema 2: The Time-Image*, trans. by Hugh Tomlinson and Robert Galeta (Minneapolis: University of Minneapolis Press, 1997); Gilberto Perez, *The Material Ghost: Films and their Medium* (Baltimore, MD: John Hopkins University Press, 1998); Daney, 'Cinemeteorology'; Burlin Barr, 'Too Close, Too Far: Cultural Composition in Straub and Huillet's *Too Early, Too Late*', *Camera Obscura*, 53 (2003), 1-25; Benoît Turquety, 'Orality and Objectification: Danièle Huillet and Jean-Marie Straub, Filmmakers and Translators', *SubStance*, 44.2 (2015), 47-65.
4. Chion, *Audio-Vision*, p. 68.
5. Ungari, 'Interview on Direct Sound', p. 156.
6. Chion, *Audio-Vision*, p. 106.
7. Chion gives various possibilities for relationships between sound, space, and image depending on the kind of sound (ibid., p. 79).
8. Deleuze, *Cinema 2*, p. 246.
9. Ibid.
10. Daney, 'Cinemeteorology'.
11. Barr, 'Too Close, Too Far', p. 9.
12. *Tell It to the Stones*, ed. by Busch and Hering.
13. Albera, 'Sickle and Hammer, Cannons, Cannons, Dynamite!', p. 117.
14. See Heberle and Funke Stern, 'The Fire Inside the Mountain', p. 254.
15. Jean-Pierre Duret, 'At Work with Straub and Huillet: Thoughts and Reflections from their Collaborators', in *Jean-Marie Straub & Danièle Huillet*, ed. by Fendt, pp. 127-38 (p. 137).
16. Daney, 'Cinemeteorology'.
17. Duret, 'At Work with Straub and Huillet', p. 138.
18. Perez, *The Material Ghost*, p. 284.
19. Lylov and Marhöfer, 'A Thousand Cliffs', p. 377.
20. Ibid., p. 380.
21. Ibid., p. 377.
22. Roud, *Jean-Marie Straub*, p. 22.
23. This count excludes the insertions of black film in both parts and the three-minute sequence of

black and white archive footage (no fewer than forty-three shots in total) which precedes the final shot of Part B.

24. Chion, *Audio-Vision*, p. 75.
25. Perez, *The Material Ghost*, pp. 320, 310.
26. Luisa Greenfield, 'History Lessons by Comparison', in *Tell It to The Stones*, ed. by Busch and Hering, pp. 268-92 (p. 279).
27. Inga Pollmann, 'Invisible Worlds, Visible: Uexküll's *Umwelt*, Film and Film Theory', *Critical Inquiry*, 39 (2013), 777-816 (pp. 806-08).
28. Daney, 'Cinemeteorology'.
29. Ibid.
30. Lylov and Marhöfer, 'A Thousand Cliffs', p. 387.
31. Christian Metz, 'Aural Objects', trans. by Georgia Gurrieri, *Yale French Studies*, 60 (1980), 24-32 (p. 29).
32. Deleuze, *Cinema 2*, pp. 235, 236.
33. Turquety, 'Orality and Objectification', p. 48.
34. Annett Busch and Tobias Hering, 'Opening', in *Tell It to The Stones*, ed. by Busch and Hering, pp. 10-27 (p. 12).
35. Alice Maligne, 'Questions à Harun Farocki', *2.0.1: revue de recherche sur l'art du XIXe au XXIe siècle*, 1 (2008), 61-70 (p. 64). See also Harun Farocki, 'Stop Coughing!', in *Jean-Marie Straub & Danièle Huillet*, ed. by Fendt, pp. 154-55.
36. Harun Farocki, letter to Jean-Marie Straub, 6 October 1977: 'Februar 2018: Ein Brief an die Straubs (Oktober 1977)' <https://www.harun-farocki-institut.org/de/2018/02/10/februar-2018-kinder-die-das-boese-und-die-schlechtigkeit-anzieht/> [accessed 9 August 2021].
37. See <https://www.harunfarocki.de/de/filme/1980er/1983/jean-marie-straub-und-daniele-huillet-bei-der-arbeit-an-einem-film-nach-franz-kafkas-romanfragment-amerika.html> [accessed 14 January 2022].
38. See Louis Skorecki, 'Qui est Farocki?', in *Cahiers du cinéma*, 329 (1981), 8.
39. Maligne, 'Questions à Harun Farocki', p. 64.
40. See <https://www.tate.org.uk/art/artworks/farocki-workers-leaving-the-factory-in-11-decades-t14332> [accessed 26 October 2021]. In the installation images Straub-Huillet's *Too Early, Too Late* is on the third monitor from the right.
41. See <https://www.harunfarocki.de/films/1970s/1979/the-taste-of-life.html> [accessed 26 October 2021].
42. Perez, *The Material Ghost*, p. 312.

CHAPTER 6

❖

'Guardami!': *Sicilia!* and the Claim on Attention

Brendan Prendeville

> At the risk of being a bit pompous, political cinema is the one that ends with saying: 'Sickle and hammer, cannons, cannons, dynamite!' [...]
>
> So the people who make this film, with that ending, will not stop there. They will add more; by asking Beethoven for a gift, they will add the idea of convalescence.
>
> And if one of these two aspects were to be missing, it would not be a political film.
>
> — JEAN-MARIE STRAUB[1]

Two films made about, respectively, the filming and the editing of *Sicilia!* (1999), provide insights into the collaborative practice of the filmmakers, tracing their decisions, recording conversations.[2] At one point in Jean-Charles Fitoussi's account of the filming, Straub, watching the rushes, finds in the lighting of a shot of the character Silvestro standing by the window in his mother's house a 'little something' in common with Robert Bresson's *Diary of a Country Priest* (*Journal d'un curé de campagne*, 1951). Mention of Bresson's famous work crops up in the long discussion Huillet and Straub had with François Albera in 2001, on the subject of political film. They recollect Jean-Luc Godard's ambivalent reaction to *Chronicle of Anna Magdalena Bach* (1968), a film which, Straub observes, would never have been made had it not been for *Diary of a Country Priest*. Godard said their film needed something added to signal a political meaning, and Straub asked if he meant he should put 'Everything is political' at the end, in counterpoint to the *Diary*'s concluding 'tout est grâce', to which Godard eagerly agreed, taking Straub's sardonic remark as a serious suggestion. 'Everything is political' is in any case a truism, Straub adds.[3] It is also a reductive formula unless the 'everything' is understood to amplify and complicate the meaning of 'political', as in 'political film': 'No political film without morality, no political film without theology, no political film without mysticism', Straub insists.[4]

No political film without grace: the films of Huillet and Straub make claims on our attention, in the sense given that faculty by Simone Weil, who saw attention as bound up 'not with the will but with desire — or, more exactly, consent'. 'What,' she asks, 'could be more stupid than to tighten up our muscles and set our jaws about virtue, or poetry, or the solution of a problem. Attention is something quite different'. 'Pride,' she adds, 'is a tightening up of this kind. There is a lack of grace [...] in the proud man'.[5] The 'difficulty' of the films of Huillet and Straub is not of the sort that might induce a tightening of the muscles, but arises rather from all that there is to take in, with a way of filmmaking in which everything counts, in sound, image, and sense. In the case of *Sicilia!*, excerpted dialogue from Elio Vittorini's novel *Conversation(s) in Sicily* (*Conversazione in Sicilia*) provides a script whose conflicting themes afford a political perspective wider in scope than the stock label 'Vittorini's anti-fascist novel' suggests.[6] The novel was indeed anti-fascist, covertly enough to escape censorship on its first complete publication in 1941, but Vittorini probes beneath fascism, of which he had until the Spanish Civil War been himself a leftist adherent. *Sicilia!* is, in any case, filmed in the present day, and makes no explicit reference to Italy of the fascist era. Vittorini's novel itself demands alertness of the reader, as a modernist experiment in narrative whose thematic strands Huillet and Straub reinterpret in terms of vision and sound, in ways that I will try to trace, in my report on watching *Sicilia!*

Voices in Time

Attention is durational. Modern philosophers, most notably Henri Bergson, have addressed the elusive subject of the relationship between time and consciousness, and, in doing so, have necessarily arrived at the topic of attention, as Bergson himself does in *Matter and Memory* (*Matière et mémoire*, 1896).[7] Film is itself a temporal object, and as with a performance of music or a staged drama, the attention we give extends in parallel over the given span, and so, as we watch, our very process of attention, as a species of time-consciousness, may find itself reflected back to us; this indeed is what occurs, through a multiplicity of distinctive means, in *Sicilia!*

We can draw a parallel between one use of sound in the film and an example of time consciousness given by Wilhelm Dilthey, who, like Bergson, reflected on the subject:

> The sequence of a continuous sound, such as that of a rolling cart on the street beneath me, is not composed of one indivisible, unextended moment that is present and others that are past. Rather, the sequence is to be found in our actual perception.[8]

In *Sicilia!*, sequences of sustained continuous sound play an important structural role, most prominently the sound of the train, heard from where the travellers converse. Shifts in registration of this sound prompt awareness of a continuity that might otherwise pass unnoticed, as background. In the first train sequence, the two policemen leaning on the window in the corridor have to shout over the noise of the rails; to the effect that when the scene cuts to the compartment, and the 'Great Lombard' closes the door, we sustain awareness of the, now quieter, train sound, and have an expectation to hear it established.

Soon after, at the halt in Catania, ambient sound alone takes up the narrative, in the first of such passages without dialogue: the sound of a train arriving and stopping accompanies a shot of the platform, the sea beyond; birds take flight from the tracks, brakes screech, there are voices. The journey resumes with an inland view of Catania, receding, to the sound of the rails. Not long after, a passage that is altogether silent tracks the passing landscape from the train. The audio recorder and the camera register these determinate, transient events, like Dilthey's cartwheels running over the ground; the continuity is in our sustained attention.

During most of the film, we watch people speaking, and so we must listen as attentively as we watch, *Sicilia!* being a journey of voices. It is comprised of conversations, and, as in other of their late films, Huillet and Straub gave much care to the rehearsal and performing of vocal delivery, here working with a group of amateur actors from Buti, where the script was first performed, in 1998, the filming being done later in the year.[9] As others have observed, the film is a piece for voices in the musical sense, and in this it follows the invitations of the text.[10] Vittorini wrote that a performance of Verdi's *La Traviata* instilled in him the ambition to achieve effects equivalent to the operatic alliance of words and music.[11] In *Conversations in Sicily*, he has Silvestro ask the policeman who pretends to be a land agent if he knows that he has a fine baritone voice, and in the film the character leans back in comic ecstasy as he imagines himself performing in *Falstaff* or *Rigoletto*.

Both Vittorini in his dialogues and the actors whom Huillet and Straub coach in delivering them exploit the particular affinity between spoken Italian and song. This is notably true of Angela Nugara, in the role of the mother. It is her voice, in fact, that we hear before the action begins, singing 'Sicilia bedda', a buoyant hymn to Sicily, 'my homeland'.[12] There is an irony in prefacing the film with this song, in that Silvestro's first conversation is with an immiserated labourer, named only in the book as 'the small Sicilian'. Between the song and this opening encounter comes a passage of undulating gravity from Beethoven's String Quartet in A minor, Op. 132, inaugurating the series of conflictual, or dialectical, transitions that is to come.

The opening shot shows Silvestro from behind, sitting at the dockside. His back is turned to his interlocutor, the Sicilian, and their consequent need to raise their voices accentuates the sense of social distance thus signified. In starting at this point, the film differs from the book, in which this conversation occurs in the third of the short chapters. The film also stops short of the book's conclusion, to the effect that it both begins and ends with an encounter between Silvestro and a Sicilian who apprehends him as in some sense a foreigner. The first supposes him to have come from America, hence to be envied; the second regards him as a tourist, to be tricked. The contrast is significant, as we will see, for its bearing on social justice. As with any adaptation from literature to screen, but especially in an approach to film where everything counts, in vision and sound, the specific bodily presence of the performers, their gestures and intonation, all carry meaning independently of the text and supplementary to it.[13] Silvestro, the book's first-person narrator, here gives voice purely as an interlocutor, incarnate along with the other characters. His recurring presence itself supplies the narrative thread linking the successive encounters; we see others in their difference from him, his changing demeanour in response to them. The opening sequence cuts between his jacketed back, silhouetted against the sunlit water, and the Sicilian, more cheaply clothed, facing the light, against a wall. To see them thus is to apprehend their relative situations concretely: one bound to his place, to his fate, the other free to travel.

In response to Silvestro's remarks and questions, the Sicilian voices a bitter lament, telling of his impoverishment. His labour is to pick oranges, and in pay he receives oranges to sell, which, he says, nobody wants: 'nessuno ne vuole'. In English, the emphasis would naturally fall on 'wants', but in Italian, at least as spoken here, it falls more devastatingly on 'nessuno', nobody, in a big open-vowelled sound in the second syllable that the performer, Carmelo Maddio, fully exploits. Vittorini's text, with its force of repetition, is an aria in waiting. Here it is, with the performer's stresses and breath pauses indicated:

> Nessuno ne vuole. | Veniamo a Messina, a piedi, | e nessuno ne vuole... | Andiamo a vedere se ne vogliono a Reggio, a Villa San Giovanni, | e non ne vogliono... | Nessuno ne vuole. [...] | Andiamo avanti, indietro, paghiamo il viaggio, non mangiamo pane [...]. | Nessuno ne vuole... | Come se avessero il tossico... maledette arance.[14]

As if they were poisoned, accursed oranges, he ends his lament, having gone, he says, to Messina on foot and having travelled to all these other towns, back and forth and paying for the trip, no bread to eat, and *nobody* wants them.

Following Vittorini's design, each of the next scenes, on the train, contrasts significantly with the one preceding. What follows the orange-seller's tale of barren journeyings is a conversation between two travellers on vacation. A pair of dark-suited men, turned to lean on an open window in the train corridor, comment on the orange-seller's outcry as evidence of social disorder. Vittorini gives this pair, who are policemen returning on leave to their native Sicily, the names 'coi baffi' and 'senza baffi' — with moustache and without moustache. Given this comic naming of a matching pair, and his description of them as 'two baritones', we might be put in mind of *opera buffa*. He scores their dialogue in brief corresponding statements, of equal length, where each reaffirms or reiterates the other's remarks. In the film — in which indeed one is with moustache, the other without — not only the authoritarian assertiveness of their comments, but also their penetrating voices, contrast with the naked emotion of the orange-seller; as Vittorini specifies, one of them has a singing delivery, 'cantante e sinuosa'.[15] At times, they turn to each other like mirror images in paired complaint. No-one has any respect, they say; 'My grocer, in Lodi' says one; 'And in Bologna, a lawyer' says the other, moustached one, with singsong emphasis — 'E a Bologna, un avvoca*aaa*to'. People despise them, they say, 'because we're Sicilian'.

The fact of their being Sicilian is a subject of the next conversation, which takes place in a compartment of the train where Silvestro faces three others, in the middle a man wearing a dark suit and hat. Light from the window models this man's strong features in relief. The sculptural effect, an achievement of William Lubtchansky's black and white cinematography, accords with the calm and resolute diction and demeanour of the actor, Giovanni Interlandi. Here, the turn away from an insecure authoritarianism to a different quality of command is signalled by the character's action in closing the door of the compartment and referring to the stink ('puzza') of the pair in the corridor. Policemen are held in worse regard here in Sicily than elsewhere, Silvestro observes in response. We will already have heard 'with moustache' complain that his mother is so ashamed that she tells people he is an employee at the Land Agency: 'impiegato al Catasto!', he says, in his singsong voice, turning his head and nodding with the emphasis.

As against the policeman's counterfeit, the character whom in the book Silvestro calls the 'Gran Lombardo', the Great Lombard, speaks of and for himself. His face framed in close-up, turned to the window and lit in profile against the dark seat, he begins, 'Sono di Leonforte', I am from Leonforte. This is a storyteller's opening, proper to the tradition in which, as here, a traveller has a series of encounters with people who have a tale to tell.[16] The Gran Lombardo, then, as the book has it, 'raccontò di sé', tells his tale.[17] He speaks of feeling like a king when he rides his land on horseback, of his three beautiful daughters, and yet of his preparedness nonetheless to relinquish horse and land in a quest for higher duties, beyond the injunctions not to steal, not to kill: new duties, such that he should feel at peace with other men (biblical allusions recur throughout the book). Giovanni Interlandi delivers his long declaration at an even pace, with special accentuation only of 'altri doveri', other duties.

With the Gran Lombardo, Vittorini introduces the complex and ambivalent theme of the father, to be played out in Silvestro's conversation with his mother, the only woman save one in the film (the other being the orange-seller's wife, who turns aside the orange that not even she wants). When the Gran Lombardo has finished speaking, the camera rests on his face, which is turned in silence in the direction of Silvestro. Such silent intervals, differing in length, end all the scenes; they mark phases in the onward journey, 'the wheel of my journey', Silvestro calls it in the book, remarking at one point that it has stopped, then that it has begun again.[18] After the halt at Catania, empty seats face Silvestro until, after a while, the moustached policeman enters and occupies the former seat of the Gran Lombardo.

On his journey, then, Silvestro, having met first a poor man, then a man who would give up his wealth in search of a 'fresh conscience' to 'be at peace with other men' now encounters a man who suspects everyone and dissimulates. He soon lies that he is an employee of the Land Agency. In the film, the character's strange mannerism of tilting his head back, opening his eyes wide and looking as if from behind the barrier of his collar and three-piece suit evokes by contrast the direct gaze of the Gran Lombardo, whose place he has taken. When Silvestro deflects the policeman's insistent prying about why he is going to Siracusa, by asking him if he knows he has a fine baritone voice, there is a moment of spontaneous human exchange between them. It ceases when Silvestro observes that even singing in the street would be better than being an employee (of such a kind). The policeman's expression becomes uncertain, he says 'Ah [pause] forse', perhaps; as the scene ends he resumes his former demeanour, and asks Silvestro what his business is in Siracusa.

There immediately follows the sequence in which the seaward view from the train passes in silence, an indication that Silvestro's onward travel is ending, and a prompt to retain the sense of its trajectory. Tales and fictions have perennially been threaded on the string of a journey across land or sea. In *Scarlet and Black* (*Le Rouge et le noir*), Stendhal called the novel 'a mirror travelling down a road' — a proto-cinematic image.[19] The train journey has a more specific importance for this narrative, however, in that trains feature significantly in Silvestro's conversation with his mother, his father having been a railway employee, and at one point he recalls, to her annoyance, his childhood memory of the sound of shunting trains.

The next sequence again frames a view of landscape, but now it is mountainous, and, after a few moments, it is the camera that moves, where formerly the train had moved the camera, as with Stendhal's travelling mirror. Sound, which has now resumed, tracks in accord with the direction of the camera. There is a sound of machinery, perhaps agricultural, as the camera pans slowly, from a tree-covered hill at left nearby, along the far side of the valley below; then, as it travels across the hillside town in the distance (Grammichele), and round past a road and a cemetery, to rest on a tree close by, we hear cicadas, and then birds. The camera returns to rest on Grammichele. This trajectory, filmed in overcast conditions, is then repeated, filmed in sunlight. While panoramic sequences are sufficiently a feature of Huillet and Straub's filmmaking to have been given the label 'plan Straubien' ('Straubian shot'), they vary in meaning and function according to context. Here, they mark a transition in Silvestro's journey, from overland travel to a journey in a different sense. In the book, the narrator says:

> 'How about that [*Ma guarda*], I'm at my mother's', I thought again, and it was as if I had arrived there spontaneously, just as spontaneously as one finds oneself in a certain place in memory — or even more fantastical, as if I had begun travelling in the fourth dimension.[20]

'Guardami!'

With the panoramic tracking shots, in their repetition, their coming to rest on a view of buildings very different from the apartment blocks glimpsed from the train after leaving Catania, the film registers a deepening or layering of time. We apprehend the geological time embedded in the mountain landscape, evidence of cultivation and habitation, nature and human history intertwined in the *longue durée*: mountain ridges, terraced fields, cicadas, a pylon. The panoramic sequences preface Silvestro's re-entry into the stream of his own life, past and present, through the conversation with his mother, where he joins her in tracing the intersection of their life histories with those of others. Later on in Vittorini's book, after Silvestro and his mother have finished talking over his recollections and hers, and they have left her house as she makes her visits (an episode not shown in the film), he rests on a wall, feeling tired and thinking of his father's frailty, an object of complaint from his mother:

> I had journeyed away from being calm in my hopelessness, and I was journeying still, and the journey was also a conversation, it was present, past, memory, and fantasy [...] I leaned on the wall and thought of my blue-eyed father when he was tired.[21]

The panning movement of the camera over the mountain landscape formally prefigures the circling between past and present in the dialogue that follows, between mother and son. It is a circle of interpretation, in which the participants attempt to reconcile and understand newly-encountered, or troubling, or differently-remembered parts of the past, and their bearing on the present.

This is an enactment of the hermeneutic circle, as reintroduced into modern thought by Dilthey: in any context whatever, our comprehension takes a circular path, from part to whole and back.[22] A commentator on Dilthey observes that the concept is borne out in everyday experience, where 'there are no absolute starting-points [...] because we always find ourselves in the middle of complex situations which we try to disentangle by making, then revising, provisional assumptions'.[23] Storytelling is our readiest means of disentanglement, and in *Sicilia!* the mother narrates the past in ways that at times cut across the son's sense of how things were.

Here, at the mother's house, everything takes place mainly in a single room. Huillet and Straub have choreographed each phase of the conversation, framing Silvestro and his mother, together and (more often) separately, in accord with the lines they speak, and in their occupation of different parts of the space. In his film about the making of *Sicilia!*, Fitoussi records the painstaking search to establish a single position from which to film the actors, wherever they are situated (see also the interview with Huillet and Straub in this volume, Chapter 11). Fitoussi prefaces this section of his film with a clip of Robert Bresson contending that: 'There is just one point in space from which something must be seen, and it's a question not of a viewpoint but of a vision [...]. In certain films, things are seen through several eyes' (i.e. to their detriment).[24] The consequence of finding the just-right position in the room where most of the conversation takes place is that, as with the panoramic sequence, the camera serves as proxy for the viewer, in conjuring what cannot be directly shown, namely the surroundingness of the space itself, as habitation.

Here — and this accords with the film's aspect ratio, akin to easel painting — we detect the filmmakers' pictorial sensibility: in particular, an affinity with a realist tradition in which a painting may invite apprehension of what is not, or cannot be, directly shown.[25] In an interior by Pieter de Hooch, for instance, or a still life by Cézanne, the incomplete or fragmentary aspects that comprise the painting enlist the viewer in a hermeneutic search, arriving at a whole through the indications of the parts and apprehending the parts afresh in the light of the whole. Thus in de Hooch, doors opening from an interior intimate unseen spaces of the dwelling; in a Cézanne still life, such as the late (*c.*1899) *Apples and Oranges* (in the Musée d'Orsay, Paris, and featured in *Cézanne: Conversation with Joachim Gasquet*, 1990), the pictorial whole is not an immobile given, but rather continually eludes and retrieves itself, by way of the assertive parts, in their mutual jostling, their tensions, and affinities. The viewer thereby becomes an interpreter, not in the sense of drawing out an exportable 'meaning', but rather by analogy with the instrumentalist interpreting say, a Beethoven quartet. To interpret, in the case at hand, is simply to watch, attentively, in ways signalled by the film, where watching of course incorporates listening.

In the filming of the conversation with the mother, watching becomes itself a theme, as in the text, but necessarily in more manifest ways. After an initial scene in the kitchen, where the mother, Concezione, cooks a herring on a brazier, the camera frames mother and son at the dining-room table, looking from Silvestro towards his mother. The camera then shifts to the position from which it can command different spaces in the room, and it is placed symmetrically between Silvestro and his mother, turned at first to frame Silvestro, his arm over the back of the chair. The simplicity of the setting, the furniture, the bottle of wine, and the cut loaf and jug at the centre of the table, with the strong and finely realized tonal contrasts, all summon echoes, again, of painting — signalled already by Concezione's hand turning the herring on the griddle. Echoes, that is, of Dutch still life, or the Le Nain brothers' depictions of peasants at table (such as the Louvre *Peasant Family*), or Cézanne's paintings of *Card Players* from the mid-1890s, notably the versions with two figures (such as the one in the Courtauld Institute Galleries).[26]

This very invitation to dwell on what we see intensifies awareness of the persisting incompleteness of our vision. After the first sequence in the living room, Silvestro and his mother only fleetingly share the frame, and we often see one while hearing the other. For this reason, and as the two are placed successively in different parts of the space, at its opposite limits, the positioning of the camera provides the constant through which we continually intercept and interpret the changing trajectories of looks given and received. Sometimes, the look might be inward, or at nothing actually there. One of these moments occurs when Concezione, recalling her father leading the cavalcade of St Joseph on horseback, walks from the table to the window, while the frame holds Silvestro following her movement. Her upper body passes briefly in front of the camera, her shadow crosses him, and we hear her say 'vedi!', look! (Figure 6.1). Whereas in the book the mother brings Silvestro to the window with her, in the film her face alone is at the window, in close-up profile, as, looking into the past, she describes the cavalcade winding its way with lanterns and sounds and sometimes passing out of view, her father at its head, 'like a king'.

It is immediately after this elaboration on vision, and a brief exchange with Silvestro, that the mother appears in three-quarters view at the left of the frame, leaning against the window. Her eyes are at first closed, her head bent, so that it is in the moment of raising her head and opening her eyes that she says, 'But why do you look at me?', an expressive congruence of act and words. 'May I not look at you?', Silvestro replies. Whereas in the book this exchange occurs at the table, and the mother says, 'Yes [...] if you want to look, look, but finish eating', here there is no 'finish eating', and the statement becomes an injunction, 'guardami!', 'look at me!'.[27] Given the statuesque framing of Angela Nugara by the window, this is an injunction as much to the viewer as to Silvestro (Figure 6.2). Nugara has a strength of presence that indeed summons our attention. It is remarkable how different Gianni Buscarino, playing Silvestro, appears in scenes with the mother in comparison to previous scenes, he seeming now much younger. As the camera cuts, at this point, from Nugara's commanding 'guardami!' — this delivered with an emphatic nod of the head — to Buscarino's returned gaze, the bright light falling on his features softens them, as against the strong *contre-jour* modelling of Nugara.

FIG. 6.1. Danièle Huillet and Jean-Marie Straub, *Sicilia!* (1999, courtesy of BELVA Film).

FIG. 6.2. Danièle Huillet and Jean-Marie Straub, *Sicilia!* (1999, courtesy of BELVA Film).

The contrast is all the more evident since it is at this point that the emotionally taxing parts of the dialogue begin, as Silvestro, seated, asks why his father has left, to which the mother, standing by the window, responds.

While congruence of speech and gesture is clearly something Huillet and Straub have consistently sought, Angela Nugara here attains it with exceptional vividness, taking full advantage of the forceful lines that Vittorini has given for her character to deliver. In this charged part of the dialogue, Silvestro and his mother are not only at opposite sides of the room, but the former is also seated while the latter stands, so that Silvestro must look up as his mother delivers a devastating account of his father's failure to assist her in childbirth. He didn't even want to *look*, she says, and when the baby's head appeared, and she demanded his help, he raised his arms to heaven and began to invoke God as if he were reciting his tragedies (the father performed tragic scenes for other railway workers). Nugara delivers the long line in a single breath, rising to an expressive stress on 'Dio', tilting her head back demonstratively as she does so; immediately, we hear a glass fall over, and Silvestro's exclamation, 'Oh'. After the mother ends the recollection, the view cuts to Silvestro, his face pressed down towards the table, his right hand on top of his head: a mimetic identification with his father, who could not bear to look. Throughout the exchange that follows, Silvestro, looking up towards his mother, acts as his father's advocate, almost as a supplicant, reacting and responding, where she most usually is assertive. The disparity is pronounced when, after his mother says that the father came to her aid only after she threw a bottle at him, Silvestro, tilting his head as he looks up, urges her to recognize that, after all, his father helped, and did not lack courage, but had something more. 'What something more?' she implacably replies, 'he wasn't a man like my father', who was, she says elsewhere, a great man who could plough the land eighteen hours a day, and did everything when the mother gave birth.

With each distinct phase of the conversation, corresponding generally to a chapter in the book, the actors change their respective locations in the room and their position in relation to each other. As they do so, a dispute continues between them, regarding the dreamer–father and the *cavaliere*–grandfather. It should be noted that this contrast is complicated by the way in which the mother's description of her kingly father recalls the 'Gran Lombardo', also like a king on horseback, but in his case not content in this role. After the mother has brought a 'winter melon' to the table, the still life it comprises with bottle, jug, loaf, and glass invokes reverie. Silvestro's hands and face appear, grasping and smelling the melon (Figure 6.3), and eventually this draws him, now framed standing by one end of the table, into a chain of childhood recollections concerning the railway, which the mother cuts short, due to the association with his father. Angela Nugara, shown standing at the opposite end of the table, very straight-backed, says angrily 'Cut the melon!', making a vigorous cutting motion with her right arm. Yet when they are seated again at the table, and Silvestro prompts his mother to say what happened about his father, her husband, she discloses unresolved, contradictory emotions. She angrily lampoons her husband writing poems to the 'dirty wives' of linesmen, calling them queens, even queen-bees (Nugara: '*aaapi-regine!*'). In recalling those gatherings

FIG. 6.3. Danièle Huillet and Jean-Marie Straub, *Sicilia!*
(1999, courtesy of BELVA Film).

organized by him, however, her anger gives way to a reverie of her own, as, looking towards the window, she speaks of him as the life and soul of the party. Her 'Cut the melon!' gesture now appears in retrospect as the willed severance of a latent, but persistent, attachment.

In the exchanges that follow, the mother sits by the fireplace, while Silvestro stands, first in front of the table, then by the window, where she had stood. This positioning enables the performers to convey the alteration that has taken place, the mother less in command, the son probing her defences. At first, he draws from her the deep cause of her anger with his father, namely that the 'dirty cows' he brought into the house looked down on her. 'He let them think they were better than me! And they looked at me as if they were much better than me!'[28] Nugara delivers this looking up towards Silvestro: 'Lui', 'he', she begins, pauses, then runs the next sixteen words together, in one breath, with rising pitch and emphasis, up to 'come fossero', 'as if they were', then a pause, 'molto più di me', 'much better than me', throwing everything into the first syllable of 'molto'. She looks down, the camera stays on her, then frames the window corner, to which Silvestro moves.

From this position, his mother having disclosed her vulnerability, Silvestro elicits from her the recollection of her own lover, a stranger who turned up one day, and who would travel far on foot to come to see her. It is now that the conversation opens from the confines of the family towards the wider world. Asked why the man eventually ceased visiting, the mother says that he worked in the sulphur mines, there was a strike, and strikers were killed by the gendarmes. Nugara performs the mother re-living the experience, including the lover's telling of his journey, and certain special moments — his 'Benedetto Dio!', praise God, in smelling the bread

FIG. 6.4. Danièle Huillet and Jean-Marie Straub, *Sicilia!*
(1999, courtesy of BELVA Film).

she gave him; the honeycomb he gave her once, which 'perfumed the whole house'. At these points, Nugara looks up; more often her gaze is down, living through the memory. Dilthey brought the concept of *Nacherleben*, re-experiencing, into philosophy; it has a family relationship to hermeneutics, but bears specifically on feeling, and, as empathy, it grounds social relationships, mutual understanding.[29] As the mother now re-experiences a past love, her son responds with empathy, asking why the lover eventually did not come back, and she replies that he must have been killed; 'I think so, because otherwise wouldn't he have returned?', Nugara delivers this as follows, in close-up, looking towards the light (Figure 6.4), as to an irrecoverable past, spacing her words with intakes of breath, imparting a sense of lingering regret: 'Così credo | perche altrimenti | non sarebbe | ricomparso?'

Not to Offend the World

A panorama of the mountain landscape, ending as before on Grammichele, marks Silvestro's passage from his mother's house to the world at large: to a small square in the town, where a knife-grinder stands before the steps of a church, his piercing cry, 'Arrota, arrota!' ('Sharpening, sharpening!') resonating in the enclosed space of the piazza. In the novel, Silvestro comes upon the knife-grinder after seeing and following a kite, and this prompts memories of childhood: 'I asked myself why, after all, the world was not *A Thousand and One Nights*, the way it was when I was seven'.[30] The strange figure of the knife-grinder, improbably demanding swords and cannons to sharpen, appears as if in answer to this thought.

Silvestro now changes in demeanour yet again: as if in the spirit of a seven-year-old, he enters into a sort of playground game with the knife-grinder. They match each other's lines, not like the two policemen in the train, but rather in a spirit of invention, and far from reflecting each other, as did the policemen, they appear mutually incongruous. They face each other but stand spaced apart, unknown to each other as they are, and declaim their exchanges. These concern the world, its wrongs, and justice: justice violated when, according to the knife-grinder, he has overcharged Silvestro because he is a stranger, a *forestiero*. This is the fourth and final time that the subject of what is owing to the other has arisen. The 'small Sicilian' at the beginning of the film was paid for his labour in oranges he could not sell; the Great Lombard sought to be at peace with other men; Silvestro's mother gave bread to the vagrant who became her lover. We have passed from the inaugural evidence of destitution to its remedies through conscience and then empathy; we now arrive at the demand for justice. This demand is for a justice that bears no relation to state power, or the views of the two policemen, 'coi baffi' and 'senza baffi'; it is a revolutionary communist demand, as the knife-grinder's last words in the film will affirm. As against the literally mute conclusion of the book — 'I left the house on tiptoe' — this final encounter features a highly vocal character whose ebullience stands in deliberate contrast to the abjection of the 'small Sicilian'. Unlike the latter, he stands facing Silvestro, on a footing of equality, as on the ground of justice.[31]

In the book, the knife-grinder is an extravagant figure, and the staging of his role in the film requires of Vittorio Vigneri a larger-than-life performance, in voice and gesture. After apologizing to Silvestro, the knife-grinder pirouettes, clasps his arms above his head, and exclaims 'E bello il mondo!', the world is beautiful. What follows, in duet form, is a litany of the world, from the knife-grinder's 'Light, shade, cold, heat, joy, non-joy' to Silvestro's 'Sickness, recovery. I know, I know. Death, immortality and resurrection', after which the knife-grinder raises his arms and gives voice to primary sounds of the human world: 'Ah, e oh! Ih! Uh! Eh!'

The knife-grinder apologizes again, as one who has 'offended the world'; Silvestro makes light of this, and the knife-grinder removes his hat, brings it to his chest and says, 'Grazie, amico', and Silvestro bows. From this fraternal greeting, the knife-grinder passes to the imaginary call to arms that ends the film (though not the book): 'Ah! If there were knives and scissors, awls, picks and arquebuses, mortars, sickles and hammers, cannons, cannons, dynamite'.

As they stand facing each other, a second passage from the Beethoven quartet takes over the soundtrack, in a final dialectical turn, from clamour to concert. The 'gift' Straub asked of Beethoven comprises interweaving motifs of yearning beauty, the long, slow instrumental lines closely harmonized, so that our listening takes in the players' rapt attention both to each other and to the summons of the music.[32]

Notes to Chapter 6

1. Albera, 'Sickle and Hammer, Cannons, Cannons, Dynamite!', p. 115.
2. *Où gît votre sourire enfoui?*, dir. by Pedro Costa (2001); *Sicilia! si gira*, dir. by Jean-Charles Fitoussi (2001).
3. Albera, 'Sickle and Hammer, Cannons, Cannons, Dynamite!', p. 122.

4. Ibid., p. 109.

5. Simone Weil, *Gravity and Grace*, trans. by Emma Crawford and Mario von der Ruhr (London: Routledge, 2002), pp. 118, 116-17.

6. *Conversazione in Sicilia* first appeared in instalments between 1938 and 1939 and was first published in its entirety in 1941. I cite from Elio Vittorini, *Conversazione in Sicilia,* ed. by Robert C. Powell (Manchester: Manchester University Press, 1978); and *Conversations in Sicily*, trans. by Alane Salierno Mason (Edinburgh: Canongate, 2003).

7. Henri Bergson, *Matter and Memory*, trans. by Nancy Margaret Paul and W. Scott Palmer (New York: Zone, 1991). See pp. 104-05.

8. Wilhelm Dilthey, *Introduction to the Human Sciences*, ed. by Rudolf A. Makkreel and Frithjof Rodi (Princeton, NJ: Princeton University Press, 1989), p. 385.

9. See Ramos-Martínez, ' "Actors Simply Explode" '.

10. Notably James Quandt, 'Operatic Tenor: Straub and Huillet's *Sicilia!*', *Artforum*, 9 (2016) <https://www.artforum.com/print/201605/operatic-tenor-straub-and-huillet-s-sicilia-59536> [accessed 2 November 2021].

11. Guido Bonsaver, *Elio Vittorini: The Writer and the Written* (Leeds: Northern Universities Press, 2000), p. 90.

12. Identified for me by Giulia Pollicita.

13. On this point, and other issues, notably political, concerning adaptation from literature to film by Huillet and Straub, see Rancière, *The Intervals of Cinema*, pp. 103-26.

14. Vittorini, *Conversazione in Sicilia*, p. 36; *Conversations in Sicily*, p. 20.

15. Ibid., p. 37; p. 21.

16. The corresponding passage in the novel is in reported speech, the narrator being the principal storyteller: ibid., p. 45; p. 30.

17. Ibid.

18. Ibid., pp. 135, 137; pp. 135, 137.

19. Stendhal, *Scarlet and Black*, trans. by Margaret Shaw (Harmondsworth: Penguin Books, 1978), p. 365; Stendhal owed the idea to the seventeenth-century writer César Vichard de Saint-Réal, whose phrase he quotes in the epigraph to Part 1, Chapter 13.

20. Vittorini, *Conversazione in Sicilia*, p. 57; *Conversations in Sicily*, p. 48.

21. Ibid., p. 119; p. 116.

22. See Wilhelm Dilthey, *Selected Writings*, ed. and trans. by H. P. Rickman (Cambridge: Cambridge University Press 1976), pp. 228-31.

23. H. P. Rickman, in Dilthey, *Selected Writings*, p. 11.

24. *Sicilia! si gira,* dir. by Fitoussi (2001).

25. In European oil painting between the seventeenth and nineteenth centuries, 'easel painting' refers to the small-scale portable canvas typical of genre, still-life, and landscape.

26. I think also of the complex role played by objects in Bresson's films, from *Pickpocket* (1959) to *L'Argent* (1983).

27. Vittorini, *Conversazione in Sicilia*, p. 71; *Conversations in Sicily*, p. 62.

28. Ibid., p. 89; p. 82.

29. See Dilthey, *Selected Writings*, pp. 226-28.

30. Vittorini, *Conversazione in Sicilia*, p. 136; *Conversations in Sicily*, p. 136.

31. Rancière writes of the aporiae of emancipation and justice as being the consistent theme of Huillet and Straub's 'politico-cinematic approach' from 1979 onwards: Rancière, *The Intervals of Cinema*, pp. 103-26.

32. Beethoven inscribed this third movement of Op. 132 'Holy song of thanksgiving of a convalescent to the Deity, in the Lydian mode', in gratitude for recovery from a serious illness. Hence Straub's allusion in the passage quoted above, as epigraph.

CHAPTER 7

❖

Into the Woods:
The Green Spaces of Huillet and Straub's
Workers, Peasants and *The Return of*
The Prodigal Son — Humiliated

Jane Madsen

Introduction

Lasting a little over a decade, in the Buti *comune* near Pisa, Huillet and Straub established a working relationship with the Teatro Francesco di Bartolo, a non-professional left-wing theatre group, developing and directing theatre performances subsequently made into films. When Huillet and Straub began working with the group the filmmakers seemed to abandon a way of working developed over decades. In previous films they worked with a combination of actors and non-actors and carefully selected sites and landscapes determined by texts, history, and architecture. In the films *Workers, Peasants* (2001) and *The Return of the Prodigal Son — Humiliated* (2003), based on Elio Vittorini's novel *Women of Messina* (*Le donne di Messina*), the actors are for the most part in green glades in the woods. Unlike the film *Sicilia!* (1999) made immediately before, in *Workers, Peasants* and *The Return of the Prodigal Son — Humiliated* there is no representation of manual labour or the places it occurs. The work of theatre itself aside, the woods are not sites of production, the workers and peasants are de-located in the glades and images of unadorned green nature. The green spaces thus raise new questions for seasoned readers of Huillet and Straub's films.

At Buti, the deployment of regional differences between actors as an estrangement device, used by Huillet and Straub in a number of previous films, is suspended and the work with the text foregrounded. This raises further questions for interpretation. Extracts of Vittorini's novel are recited in an unadorned style, the workers and the peasants speak about the work of survival after World War Two, restoring and cultivating the land, making it productive, their circumstances conditional on the immediate past. While the war itself is not mentioned, the importance of being anti-fascist is underlined. The films based on *Women of Messina* revive the interest in the politics of renewal in the decades immediately after World War Two already seen in Huillet and Straub's films made from work by Heinrich Böll, Bertolt Brecht, and Cesare Pavese.

Text and Testimony

In both the films under consideration here twelve actors representing the titular workers and peasants are arranged in small clearings in a valley in the woods near Buti. Performing in the woods connects these films to the *maggio epico* folk theatre of Tuscany dating back to at least the eighteenth century. *Maggio epico* is performed as sung recitation. According to Dario Marconcini, in Armin Linke's documentary about Huillet and Straub's working relationship with the Teatro Francesco di Bartolo, the *maggio* or May dramas were performed outside by peasants, 'when nature is in full bloom, in squares or in clearings in the woods. They were sung by peasant farmers, who learnt these stories by heart'.[1] Jo Ann Cavallo states more specifically that the performances were 'ideally at the edge of a forest, or near trees that provide some shade from the afternoon sun, and preferably on an incline that serves as a natural amphitheater'.[2] This might suggest a connection between the topography of the Buti woods as they appear in the films and the *maggio epico*, especially those scenes where the actors are represented against steep earth banks in the valley, perhaps also suggesting that the woods were common land. Although *maggio epico* as situated performance is not mentioned by Huillet and Straub, it is local knowledge brought by the actors, just as, for his part, Vittorini would have been aware of the folk theatre from Sicily, *opera dei pupi* (puppet theatre). Folk forms such as the *maggio epico* were championed from the late nineteenth century because they represented 'something revolutionary compared to "bourgeois" theatre'.[3] The text and the voice are central to both folk forms though *opera dei pupi* improvised dialogue around a scenario and *maggio epico* strictly conformed to the text which was performed using the 'same tonality throughout'.[4]

Huillet and Straub not only put the text resolutely at the centre, but literally into the actors' hands as they speak in the woods. In *Workers, Peasants* and *The Return of the Prodigal Son — Humiliated* the actors both recite some parts from memory and read from scripts marked up in highlighter and red pencil (Figure 7.1).[5] Straub described the actors' relationship to the annotated script as:

> 'Memoria/lectura': what was learned by heart by the actors and what they read. The whole film is so structured: as if they had taken notes to justify themselves so many years later after what had happened. They had everything written out, and we chose at certain moments to have them recite things by heart, and others, in contrast, to have them read the text like a memorandum, as if they were in front of a judge.[6]

Marconcini regards the relationship to the marked-up texts as Brechtian, 'not being a character, but being the desire to passionately recount what is happening in the scene'.[7] The films *Workers, Peasants* and *The Return of the Prodigal Son — Humiliated* document the theatre company at work as much as they do the text. The cinematographer Renato Berta described the location as follows: 'There was such a silence in the woods, and the distance between the camera and the actors meant that it was possible to have a real rapport with the text'.[8]

In *Workers, Peasants* and *The Return of the Prodigal Son — Humiliated* actors tell their stories to the empty space of the woods in front of them, but the text speaks of locations not represented in the space. The presence of the script is the

FIG. 7.1. Danièle Huillet and Jean-Marie Straub, *Workers, Peasants* (2001, courtesy of BELVA Film).

primary evidence of the actors' work. The minimal gestures performed include raising, lowering, and turning pages of their scripts and shifting their gaze. Gilles Deleuze says that in cinema the 'speech-act creates the event, but always placed crosswise over tectonic visual layers: there are two trajectories crossing each other. It creates the event, but in a space empty of events'.[9] This suggests that the event is materialized by speech as an *act*, yet this does not happen because the voices slide past, presented in glades whose only layers are different shades of green. The passages of direct speech selected from Vittorini's novel are spoken as testimony, as though memory was being tested. Straub explained: 'they are in a physical space, in a place where they are undergoing a trial, a trial in the sense of being before a court'.[10] The actors speak in a declamatory but not dialogic style, movement is minimal except when adjusting their gaze up, down, or beyond the camera from one fixed point of their focus to another, becoming almost somnambulant, reaching a point Huillet described as 'extinguishing themselves'.[11] Jacques Rancière describes the performers in *Workers, Peasants* as 'massed choirs', and argues that cinema is 'bound to the visibility of speaking bodies and the things they speak of' and that the politics of Brechtian dialogue is the 'ability to hold opposing arguments in balance'.[12] The actors do not participate in gestural acting as embodied characters. The occasional gestures are disruptive jolts, such as when Spine first appears half-way through *Workers, Peasants* — in a sudden gesture he draws his arms to his body, stamps his foot, raises and lowers his arms before claiming: 'And I who believed in the story of the Prodigal Son!'. The voice and bodies of the actors perform in a state of extreme separation. The actors are de-located in the woods as bodies who speak, but not to each other.

Text and Fragmentation

Huillet and Straub's use of Vittorini's text and the approach to location may be understood in the context of their earlier Hölderlin films (see the Introduction to this volume). The Empedocles films continue their engagement with unfinished, reworked, or revised texts which began with their Schoenberg and Kafka films: Hölderlin's *The Death of Empedocles* exists in three incomplete versions from 1798 to 1799; Huillet and Straub's film *The Death of Empedocles* (1987) was edited as four separate versions, 'Berlin', 'Paris', 'Cricket', and 'Lizard', from different takes; *Black Sin* (1989) was based on the last, fragmentary version of the play. The five films correspond to the inherent uncertainty of Hölderlin's textual reworkings. Vittorini's *Women of Messina* was first published in 1949 then revised and republished in 1964. As Webster Schott writes in his foreword to the English translation of the novel: 'It is the kind of novel a man writes once in a lifetime, never finishes to his satisfaction, and surrenders rather than completes'.[13] The films make use of only a handful of episodes from the novel: *Workers, Peasants* is based on Chapters 44-47; *The Return of the Prodigal Son* comes from alternative takes from *Workers, Peasants*: shots 40-46 and shots 63-66, the latter focusing on the peasant Spine, who returns to the group after having left with a cart during the winter. *The Return of the Prodigal Son* was released as a single entity with *Humiliated*, which adapts scenes later in the novel when outsiders threaten to undermine the nascent collective. The full title is *Humiliated: ... that nothing produced or touched by them, coming from their hands, proves free of the claims of some stranger (Workers, Peasants — continuation and end)*. *Incantati* (2003) is a separate version of the ending of the last scene of *Humiliated*.[14]

A possible further model for this proliferation of versions may have been Cézanne's Mont Sainte-Victoire paintings — there is no one definitive version, only the multiple reworkings of an idea (see *Cézanne: Conversation with Joachim Gasquet*, 1990). In addition, it may be the case that Huillet and Straub were using these texts as 'open works', as identified by Umberto Eco in *The Open Work (Opera aperta)*, where: '"informal" is a rejection of classical forms [...] the informal, like that of any open work, does not proclaim the death of form; rather it proposes a new, more flexible version of it — *form as a field of possibilities*'.[15] This engagement with open-ended texts offers in turn a model for the open historical and geographical situation already noted in *Workers, Peasants* and *The Return of the Prodigal Son — Humiliated*. Vittorini's title *Women of Messina* indicates the women are from the Sicilian port and the reader is left to assume the narrative is in Sicily. However, the beginning of the novel charts a geographical montage of displacement:

> I am from Apulia and could find no peace until I began this run back and forth from Molfetta to Milan [...]. Or I am from Milan and did not want to stop [...]. Or I am a Ligurian from Bracco [...]. I am from Emilia from the Val di Taro region [...]. Every day new people join this back-ing and forth-ing; new unemployed, new veterans; and of the earlier ones there are few indeed who have found a place to stop in.[16]

Vittorini creates the characters as geographical every-men and every-women who arrive at an unspecified war-worn village in the mountains. In the film this sense of displacement puts the characters already in the location of the woods. The worker Carmela's testimony, both in the novel and the film, is a ledger accounting for people coming and going from designated, located, and named places which gives a sense of elsewhere, but in the film they are shown de-located, displaced in an undocumented place. These nondescript woods at Buti become an expression of this uncertainty of place, or non-place, in *Workers, Peasants* and *The Return of the Prodigal Son — Humiliated*.

The actors wear relatively ordinary clothing, making little distinction between workers and peasants, and the additions to the group Spine, Fischio, Toma, Giralda Adorno, Siracusa, and Ventura who is also called 'Ugly Mug' ('Faccia Cattiva'). In *Humiliated* attention is drawn to the red scarves and black berets and caps worn by the three partisans, and the very few props used are their guns and the bottle of beer drunk by Carlo the Bald. These are the only times props are used and they are associated with the disrupters who almost destroy the co-operative built by the workers and peasants. The testimonies recounted in the woods are the recent past, and not told as representations of the seasonal tradition of peasants passing the winter months in storytelling. They outline details of surviving the winter — measuring every morsel of food, deciding when to slaughter a lamb or goat, making ricotta. As they recount their endeavours, each must face how they fit in and become part of the community, especially the insecure outsider, Ventura, who speaks of how he has been changed by being part of the group and planting food:

> And the green altering the folds of our earth, with the growing of the wheat, was under my gaze as if I were changed. And also the smell of the smoke of milk and underbrush, when they began making the ricotta, was as if I were changed.[17]

For Rancière the story of the ricotta-making, further elaborated by Widow Biliotti, is transcendent and ecstatic, 'a communist Eucharist ... like a consecration of the community';[18] Straub has himself indeed contended there is 'no political film without theology, no political film without mysticism' (see Chapters 1, 6, and 9).[19] These two comments suggest the means and necessity of belonging to the collective, irrespective of its specific location.

The collective they create is a fragile one — the unifying harmony they worked for is disrupted in *Humiliated* when Carlo the Bald arrives, shattering the hope of their new utopia, threatening to extort taxes on the land they do not own. Later the hunters/partisans pour scorn on the meagre returns yielded by the peasants' labour, making their communitarianism seem futile. The Vittorini text gives an image to Gramsci's identification of the disparity between the peasant and an industrial worker: 'The agricultural labourers to this day are for the most part peasants without land [...] and not the workers of an agricultural industry developed through concentration of capital and the division of labour'.[20] The workers and peasants are not able to reconcile their fundamental differences, but the change described by Ventura though his closeness to the land in growing and producing food is testimony to their shared experience of survival.

From Landscape to Nature

The green locations in Buti, described as 'undifferentiated' by Claudia Pummer, are evidence of the emergence of nature from materialized landscape in Huillet and Straub's work.[21] Previously, landscapes in *Fortini/Cani* (1976, see Chapter 4) and *Too Early, Too Late* (1981, see Chapter 5) held and represented history, described by Deleuze as 'stratigraphic landscapes' where 'the earth stands for what is buried in it'.[22] The panning shots across the Apuan mountains in *Fortini/Cani* where massacres of partisans occurred during World War Two, and the tracking shot in Egypt along a road beside a canal in *Too Early, Too Late* suggest a sensory history and empty landscapes replete with meaning — according to Deleuze 'the archaeological, or stratigraphic, image is *read* at the same time as it is seen'.[23] The open vistas of these durational landscapes exposed in bright sunlight with great depth of field suggest they are to be read. Renato Berta recalls discussing with Straub the idea of filming alternative takes across the Apuan mountains in *Fortini/Cani* with different starting- and end-points, however in the finished film both were used together as iterative manifestations of history which became a 'double panorama' rather than simply two takes.[24] Despite their materiality these landscape images are part of the visual montage of sound, text, and voice. Deleuze said that in Straub (and Huillet) the 'visual image [...] is the rock' but the rock does not exist on its own and cannot be separated from the place of its history.[25] Edward Said, with reference to the struggle over territory, claims that history determines landscape through two socially constructed entities: 'memory and geography'.[26] A site becomes its cultures of resistance. Said further asserts that 'geography [...] as a socially constructed and maintained sense of place' is emphasized through contested historical narratives.[27] *Too Early, Too Late* is a meditation on these themes of place and history; as Huillet comments, 'no one has ever shot landscapes in a film and then held and, as it were, caressed them. As if they were precisely characters'.[28] Huillet and Straub's films have long participated in retrieving historical narratives from the geographies they film.

The arrangement of the figures in the green woods in the Buti films, however, breaks with spatial depth especially in the case of the shots of the figures against the earth banks. This can be interpreted by considering the compression of space in the picture plane and the progression from historical landscapes to nature which emerged from 1986–90 when Huillet and Straub turned to Hölderlin. Nature begins to encircle and enclose the figures performing in secluded locations. The films *The Death of Empedocles* and *Black Sin* located in Sicily, the site of both the historical and dramatized narrative, and bound to Mount Etna where Empedocles supposedly died, were immediately followed by *Cézanne: Conversation with Joachim Gasquet* (1990) which includes footage from *The Death of Empedocles* (Figure I.1). Huillet's and Straub's admiration for Cézanne can be seen in the treatment of space in the locations at the foot of Mount Etna. In *The Death of Empedocles* the actors are surrounded by nature and the registration of the sky and trees maintains the classical pictorial space of seventeenth-century figurative painting: foreground, middle distance, and background.[29] By the end of the film the five-minute shot of Mount Etna compresses the space so that the grassy foreground is flattened against the foothills and sky, as with Cézanne's Mont Sainte-Victoire series, and Empedocles's off-screen voice speaks of the rebirth of nature, suggesting he has already disappeared into the volcano and become part of the earth.[30] The compression of space and the turn to nature coalesce in this one single shot. Barbara Ulrich suggests that 'the renewed reconciliation of humans with nature [...] is the deepest concern of all of Straub and Huillet's work'.[31] Straub, of course, sees this in political terms, suggesting that *The Death of Empedocles* is 'Hölderlin's communist utopia. You couldn't make a better democratic declaration'.[32]

The connection to the possibilities of a communist utopia is also at the heart of the Vittorini films made at Buti. As critical and engaged observers, Huillet and Straub have always avowed their communism while at the same time presenting the limitations and failures of post-World War Two communist aspirations. Vittorini himself was an activist and communist and the novel *Women of Messina* explores lives being rebuilt in Italy from 1945/46 onwards. In *Workers, Peasants* the stories of how they got through their first winter together bear witness to their testimonies of survival individually and as a group. The necessity of belonging to the collective connects with Vittorini's view of Marx: 'the liberation of the individual cannot be a phenomenon of a single individual. He taught the necessity of collective means to reach individual freedom'.[33] The collective, communitarian war-torn survivors, ekes out subsistence living in a semi-derelict, abandoned village and tells its stories to these small green spaces. The green glades in the woods bear witness to the drama of the text recounted by the actors, but don't themselves situate them historically or geographically.

Into the Woods

At Buti, these undefined green spaces of nature are generalized temperate European woodland. Nothing ties these glades to the history, politics, and poetics of landscape from Huillet and Straub's previous work. The greenery of the woods has an any-woodland-whatsoever quality, a green non-place of generic nature, almost random, its nondescript quality makes these green locations unsettling and puzzling. The trees common to this woodland are spindle, elder, dogwood, ash, though no substantial, mature trees are shown. According to Berta, at Buti they would film about fifteen metres from the house where they stayed.[34] These woods have been described as 'living nature'.[35] They are an edgeland on the fringes of suburban life, the kind of nondescript, unestablished liminal woodland found near many European towns and villages.[36] This kind of woodland blurs the boundaries between urban and rural; the urban nature writer Richard Mabey describes it as 'spontaneous' and 'unofficial'.[37] In *Workers, Peasants* the wooded locations are green barriers, the sky and horizon are out of frame until the final shot pans across woodlands and a line of hills. The opening shot of *Workers, Peasants* is a 360-degree pan running for two and a half minutes starting and ending with a tree trunk in centre frame — it moves across a creek at the bottom of a valley, past mossy stones, with steep slopes covered in leaf litter dropped from the straggly trees, the ground scattered with

FIG. 7.2. Danièle Huillet and Jean-Marie Straub, *Workers, Peasants*
(2001, courtesy of BELVA Film).

etiolated ivy, weeds, and ferns shaded by the tree canopy. The continuous aural
background comprises sounds of running water from the stream, birds chirruping,
insects buzzing. By filming a complete revolution of the camera, the space of the
woods has no beginning and no end. It can be read as an establishing shot and that
this will be the frame of reference for this film. The second shot of *Workers, Peasants*
emerges in the middle of the woods: three peasants are in shadow in front of an
earth bank (Figure 7.2) instituting the limitation and the scale of the performance
space the actors will occupy.

In his discussion of *Workers, Peasants*, Rancière describes this convergence of
narrative and green space as eco-communism:

> At this moment, the relationship of bodies to space becomes more and more
> this relationship to an inhuman nature, an inhuman nature that is the basis
> of another idea of culture. We move to a peasant or ecological communism,
> opposed to the communism of Soviet engineers. After all, this nature has
> no pastoral qualities. It is an ancient nature [...] an ancient philosophy of the
> elements of nature — water, earth, fire, air — and their conflict.[38]

The four classical elements of ancient philosophy to which Rancière refers are
contained in Empedocles's poem *On Nature*. The concept of eco-communism in
Huillet and Straub's work, suggested by Rancière, is further elaborated by Daniel
Fairfax as the retrieval of communism for a post-Soviet age in a new century that
more or less began with the global financial crisis, austerity, and temporary coalitions
on the left.[39] However, processes of political and cultural reclamation had begun to
be represented in the films of Huillet and Straub from the late 1970s, especially in
From the Cloud to the Resistance (1979) which was based on a text by Cesare Pavese,

a friend of Vittorini and a fellow communist. Rancière argues that by the time *Workers, Peasants* was made there was a political and poetic transition: 'from Brecht to Hölderlin or, if you prefer, from a dialectic *dispositif* to a lyrical *dispositif*'.[40] This aestheticized concept suggests their work progressed between two points as either/ or, but in practice Rancière's 'lyrical *dispositif*' becomes a homogenizing concept as 'peasant's communism'. The retrieval of the *maggio epico* peasant folk theatre may provide an alternative to Rancière's 'ecological communism'. Straub finds Rancière's position misleading:

> I can't comment on Rancière. I don't even quite understand what he means. [...] Besides, *Operai, contadini* is not only about peasant communism. It is also a love story between Ventura and the woman. A love story based upon mutual respect. These are people that built a community after the war.[41]

The love story between Siracusa and Ventura is a significant element in the second half of *Workers, Peasants*. Straub comments on the absence of the representation of work: 'had we shown them in cultivated fields it would have been flat and illustrative'; moreover, only showing the peasants would create an uneven balance since the workers' sites of labour would be absent.[42] Instead, Huillet and Straub chose the woods, a place that is not agricultural and not industrial.

In a curious and unsettling coda, the film *The Return of the Prodigal Son — Humiliated* ends with the only interior of the film: Siracusa hovers displaced inside the threshold of a house, she opens the door to Carmela, shown in front of a green, leafy background, who says people are leaving the village for Bologna and Modena. This is followed by an awkward exchange between Siracusa and Ventura who lies and sits on a bed, speaking the film's last lines, repeating: 'What more can I say!' three times. In the final shot Siracusa sits on the doorstep barefooted, in a pose of defeat, she raises her head, sighs, clasps her hands, then drops her arms by her side, fists clenched; the camera tilts down flattening the picture plane into a relief framing her feet, the folds of her dress, the step, and gravel with insects moving and weeds growing through the cracks (Figure 7.3). Nature's capacity for reclamation and renewal is evoked in this shot: 'every patch where the concrete has not actually sealed up the earth is potential home for some living thing'.[43] The feet, the skirt, and the soil are strikingly similar to the scene in which Empedocles first appears in *The Death of Empedocles* (Figure 7.4), and one senses that the similarity must be intentional. This scene in *Humiliated*, repeated as a separate short film (*Incantati*), reinforces Straub's comment about the significance of the love story between Siracusa and Ventura as a narrative that humanizes the post-war efforts of reconstruction in Italy, but as part of nature too. This scene underscores the disappointment in failing to hold their collective together, suggesting the potential of reading *Workers, Peasants*, *The Return of the Prodigal Son*, and *Humiliated* as 'open works'.

In his desire to idealize the greenery of this environment, Fairfax describes the Buti woods as 'untouched nature: the luscious grove in which *Workers, Peasants* is played out' and asks if the Eden-like quality of nature is 'nostalgic yearning for a prelapsarian past in the "post-Brechtian" work'.[44] Yet, Fairfax sees the woods as

FIG. 7.3. Danièle Huillet and Jean-Marie Straub, *Humiliated*
(2003, courtesy of BELVA Film).

FIG. 7.4. Danièle Huillet and Jean-Marie Straub, *The Death of Empedocles*
(1987, courtesy of BELVA Film).

something more than they are, overlooking commonplace elements which locate the woods as edgeland in the uncertain, indeterminate place where a town finishes or is yet to colonize. The Buti woods are not 'untouched' — in the second shot of *Workers, Peasants* Widow Biliotti sits on a broken, moss-covered water trough and at the feet of Pompeo Manera there are some cut paving stones and a black plastic pipe runs behind them. Later Toma, Siracusa, and Ventura stand in front of a dry-stone wall overgrown with weeds, and there are clearly defined pathways. There are indeed at least eleven shots showing the black plastic pipe, the kind used for water overflow or small-scale irrigation. There are too many shots of the pipe to be accidental or a chance occurrence — they would have been immediately noticeable in the location search (Figure 7.5).[45] The black plastic pipe tends to be most obvious in the shots of the workers, an industrially made element which acts as a small, incidental sign suggestive of their work in factories. The pipes cannot be overlooked as something out of place, instead they are an intentional disruption, a Barthes-like 'punctum' and a reminder that the town is nearby (see also Figure 7.1).

The trees in the woods at Buti are only partly shown since the camera frames the actors at ground level. In previous films trees have been filmed for their poetic agency: in the last shot of *The Bridegroom, the Actress and the Pimp* (1968) wind swirls through a tall tree suggesting the transience of life; on a football field near the beginning of *Not Reconciled* (1965) a single poplar is lined up in the centre of the goal; in *From the Cloud to the Resistance* a goddess sits in a large tree; and the Arolla pine at the edge of the amphitheatre in *The Antigone of Sophocles* (1992) is a visual axis; according to Huillet, 'we thought: if this tree dies, we cannot make the film, because this tree was also Antigone'.[46] Throughout *Workers, Peasants* the narrative

FIG. 7.5. Danièle Huillet and Jean-Marie Straub, *Workers, Peasants* (2001, courtesy of BELVA Film).

is told through the gritty, mundane materiality of survival, but in the last speech of the film trees are given lyrical, but importantly not visual, significance through the words of the peasant Pompeo Manera when he tells of transporting and replanting laurel trees, of the toughness of the laurel to grow between stones and to survive in unlikely places, alluding to the classical references of the laurel as the symbol of peace and victory:

> Laurel is not a plant that really and truly becomes a tree, and really and truly becomes a grove, and gives timber, though it is most advisable as a start wherever you want to reforest. It's the one that most quickly takes root and most quickly spreads. [...] Everyone spoke of wayfarers who had passed by with a laurel branch in their hand.

Filming the 'near'

In the woods, the compression of the space where the actors read and recite occurs through using fixed focal length lenses which foreshorten visual depth since each prime lens has a limited span of focus. In the first half of *Workers, Peasants* the rhythm of shots is one where three peasants or three workers are shown, followed by medium shots framing two people and medium close-ups of one person speaking. The camera appears to get closer to the figures in the frame because the changing focal length of the lenses used shows their head and shoulders in focus while blurring the background greenery or earth bank. This is partly explained by Straub's comment about expanded landscape against the performance spaces in *Workers, Peasants*: 'we are no longer dealing with the distant but with the near'.[47] In the Buti woods the characters are primarily in shadow, while occasional shafts of sunlight fall on them as if by accident, the perspective and depth of field that bright sunlight gives to film is mostly absent. This *near*-ness means that the readable quality of the 'stratigraphic' has been eliminated and 'reading' these wooded glades is not possible, they are intentionally 'un-readable', resistant and austere despite their rich greenery.

In *Workers, Peasants* the stories carefully denote and map place, especially in Carmela's testimony where she identifies in detail the towns and cities where people came from and went to. However, to return to the point made above, there is no correspondence between these places and the generalized nature of the woods. The actors are frequently depicted against earth banks where there is no depth of field and no relationship to the land as a site of production. The characters are dislocated or de-located in these green glades; there is no representation of their labour, work becomes an abstraction only existing as it is reported by the actors telling their stories. The last shot of *Workers, Peasants* remains ambiguous — a 180-degree pan which finally opens out from the woods moves from the top of a corrugated iron shed across wooded hills, a wide blue sky above finishing at a fence line but without showing any agricultural land and does not establish the locations in the woods. The limiting effect of fixed focal lenses in *Workers, Peasants* and *The Return of the Prodigal Son — Humiliated*, coupled with the use of 35mm colour film stock, saturates the photography with artifice and disorientation creating a sense of unease in deciphering the green spaces in the woods.

FIG. 7.6. Danièle Huillet and Jean-Marie Straub, *Humiliated*
(2003, courtesy of BELVA Film).

In *Workers, Peasants* and *The Return of the Prodigal Son* — *Humiliated* the spaces
are filled with verbalized memory as testimony, but, as I have argued, the wooded
locations do not become history as 'memory and geography' — the woods remain
non-places. In the green glades there is nothing to tie the spaces to the history of the
stories, unlike the intensity of history held by the mountains in *Fortini/Cani*. In shot
34 of *Humiliated* (Figure 7.6) Ventura is shown pressed between the layers of greenery
as though barricaded by the compression of space itself. Some of the camerawork
in *Workers, Peasants* is out of character with Huillet and Straub's previous films: on
several occasions there is an awkward and baroque movement zooming out and
panning from one group to another which joins the groups of workers and peasants
together in wary interchange as they try to understand each other's roles. These
disruptive zooms break the visual division of placing the workers and peasants in
separate shots, described by Manuel Ramos-Martínez as 'oppositional framing'
suddenly and deliberately linking the groups together in a single take — a defiant
and deliberate political act of unification.[48] Further situations build to bring the
workers and peasants together, in shots 15 (Figure 7.7) and 38 of *Humiliated*, the
widest shots from the films *Workers, Peasants* and *The Return of the Prodigal Son*
— *Humiliated*, the twelve figures are shown together standing in groupings under
trees unified by their defence against their humiliation by the outsider Carlo the
Bald. Later, shot 43 (Figure 7.8) shows seven of the workers and peasants standing
on a ridge in the woods looking down as they defend their co-operative from the
cruelty of the hunters/partisans' criticism. These external figures are intruders
and interlopers who have entered uninvited. They are visually and narratively

FIG. 7.7. Danièle Huillet and Jean–Marie Straub, *Humiliated* (2003, courtesy of BELVA Film).

FIG. 7.8. Danièle Huillet and Jean–Marie Straub, *Humiliated* (2003, courtesy of BELVA Film).

disruptive and try to divide the workers and peasants secluded in their refuge on the common ground offered by the woods.

Conclusion

The films *Workers, Peasants* and *The Return of the Prodigal Son — Humiliated* seem to depart from Huillet and Straub's previous films. The woods at Buti do not offer immediate readings as historically determined 'stratigraphic' sites despite the fact that the actors from the Teatro Francesco di Bartolo are working in a tradition which derives in part from *maggio epico* folk theatre and approach the texts as 'memoria/lectura' performance. The turn from landscape to nature, which can be traced back to the Hölderlin films shot in Sicily, is intensified by the compression of space in *Workers, Peasants* and *The Return of the Prodigal Son — Humiliated*. The political space of *near*-ness between the workers and peasants is constructed in the displaced green spaces occupied by the actors in the undifferentiated woodland.

The task of bringing workers and peasants together visually, socially, and politically is at the heart of these films and echoes the political aspirations represented by Huillet and Straub's version of eco-communism. These films are not unreadable, but they parallel the difficulty of resolving the divisions between workers and peasants in the post-war economy as represented in Vittorini's novel. The struggle of the workers and peasants to comprehend each other's social and politically-determined perspectives and the communication needed to bridge their separation is negotiated in the open, shared space of the woods.

Notes to Chapter 7

1. Interview in *The Green and the Stone: Straub and Huillet in Buti*, dir. by Armin Linke (2017) <vimeo.com/236318068> [accessed 14 January 2022].
2. JoAnn [*sic*] Cavallo, 'Where Have All the Brave Knights Gone? Sicilian Puppet Theater and the Tuscan-Emilian Epic *Maggio*', *Italian Culture*, 19.2 (2001), 31-55 (pp. 32-33).
3. Dario Marconcini in *The Green and the Stone*.
4. Cavallo, 'Where Have All the Brave Knights Gone?', pp. 37, 33.
5. Pummer says this is the first time a script has been shown in their work, though scripts were partly seen in *Introduction to Arnold Schoenberg's Accompaniment to a Cinematographic Scene* (1973) and Franco Fortini's book in *Fortini/Cani*: Pummer, '(Not Only) for Children and Cavemen', pp. 84-85.
6. Jean-Marie Straub, 'Annotated Script for *Workers, Peasants*', in Straub and Huillet, *Writings*, pp. 445-51 (p. 445).
7. Marconcini in *The Green and the Stone*.
8. Berta, 'Portfolio', p. 534.
9. Deleuze, *Cinema 2* (1989), p. 237.
10. Lylov and Marhöfer, 'A Thousand Cliffs', p. 381.
11. Danièle Huillet and Jean-Marie Straub, 'Hölderlin, That is Utopia', in Straub and Huillet, *Writings*, pp. 204-12 (p. 206).
12. Rancière, *The Intervals of Cinema*, pp. 118, 108.
13. Webster Schott, 'Elio Vittorini's Hoping and Nonhoping', in Elio Vittorini, *Women of Messina*, trans. by Frances Frenaye and Frances Keene (New York: New Directions, 1973), no page numbers.

14. The film *Sicilia!* was made immediately before *Workers, Peasants* and was the first of Huillet and Straub's films to be based on a Vittorini novel, *Conversations in Sicily* of 1941, and to work with actors from the Teatro Francesco di Bartolo. Even the apparent orthodoxy of the realist style used in *Sicilia!* is counterpointed in the additional films *The Wayfarer* (2001) and *The Knife Sharpener* (2001) made from different takes. These multiple versions created from parts encourage uncertainty.

15. Umberto Eco, *The Open Work*, trans. by Anna Cancogni (New York: Hutchinson Radius, 1989), pp.102–03.

16. Vittorini, *Women of Messina*, pp. 3–8.

17. The subtitles of the films are literal translations with different cadences from the American translation of the novel.

18. Rancière and Lafosse, 'Politics and Aesthetics in the Straubs' Films'.

19. Quoted in Leslie Hill, '"O Himmlisch Licht!": Cinema and the Withdrawal of the Gods (Straub-Huillet, Hölderlin, Godard, Brecht)', *Angelaki*, 17.4 (2012), 139–55 (p. 148).

20. Antonio Gramsci, *Selections from the Prison Notebooks*, ed. and trans. by Quintin Hoare and Geoffrey Nowell-Smith (London: Lawrence & Wishart, 2003), p. 75. Gramsci identifies the 'braccanti', landless agricultural labourers (p. 313), and 'mezzadria', primitive share-cropping (p. 283).

21. Pummer, '(Not Only) for Children and Cavemen', p. 83.

22. Deleuze, *Cinema 2*, pp. 234, 235.

23. Ibid., p. 235.

24. Renato Berta and Rinaldo Censi, 'When the Image Doesn't Exist Yet', in *Tell It to the Stones*, ed. by Busch and Hering, pp. 424–32 (p. 428).

25. Deleuze, *Cinema 2*, p. 235.

26. Edward Said, 'Invention, Memory and Place', in *Landscape and Power*, ed. by W. J. T. Mitchell (Chicago: University of Chicago Press, 2002), pp. 241–59 (p. 241).

27. Ibid., pp. 245–46.

28. Hans Hurch, '*Too Early, Too Late*: Interview with Huillet and Straub', trans. by Ben Brewster <http://kinoslang.blogspot.com/2014/08/too-early-too-late-interview-with.html> [accessed 27 July 2021].

29. For example the classical, idealized utopias of Nicolas Poussin (1594–1665) and Claude Lorrain (c.1600–82).

30. From the 1870s Cézanne painted Mont Sainte-Victoire approximately sixty times; the works from 1896 to 1906 were the most significant for modern landscape painting.

31. Barbara Ulrich, '"Hast du nicht alles mir gesagt?" and Hölderlin's *Native Reversal* as response', in *Tell It to the Stones*, ed. by Busch and Hering, pp. 140–57 (p.143).

32. Danièle Huillet and Jean-Marie Straub, 'Questionnaire on May 1968', in Straub and Huillet, *Writings*, pp. 266–67 (p. 267).

33. Elio Vittorini, quoted in Danièle Huillet and Jean-Marie Straub, 'Press Kit for *Workers, Peasants*', in Straub and Huillet, *Writings*, pp. 434–44 (p. 442).

34. Berta and Censi, 'When the Image Doesn't Exist Yet', p. 426.

35. Peter Kammerer and Patrick Primavesi, 'Work, Progress: On the Resistance of Peasants in the Work of Straub, Huillet, and Heiner Müller', in *Tell It to the Stones*, ed. by Busch and Hering, pp. 196–217 (p. 209).

36. A term coined by geographer Marion Shoard: see Michael Symmons Roberts and Paul Fairly, *Edgelands* (London: Vintage, 2012), p. 5.

37. Richard Mabey, *The Unofficial Countryside* (Stanbridge: Little Toller Books, 2010), pp. 15, 20.

38. Rancière and Lafosse, 'Politics and Aesthetics in the Straubs' Films'.

39. Fairfax, 'Straub/Huillet's Ecological Communism'. Fairfax discusses the significance of a 2009 conference in London, 'The Idea of Communism' led by Alain Badiou and Slavoj Žižek, at which Jacques Rancière was a speaker.

40. Rancière and Lafosse, 'Politics and Aesthetics in the Straubs' Films'.

41. Lylov and Marhöfer, 'A Thousand Cliffs', p. 365.

42. Ibid., p. 381.

43. Mabey, *The Unofficial Countryside*, p. 20.
44. Fairfax, 'Straub/Huillet's Ecological Communism'.
45. It appears in the first shot with the actors (shot 2) and repeatedly thereafter. See, in particular, shots 6-8.
46. Huillet quoted in Patrick Primavesi, 'Violence and the Stones', in *Tell It to the Stones*, ed. by Busch and Hering, pp. 478-93 (p. 493).
47. Lylov and Marhöfer, 'A Thousand Cliffs', p. 367.
48. Manuel Ramos-Martínez, 'Marx Immemorial: Workers and Peasants in the Cinema of Jean-Marie Straub and Danièle Huillet', in *Marxism and Film Activism: Screening Alternative Worlds*, ed. by Ewa Mazierska and Lars Kristensen (New York: Berghahn, 2015), pp. 105-23 (p. 113).

❖

CHAPTER 8

Jean-Yves Petiteau,
Itinerary of Jean Bricard:
Three Documents

Translated by Ricardo Matos Cabo

Huillet and Straub's film *Itinerary of Jean Bricard* (2008), shot by Straub alone in December 2007 after Huillet's death in the previous year, is based on an itinerary — 'a journey, where the person who is interviewed guides and introduces the researcher to a territory' — by the French sociologist Jean-Yves Petiteau (1942–2015). The text with its accompanying photographs was published in the journal *Interlope la Curieuse* in June 1994. What follows is the first English translation of this document, which sheds valuable light on the film based on it. In order to facilitate comparison between text and film, the translation remains very close to the English subtitles for the film by Misha Donat. The English text follows the layout of the French original.

The original publication in 1994 was accompanied by an essay by Petiteau and Isabelle Rolland explaining the methodology of the itinerary. This document constitutes the second part of this chapter. The third document consists of a transcription of a talk given by Petiteau before a screening of Huillet and Straub's film in Grenoble in 2012.

The original publication of the itinerary and accompanying essay contains footnotes that are often brief. These have not been expanded in what follows, although translator's notes have been added where necessary. The spelling of a number of names has been corrected.

The translator and editors of this volume are very grateful to Erik and Lou Petiteau for permission to translate these documents and include the photographs. We are also grateful to Misha Donat for permission to use his subtitles.

ITINERARY OF JEAN BRICARD[*]

We arrive at Île Coton, where I spent my youth.

We lived in La Basse-Pierre.

There used to be a port at La Basse-Pierre. It used to be the port of Basse-Pierre, but that was centuries ago.

There was a warehouse for grains and wines. The Butte de la Pierre was planted 90% with vines, the wine was transported by boat.

★ Jean Bricard was born in 1932 in La Basse-Pierre, now retired, he was the head of a company trading in aggregates on the Isle Verte, opposite Ancenis.

Because in winter there were boats, but in summer, when there wasn't enough water to join the banks, we went by foot across a ford like you have at Oudon and Saint-Florent. There were several, diagonally.

The fords were usually 2 or 3 kilometres long.

There was one here which went to Basse-Pierre from the Ancenis château.

They were demolished partly for the channel.

I knew this ford, then they demolished it.

See, I live over there.

This year there were 40 centimetres of water in the house.

There used to be willow bush which, during the war in '43-'44, you could hide in to avoid capture by the Germans.

'44, the year my uncle got caught. My uncle was shot because for 3 weeks we had the Americans in Ancenis.

The Loire was the frontier. The Germans were here on the left bank. Which made things tough. Some people were caught crossing the Loire by boat, because at night they used small boats to get to the Americans.

In a moment we're going to go and see the cross.

Christophe is the neighbour without a job, so he comes and gives me a hand.

Here are the island heads which get the most sand.

Over there the ash trees were torn out during the war. Look, you can still see the holes. They dug down 2.6 metres to get to the roots.

And just as we were working on the islands, the guys in the boat...

— 'Hey, you guys over there, you're going to eat with us at noon!' Then they'd eat a little fish passing by.

I saw salmon in '43, a whole lot heaped on the boat floor.

I saw that one year, in '43, never had so many been seen. The same with shad. There were 10 cases a day. We spread them out to send to Paris.

There were fish between '45 and '50, and then some. After that, less. Pollution. First because of the silting, then the lack of water in summer. Because people steal the Loire's water to redirect it into other spillways, the water goes elsewhere and we have to live with it.

We'll see the cabin to shelter in when it rains really hard.

When we had an hour or two, we worked around the farm. But whenever there was a chance to get out for a day, or half a day, we came to the island.

It was in there that I had my finger eaten by rats. They ate my finger while I was asleep.

You can still see where the oven was. Here there was a farm which was once a café. It was like that everywhere along the banks of the Loire, real veritable bands of people. The barges would stop.

I don't know if we'll see it, maybe it's buried, given the level of the islands when the bistro was here.

It must have been 2 or 3 metres lower. All this, landfill made up of sand and clay.

The base of the ash tree... no, of the oven, is there. But you can't see it. The water would have to be lower.

There's a wharf behind where boats would tie up. You can see the shape of the oven in the summer. There.

200 metres from here as the crow flies, over there was a farm that was destroyed by the company's barges in '68, '69, '70. Because it interfered with navigation. The sand barges were going upriver against all obstacles, and these had to be removed.

They made a dike at the head of Île Macrière that one should see from here. Now you can't see it because it's underwater.

It starts 45° to the right of Île Macrière. To shore up the island head, so the current wouldn't wash it away, they put 75 tons of rocks per metre.

Those are the rabbits. They came here. They were hiding during the flood. When they're trapped by the water, they climb onto the treetops or hedges.

We removed the ones in distress. We recovered a hundred. We put them back once the water receded.

This is at the moment when my uncle was shot. Around 13 August 1944. 50 years ago, this year.

This is the plaque. — 'Here were captured Abbot Brouard, Jules Aze and Rubbens'; they say Abbot Bricard was with them, but he wasn't with them when they were captured. They were captured before they got back to the island.

The plaque was put here so it'd be out of the water, but they were captured on the shore, on the Brevet side.

A week before, my father had hid in the willows.

We kids could go where we wanted. So, I went home and said my father was hiding in the willows. When everybody was gone, I came to tell him they had cleared off and he could show his nose.

Until I was 20, there was no question of going anywhere except to the neighbours.

At that time there was no unemployment. We weren't paid much, but there was work for all.

We went as day labour and there was work for us.

We used to hunt a bit, even without a permit, when we were young, at the hut, because we had a hut with a boat there.

Often, we'd make huts at the top of an ash tree or willow. We added straw, then got inside.

Our parents had gone to the mainland and we kept the rifle.

I'd started to shoot when I was 12 with a machine gun, because my brothers were in the Resistance.

We leave Île Coton, we start the motor, and we cross the Loire.

That was the island of my childhood.

We could've gone to see over there, where the islands are disappearing. It's a calamity.

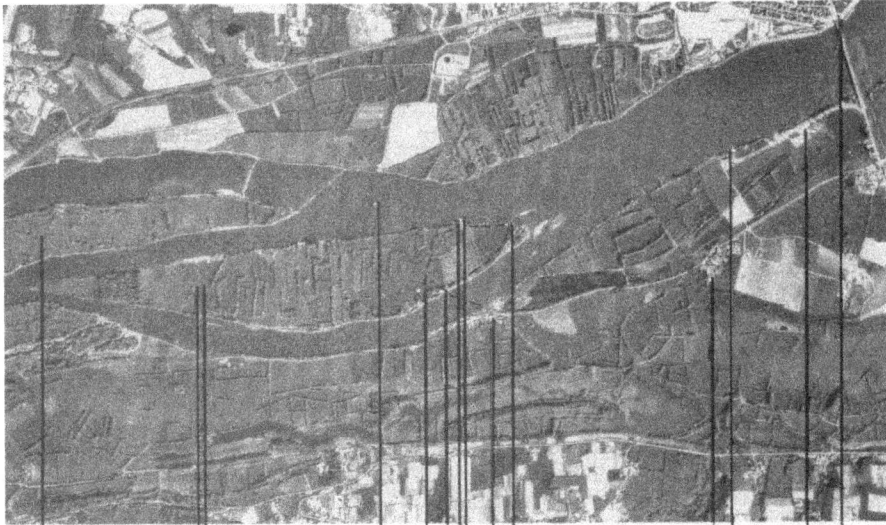

The destroyed
submerged farm

The container
cabin

The plaque of the
Fusillés de la
Résistance

The head of
Coton Island.
Shoreline

The sand
trap
(company)

Île Macrière

The hold

The rat cabin

The buried oven

Ancenis

Île Coton

Les Brevets

La Basse-Pierre

Le Strasbourg

— Itinerary — 24 February 1994.

[Text by Jean-Yves Petiteau and Isabelle Rolland]

The itinerary of Jean Bricard, 24 February 1994, here presented, was made after two interviews about his life story. ⋆

The journey was entirely recorded.

An itinerary is the creation of a journey, where the person who is interviewed guides and introduces the researcher to a territory he is familiar with, following the rhythm of his own narrative. The one who is constituting his narrative or story together with us is totally free to choose his journey, his own words, to decide on the time he will give us. Our methodological undertaking is to establish a report of this mise-en-scène. *Two people accompany the speaker, one fully records his speech, the other takes a photographic snapshot every time there is an important change in the journey or story. The aim of this* mise-en-scène *is to relate the different levels and reference points that give meaning to each story.*

⋆This work was part of a research project led by the Conservation Centre for the Banks of the Loire and its Tributaries [Le Conservatoire des Rives de la Loire et de ses affluents] (person responsible: N. Le Nevez) with the students of the Nantes School of Architecture [École d'architecture de Nantes] (teachers: M.-P. Halgand and J.-Y. Petiteau).

'The valley spirit never dies. It is named the mysterious female. And the doorway of the mysterious female is the base from which Heaven and Earth sprang. It is there within us all the while; draw upon it as you will, it never runs dry. The spirit descends into the valley and rises again, it is the breath; spirit and valley embrace one another, this is life.' Lao Tzu (ch. VI).[1]

An itinerary is not the result of a totally predictable ritual, because its meaning is the result of a negotiation between the researcher and the person who is interviewed. When we met — in December 1993 — Jean Bricard and his family were about to move from the ground floor of their house in Les Brevets to take shelter on the upper floor.

We had agreed to meet when the level of the water went down: the date we set for this interview was significant. It was the time for a rebirth after the flood; the time to speak; it was also the time to rediscover the land.

The first interview, on 31 January 1994, took place on the 'Strasbourg', an old barge owned by his company. He cut the interview short and proposed another initiatory approach to us, where his remarks would be articulated around 'making'. This spontaneous itinerary began with the passing of a tractor on a boat from the continent to Île Coton. As if history demanded the sharing of a sensible experience to be deciphered.

Along the way, he recalls the main facts and actions that affected him during the floods.

The 'Strasbourg', moored upstream of Île Coton near the sand trap, will remain the meeting point to relate each phase of his life story. A place of memory of his professional life, this boat marks his attachment to the river. The place where he was born, where he returns to, the home port for this 'community' of river dwellers.

Inhabiting the shore, but on the water, the boat seems to watch over the return of the one who sails. Like the ancient ferryman, it observes and evaluates each variation in the flow, or level of the water.

The banks of a river only reveal themselves when you walk along them, when you traverse them, when you approach them. Their existence depends on what created them, the water and the current. 'Thales declared the earth to be sitting on water.'[2]

Today this proposition still raises the question of representation: the river and the sea impose their surface on what surrounds them, as a reference.

The permanent variation of the water level is also the mark by which we measure any change in the shoreline. Its instability is both readable and measurable. It is this instability that allows the layout of the land to be traced on the horizontal plane.

The banks are not only the edge that the river licks, but are also themselves a territory, the reading of which is inseparable from the movement of the water. Therefore, the mobility of the river dwellers follows that of the river and constitutes the edgelands, where the border is established and reproduced.

The landmarks are never static, but signal a journey. The Vallias[3] do not live only in an enclosed country, it is a 'movement space'.[4] The river seems to impose its rules on any attempt at representation. These rules require a knowledge of its moments and forces.

Jean Bricard is a guide not only because he is descended from several generations of river dwellers and because he has used the Loire from 'a young age', but also because of his professional activities: the riprapping of the banks, of the island heads, the digging of the channel.

The natural character of the river is not unambiguous. Its wild river quality is dependent on the vigilance of the locals who use it, and thus keep looking after it.

Everything that moves him in his daily life and culture is related to the maintenance of the river, and that is why the actions he comes up with never result from an abstract analysis, but from a confrontation with a problem or an object that changes every time, the meaning of which only becomes clear as we go along.

When it comes to crossing a river or sailing upstream, navigation is rarely parallel or orthogonal in relation to the shore. Cunning and tactics are needed to outwit the traps.

Each move involves an angle of attack and an oblique approach. The gaze must both recognize the obstacles and deal with the mobility of the territory. The laws of representation result from this balance of power. To establish a perspective, the survey must consider elements that change. The relation between these elements and the combination of their multiplicity forms a gaze that allows for representation.

The question of representation forces us now to make a detour. It is necessary to escape from the knowledge that allows us to transcribe or to create an order to find what constitutes it from the start. To approach this question in its specificity, we must tackle the issues that are at the basis of how one experiences the territory, whatever that may be.

'Escaping the imaginary fantasies produced by the eye, the everyday has a certain strangeness that does not surface, or whose surface is only its upper limit, outlining itself against the visible. Within this ensemble, I shall try to locate the practices that are foreign to the "geometrical" or "geographical" space of visual, panoptic, or theoretical constructions.'[5]

As with the walker, the gaze of the navigator is carried by his body; it is the body that imparts an intention, a strategy to any process through which the movement is articulated.

'Thus, Thales had seen the unity of all that is, but when he went to communicate it, he found himself talking about water!'[6]

Here it is not only the current that shapes the space, but also the movements of the river that organize the territory.

The mobile generates the immobile.

'The divine intelligence moves through the water with rapidity.'[7]

What is paradoxical in this itinerary is that what is at the bottom is described with the same precision as what is on the surface. At the bottom of the water, the fords reproduce the obliquity of a crossing. These crossing lines touch the shore from one side to the other, establishing the expectation of a relationship of alterity.

The surface of the earth is not that of the humus but of the river, whose level is the standard of measurement. The height of the water, the speed of the current, and the measure of the flow are the most tangible qualities that allow us to grasp reality. The accuracy of the numbers is based on a ratio. The zero of the rivers, the reference point for all measurements, is not sea level but the surface of the Loire at the lowest water level. From this point, we count day by day the draught or the flood, the flow of water, the x and y axes of the landscape.

When Jean Bricard talks about the area he belongs to, he lists the villages and places of pilgrimage along the south bank between Saint-Florent and Champtoceaux. Not only does this space run along an axis, but the survey of its route is the only measure of its extent. A sort of slow-motion travelling shot where vigilance and memory are articulated on a path.

List of names, declination of numbers. Numbers always imply a relationship. Encounter and coincidence establish a fraction, a space of measurement and designation.

'Pythagoras said that there was nothing more sacred than the number, and after the number, the first rank belonged to the one who had given names to things.'[8]

When the river regains its strength, it takes over time as it drowns the banks.

This time is not only that of the seasons, winter or spring flooding, low water in summer. Different seasons in the years, where nothing that happens is identical; floods in and out are an expectation, a predictable and unpredictable event.

The cycles on which memory is grafted obey another temporality, that of the memorable floods. History is built on these exceptional phases. These events are all present at once in the memory, they are anticipated like the iterations of a cycle, but even more so as an initiation ritual through which the community meets and recognizes itself.

The new river dwellers experience the first floods, the group closes in, and networks of mutual aid are formed (to take the children to school or to allow the dead to cross on their last journey).

The flood is not only the resurgence of a primitive anguish, but also the expectation of a deliverance (from the earth and from order), of an original rebirth (baptism and deluge are perhaps close to one another).

The deluge heralds the erasure of the world, but also the end of all guilt.

The laying bare of the earth or any fecundation will give back to the soil abundance and fertility, the enjoyment of oblivion and a possible rebirth of the world.

The rituals upon which a tradition is built are maintained because they are reproduced; to do this, they must not only be revisited, but also reinvented in the present.

This maintenance, or rather this reconstitution, is most often the result of instability: the anxiety of disappearance, the expectation of a return.

Diasporas are both a consequence of a form of emigration and a separation from the land of origin. Here it is not the journey that the absence is built upon, but the relative instability of the land: submersion by water, erosion of shores and islands, the silting up of the river branches.

The islands are not only a reverse side of the continent, but allow for a permanent relationship of alterity in relation to history.

Beyond the reach of land consolidation or urbanization, these lands preserve the traces of childhood.

The initiated of the islands, far from the gaze of the world (that of other adults), can maintain a 'secret society of childhood', protected from the erosion of time.

Their exploitation (planting, hunting, and fishing) undoubtedly implies effort and work; but the island, as it is not permanently inhabited, is, every day, from dawn to dusk, the object of a perpetual return.

Each time, its rediscovery reverses the values that affect the functions of daily life, because it contains all the characteristics of an imaginary space.

With each shift, the ritual changes and interferes with the time of History.

It is indeed the interplay of these interferences, where different strata of memory are combined, that the itinerary tries to make explicit.

'The frameworks of memory exist both within the passage of time and outside it. External to the passage of time, they communicate to the images and concrete recollections of which they are made a bit of their stability and generality. But these frameworks are in part captivated by the course of time. They are like those log drives that descend a waterway so slowly that one can easily move from one side to the other, but which nevertheless are not immobile and go forward. And so it is in regard to frameworks of memory: while following them we can pass as easily from one notion to another, both of which are general and outside of time, through a series of reflections and arguments, as we can go up and down the course of time from one recollection to another.'[9]

The signs and symbols which mark out the edge or the margin generally escape the attention of the walker; placed near the coppice or at the crossroads of the sunken paths, they mark for the inhabitants a relationship of appropriation and a link to the sacred.

Crosses, statues of saints, commemorative plaques, are not maintained by the clergy or the commune, but taken care of directly by each family.

'Michelet was right. If the great ancient gods are dead, the "little ones" — those of the forests and houses — have survived the upheavals of history.'[10]

It is because this territory is unstable that those who live there constantly intervene to restore the sacred reference points, and because they undergo extreme events that they keep a relationship, gift against gift.

Like the sailors who offer an ex-voto, they build up small monuments, discreet signs of an affective relationship with the sacred. 'I remember when Bernadette started to float... Then Bernadette began to float away on her own, adrift.'[11]

'By reason of these things, then, the whaling voyage was welcome; the great flood-gates of the wonder-world swung open, and in the wild conceits that swayed me to my purpose, two and two there floated into my inmost soul, endless processions of the whale, and, midmost of them all, one grand hooded phantom, like a snow hill in the air.'[12]

1. Translator's note: this rendering is a modified version of the translation of Lao Tzu by Arthur Waley (1934). In what follows, footnotes are from the original text unless indicated otherwise.
2. Aristotle.
3. A name by which riverside residents distinguish themselves from more distant residents.
4. G. Deleuze.
5. Michel de Certeau, *The Practice of Everyday Life*.
6. Nietzsche.
7. Aristotle about Thales.
8. Aelian, 2nd century.
9. M. Halbwachs, *On Collective Memory*. [Translator's note: the translation is from Maurice Halbwachs, *On Collective Memory*, ed. and trans by Lewis A. Coser (Chicago & London: University of Chicago Press, 1992), p. 182. Translation amended.]
10. M. de Certeau, *Ghosts of the City* in *Traverses* no. 40, *Theatres of Memory*. [Translator's note: the translation is from Michel de Certeau, Luce Giard, and Pierre Mayol, *The Practice of Everyday Life: Vol. 2: Living and Cooking*, trans by Timothy J. Tomaskik (Minneapolis & London: University of Minnesota Press, 1998), pp. 136–37.]
11. Jean Bricard (2nd interview) reports on his familiar relationship with the cult and its objects during a historical flood. Here the statuette of the local saint was dislodged from the cave by the waters.
12. H. Melville, *Moby Dick*.

Apropos: Jean-Marie Straub and Danièle Huillet, *Itinerary of Jean Bricard*[1]

And as Brecht used to say... who was said to have invented... *distancing*, nonsense, he never used that word... He used *Verfremdung*, which means making things strange... making people feel that things are strange every second of a film, that they are like that, but could be otherwise. That's all... They could and should be different...[2]

After the screening of *Too Early, Too Late* in a cinema in Nantes, I told Jean-Marie Straub about my fascination with the framing of a static shot, the duration of which seemed to be at the limit of what could be tolerated. This shot showed the progress of a person driving an oxcart; a person whose appearance and activity wouldn't usually raise interest. The surprise comes from this insistence on showing an ordinary person passing at a slow pace and whose presence in this territory, an ordinary countryside, would not be noticed.

I told Jean-Marie Straub about my surprise, which echoed a reference in my work about itineraries, where I rely on duration to bring out the unique quality of an everyday narrative that is usually overlooked, because it is considered a mere fragment of everyday life.

This sequence, because it illustrates nothing other than itself, seems to be directly captured from the location scouting [*repérage*]. The emotion is raw, as if it were a first appearance not yet inscribed in the register of interpretations that give it meaning.

'In the Theaetetus, Socrates asserts that philosophy begins with amazement... The relationship between amazement and questioning only emerges if something is raised as a problem: no one, in fact, questions what is unequivocal. On the contrary, what "looks at us", what arouses our interest, becomes an object of questioning. Questions only arise when there is a need for clarification, as uncertainty is unbearable. In other words, we must be in an original tension for our "a-tension" to be awakened.'[3]

Our attention focuses on this person as they cross the static shot. And the duration of the crossing creates an expectation in the viewer. The static shot, marking the beginning and the end of his progress, highlights the event that it stages.

During the preparation of an itinerary, it is the person accompanied by the anthropologist who becomes the guide. This person scouts the territory he or she is surveying. During the *mise-en-scène* of the journey, the person meets and names the landmarks that give meaning to their story. This *mise-en-scène*, which is guided by an emotional recognition, brings into evidence places and connections in the territory that escape the control of representations derived from cultural habits.

Time is the key to the protocol in place for the itineraries. Words escape the classifications of the text, they name, open up, await a response.

This location scouting escapes the perversion of scholarly analysis, creating a surprise, because it allows us to collect unknown or forgotten elements. Above all, in the act of recognition, it expresses an amazement or an emotion that echoes their original occurrence.

Danièle Huillet and Jean-Marie Straub decided to visit me the next day to find out about the itineraries I had mentioned.

I told Danièle Huillet and Jean-Marie Straub about the 'itineraries' I had made with artists and dockworkers. These were accounts, edited like a photo-novel. The exact words of the person doing the itinerary are transcribed. The editing keeps to the chronology and emphasizes the articulations that mark an emotional change.

They studied this work carefully and Danièle Huillet chose and presented Jean Bricard's itinerary to Jean-Marie with great sensitivity. The place reminded her of her childhood memories of the banks of the Loire.

They read this itinerary, which told the story of a river dweller and his attachment to an island: Île Coton near Ancenis. Resistance fighters, close relatives of Jean Bricard, were captured near the island at the end of the Second World War and were shot by the Germans.

Jean Bricard constructed this place as an ideal world. There he rediscovered the pleasure and dreams of his childhood. His friends and the boatmen of the Loire used to dock near a café that is now in ruins. He would later receive them in a hut.

Danièle and Jean-Marie borrowed this itinerary, with photographs in black and white, published in the magazine 'interlope la curieuse' and asked me to share with them the original recording of this story to discover the voice of Jean Bricard. The tape having disappeared, I tried to find Jean Bricard after this meeting.

He had just died. I met his wife, his brother and one of his friends and asked them to tell me about him. Jean-Marie Straub asked me if I knew someone local who could read the itinerary and record it. I ended up entrusting the reading of his story to a young actor, David Humeau, who had no similarities with Jean Bricard's culture or tone of voice.

Several years later, Jean-Marie Straub and Danièle Huillet contacted me to make the film.

In August 2006, Jean-Marie Straub announced his decision to shoot in September. Then came the tragic death of Danièle Huillet.

In the spring of 2007, Jean-Marie Straub decided to scout the locations to shoot the film.

I could not have participated in a location scouting exercise that would show the places that bear witness to Jean Bricard's words as if they were only the setting for a story. Jean-Marie Straub surveyed the territory of the island, book in hand, insisting on finding the pollard oaks, the holes of the roots torn out of the earth, the abandoned oven of the inn, the crossing places of the ford... where the words took shape.

Location scouting, like the involuntary memory of a place, becomes the silent part of the narrative where what we see interrogates each statement as if it were an enigma.

The narrative becomes speech again, shaping the elements of the island in the absence of the one who names them.

This location scouting, punctuated by the insistent framing and the recording of all the sounds that brush against the territory, gives rhythm to the movement and the silences punctuating the speech. Listening to the story becomes like listening to a poem.

Because the location scouting resonates together with the original speech, it is montage.

This reflexive location scouting [*repérage du repérage*] dislocates the chronology of the composition: the text is no longer a script used by the filmmaker to assemble his film. Instead, the film is like an archaeological dig, a form of listening or an origin of the text.

The cinematographic work reveals, in all their complexity, the edges or contexts that the narrative animates, disturbs, or causes to vibrate. The rhythm and duration of the cinematic unfolding [*déroulement cinématographique*] validates the premises on which the itinerary was built.

An itinerary-narrative only questions knowledge when the speech is let loose from the grip of common logic, when the time or the silence between two statements thwarts the recognition of an order or interrogates the places of resonance.

This primary composition resulting from the location scouting becomes montage. It resists the obviousness of immediately intelligible declensions and accepts being mobilized by sensorial expressions that awaken unexpected resonances.

For me, Danièle Huillet and Jean-Marie Straub displace the meaning and the chronology of editing, whether in text or in film. From beginning to end, the location scouting allows us to interrogate the origin of the presence of things and of speech. What is named is not immediately legible, and it is the resonance of the words or icon, at the place of its emergence, which frames the question of meaning in relation to its origin. Location scouting is a paradox; it is the permanent questioning of the place and time where the expression is incarnated.

'I was not a murderer who returned to prowl the scene of the crime, the place is itself a very old criminal, and has been for as long as it has revolved around the sun.'[4]

Jean-Yves Petiteau

1. Translator's note: this text is a translation of a talk given by Jean-Yves Petiteau before a screening of *Itinerary of Jean Bricard* at the Cinématèque de Grenoble on 24 February 2012. The transcript was published in *La furia umana*, 35 <http://www.lafuriaumana.it/index.php/68-archive/lfu-35/846-jean-yves-petiteau-itineraire-de-jean-bricard> [accessed 21 January 2022]. The original punctuation has been retained. For a video recording of the talk see <http://www.lafuriaumana.it/index.php/68-archive/lfu-35/834-re-itineraire> [accessed 21 January 2022]. The footnotes that follow are presented as they appear in the original text. We are grateful to *La furia umana* for permission to translate this text.

2. *L'étrange cas de Madame Huillet et Monsieur Straub*, Philippe Lafosse, Ombres/À Propos, Toulouse-Ivry-sur-Seine, 2007.

3. Ernesto Grassi, *La métaphore inouïe*, Quai Voltaire, Paris 1991.

4. Romain Gary, *Clair de femme* Gallimard, Folio, Paris 1977, p. 13.

CHAPTER 9

❖

Communist Photosynthesis

Rastko Novaković[1]

> Neither the paradoxicality of what is happening, neither the scale of what has
> already happened, nor the perspective of what awaits the world to experience
> — can be grasped by a single consciousness.
> We know firmly — ahead there will be victory over darkness.
> Ahead — there is light.
> But we are still not able to assimilate its rays, to examine the new life in these
> new rays, to move along the new paths illuminated by them.
> We foresee, have a presentiment, and have a foreboding of it.
> But this light is only now being born in the truly apocalyptic madness in
> which the universe is now enveloped.
> Humanity is stretching out to it, toward this unknown light of the future.
> — SERGEI EISENSTEIN, 1942[2]

> In the yellow of the sempiternal rose,
> Which unfolds by degrees and dilates and breathes back
> The odour of praise to the sun which keeps perpetual spring.
> — DANTE ALIGHIERI, 1320[3]

In the first part of the film *O somma luce* (2010) Jean-Marie Straub leaves us in the
dark for just over seven minutes (a couple of seconds longer in the second version)
with a recording of the first performance of Edgard Varèse's *Déserts* (Paris, 1954).[4]
The first two and a half sections of *Déserts* are thereby spliced together with the
second half of the final canto, XXXIII, of *Paradiso* from Dante's *Comedìa* (1320). The
overall shape of the *Comedìa*, which is a long and gradual movement from darkness
into light, is with Straub an irruption of light and words.

Varèse's piece brings together his ideas on how to organize sound and music (and
therefore time) away from the classical tradition, through the concepts of duration,
intensity, frequency, and timbre. *Déserts* also features interpolated tape recordings of
electronic sound which were played into the auditorium. It is this first interpolation
which produces the eruption of boos, abuse ('This is a scandal!'), and hisses from
the audience attending the premiere, adding another layer of sound. Straub brings
these un/intentional forms into juxtaposition with Dante's strict metre and rhyme.
He also honours Varèse's intention for *Déserts* to be experienced in company with
a film,[5] one that would have to be 'in opposition with the score. Only through
opposition can one avoid paraphrase... . There will be no action. There will be

no story. There will be images. Phenomena of light, purely'.[6] With Straub, the opposition is almost absolute because music and video footage stand side-by-side, the two domains separated in space and time.[7]

Despite the atonal and athematic principles of the work, Varèse spoke of it in terms reminiscent of programme music by listing various deserts:

> All those that people traverse or may traverse: *physical* deserts, on the earth, in the sea, in the sky, of sand, of snow, of interstellar spaces or of great cities, but also those of the human *spirit*, of that distant *inner* space no telescope can reach, where one is alone.[8]

Here Varèse approaches Dante, since the poet is constantly engaged in a montage of the personal and the cosmic and exploring the tension between the subjective and the objective. Moreover, in his *Inferno*, deserts are a constant refrain: 'The sand caught fire, like tinder under flint'; 'Here is no hope of any comfort ever, neither of respite nor of lesser pain'; 'Eyesight unaided — in that blackened air, through foggy, dense swirls — could not carry far'; 'Here pity lives where pity's truth is dead' (*Inferno*, XIV: 37; V: 44; IX: 5; XX: 28.). The simultaneous implosion and explosion of space finds clear expression in Friedrich Nietzsche's verses which also concern the desert: 'Many suns circle in desert space: to all that is dark do they speak with their light — but to me they are silent';[9] and 'The desert grows, and woe to him who conceals the desert within him!'.[10] And finally, for Jean Genet, the desert is a wellspring, in this dare and advice: 'Put all the images in language in a place of safety and make use of them, for they are in the desert, and it's in the desert we must go and look for them'.[11] All this by way of posing a question that the film does not answer: does the world presented by the music precede the text of *O somma luce*, or is it contemporaneous with it? In the same way we can ask: is the catastrophe, which finds Giorgio Passerone sitting on a dismembered and rusted excavator's arm (Figures 9.4-9.7), over, or is it still unfolding?

Before I turn to the cinematic treatment of Dante's text, it is useful to look at the exact nature of the source material, because it will inform our understanding of Straub's artistic decisions. Dating back to 1320, the *Comedìa* is one of the oldest texts which Huillet and Straub worked with. It is written in a proud, rich, and earthy vernacular, which Dante came to refer to as 'volgare illustre' and whose standard he took up militantly against 'the detestable wretches of Italy who hold this precious vernacular cheap'.[12] In the enemies of the vernacular, Dante sees moral failings — vainglory, envy, and avarice — and in the vernacular he sees the very origins of philosophical friendship between author and reader. The vernacular is associated with the reign of Love (rather than Latin's reign of Law), it is favoured by God because it is 'natural (and naturally humble)'.[13] As Robin Kirkpatrick summarizes, 'in its power to arouse benevolence, the vernacular resembles God himself'.[14]

Dante's belief in the power of the word borders on the mystical: he variously refers to the bone structure of the human face as inscribed with the letters 'omo' (spelling 'man' (*homo*), with the eyes standing in for the 'o's and the brows and nose for the 'm', *Purgatorio*, XXIII: 31) and of the Latin word *aueio* ('author', one who can knot words with authority) as itself formed by knotting the standard sequence of the vowels: a, e, i, o, u.[15] Here is a writer who takes his exploration of the power of words beyond the syllable to the molecular level of letters, yet never forgetting the syntactical, or narrative structure. It is hard to declaim or hear l. 126 of *Paradiso* XXXIII, 'e intendente te ami e arridi!', without feeling the full force of a phrase in which there are more vowels than consonants.[16]

Taking up the cause of the vernacular and the problems of how to elevate it to Latin involved theory (two unfinished treatises) and practice (his poetry). This brought about a revolution in syntax as part of a project, in Kirkpatrick's words, 'to expand the philosophical capacities of Italian writing'.[17] This consisted partly of 'reclothing' the Latin in the vernacular, partly in seeking 'to bestow [on the vernacular] a permanence such as, by its nature, it is bound to lack'.[18] This permanence, or stability of phrase, Dante found through language, as he himself put it *Convivio* Book One, 'binding itself with metre and rhyme'.[19]

For the *Comedìa* he devises the terzina — a new, three-line verse form (in a rhyming structure of ABA BCB CDC), elegant and propulsive (a prerequisite for a narrative poem) — which can hold both reported speech and philosophical speculation. The *Comedìa's* standard unit of metre is an eleven-syllable line, which concludes almost invariably with a stressed followed by an unstressed syllable.[20] Each canto is never more than a mere 160 lines long (much shorter than the traditional 600 lines of Virgil or Milton) which begs the question: why does Straub, who often insists on the integrity of a text (see the Introduction to this volume), decide to cut the first sixty-six lines of the last canto? This we will return to. For the three canticles of the *Comedìa* (*Inferno, Purgatorio, Paradiso*), some of the language, narrative devices, and imagery are constant, while others are specific to *Paradiso*. All of them come into play in *O somma luce* and I want to touch on them briefly below.

The 'modest voice' is typical of the *Comedìa* and is a response to the ineffable nature of the poet's experiences. It is also an acknowledgment of the natural limits of the mind, of memory, imagination, and speech.[21] Throughout, Dante acknowledges that to speak is one thing and to remember is quite another. As Kirkpatrick has commented, 'Though speech may be possible only where memory is active, the action of the memory cannot, it seems, automatically ensure that speech should follow'.[22] It is in our nature not to see clearly (when we do see), also not to see 'divine counsel' (*Paradiso*, XIII: 141).[23] It follows that it is difficult to make reliable statements, so we should proceed with 'leaden-footed' caution (*Paradiso*, XIII: 112).[24] The eyes fail, the body quivers under the weight of the theme (*Paradiso*, XXIII: 64-66), and often Dante falters and withdraws: 'my pen leaps and I do not write it' (*Paradiso*, XXIV: 25).[25]

Speech is counterposed to sight. For Dante the most fundamental act of the mind is that of seeing, and for much of the poem 'what is thought and what is seen are profoundly inextricable'.[26] Ultimately, in the last canto of *Paradiso*, his experience is revealed as greater than its recounting: 'from that point on my seeing was greater than my speaking' (*Paradiso*, XXXIII: 55).[27]

A courtesy which Dante seeks to foster between reader and poet is a joint intellectual and spiritual endeavour akin to the bond that Dante describes between himself and Virgil, his guide through *Inferno* and *Purgatorio*.[28] Throughout *Paradiso*,

Dante invites the reader into collaborative endeavour, seeking to engage the full exercise of all their faculties — rational, discursive, emotional, perceptual, and imaginative. Even though an anatomical and static description of heavenly order is one of his main concerns, dogma is not offered as a replacement for living faith and experience. *Paradiso* has a tendency to isolate statements and for the poet to interrupt himself in what Kirkpatrick has identified as self-possessed 'didactic pauses'. Contrary to the previous two canticles, here the pause is not primarily an 'agent of emotion', but of understanding.[29]

In *Paradiso*, having left Virgil in Purgatory, the poet must face tests of faith and demonstrate on his own the independent virtue of his art.[30] These tests are presented without suspense, or a possibility that he might fail, because the journey of the soul is complete.[31] The poet has been completely exposed to the truth, having come face to face with the Light of God. It is telling that Straub excises all explicit references to the Virgin, St Bernard, and Beatrice, which feature in the first part of the canto. While *Inferno* and *Purgatorio* teem with many voices and characters, several of *Paradiso*'s cantos are Dante's arias. Straub's script features only the poet's voice, thereby achieving maximum concentration as well as a partly de-Christianized character through a focus on natural imagery, without the allegorical scaffolding which an otherwise integral reading of the canto would impose.

The natural imagery is presented through the encounter of the poet with the variously 'simple', 'living', 'lofty', 'eternal', and 'supreme' light and three rainbows. This light, which moves everything, is 'self-loving' and 'self-known' (*Paradiso*, XXXIII: 124-26), 'always what it was before' (111), an 'infinite value' (81) which gives 'abundant grace' (82) without receiving. However, it does receive itself as reflected in us, and it receives our 'odours of praise' (as in the verses which open this text). The poet sees the face of God 'painted with our likeness' (131) and feeling himself photosynthetically changing (114) knows it is impossible to turn away from this light (100-02).[32] In this glow he sees the rainbow of the Holy Trinity, which should also remind us of the Rainbow of the Covenant: the earth ('commune madre', *Purgatorio*, XI: 63) is for humans and other creatures to inhabit (*Paradiso*, XII: 16-18, and Genesis 9:13).

The whole text of *O somma luce*'s personal revelation is framed as another one of Straub-Huillet's 'to those born after', like the philosopher's final speech in *The Death of Empedocles* (1987), which addresses the People not shown by the film.[33] The last line of the second terzina (72) in Straub's script addresses the usefulness of the poet's illumination to 'the future people' or 'the people yet to come'.[34] This line is isolated in Straub's instructions with a caesura before and after, which is not often found in other performances of Dante, where the performers are keen to complete the sentence which runs on for another terzina. We should not see this as a distortion of Dante, who set out to aid 'the world that lives all wrong' (*Purgatorio*, XI: 63), by writing a public poem which, as Kirkpatrick puts it, 'aims to explore the political and ethical principles on which a successful society must always depend'.[35] We should also note that, rather than sinking into quietism, the final lines set in motion the dynamic and world-changing forces of will and desire.

Straub sets the text up in an alternating rhythm between mobile (panning) landscape shots and static shots of the speaker sitting 'in love's palm' (*Inferno*, v: 127). The division of the text creates an irregular rhythm, as the shots feature between one and four terzine (Figures 9.1-3).[36] You can see an overview in the following breakdown of the film's eleven shots after the music, where 'P' stands for the shots of Passerone, 'L' stands for the shots of landscape and the numeral represents the number of terzina: P – 3, L – 2, P – 1, L – 4, P – 1, L – 2, P – 3, L – 2, P – 4, L – 2, P – 2. The landscape shots are of varying duration and cover more or less ground depending on the speed of the pans. The widescreen frame allows Straub to cover twice the angle while maintaining a stately pace to the unfurling of the landscape.[37] The first and fourth pans cover half the span (the first being the only one which Straub cuts into with the movement still ongoing), while the remaining three pans complete the full arc, and the last is the only one which also reverses, returning to the opening position. The three full arcs invite a parallel with the three rainbows in Dante's text. The cuts correspond strictly to ends of sentences in the *Comedìa* as set in modern printed editions, mostly featuring one sentence and sometimes two, apart from the last cut which falls on a semi-colon. This last shot matches a change in mood, with the poet's powers faltering as the vision slips through his fingers. Straub thereby explicitly underscores Dante's didactic pauses, matching them with static shots of the landscape or the performer sitting silently between one verse and another.

When it comes to Passerone's performance we have four records to draw on: the two versions of the film (shot over a period of four days) and two performances at the communal theatre in Buti which took place on the same night and were subsequently broadcast on Rai 3.[38] The duration of each speech (from first to last line of speech) varies: the live performances at Buti are 7 minutes 30 seconds and 7 minutes in duration respectively. Version one and version two of the film are 9 minutes 11 seconds and 9 minutes 4 seconds in duration. The film presentation is obviously significantly slower and the pauses are given more prominence. In the theatre the speaker faces the audience head-on and in the film he is at three-quarter profile. The Buti stagings thus continue the long popular tradition of Dante being performed to the community (helping it think and feel through its life together), affirming it in an uncomplicated manner.[39]

The complications arise elsewhere: 'For instance, a man would be seen struggling with a text, its material nature: meter, scansion, sound and sense', Jean-André Fieschi wrote about the films of Straub and Huillet in 1976.[40] We have seen how much Dante concentrated on all the aspects that Fieschi lists. Straub and Passerone often follow the structural strengths of Dante's design. The statements, whether full sentences or not, are marked with pauses at either end. Inserted phrases and asides (such as 'of what I still remember', in *Paradiso* XXXIII: 107) are grouped together and treated as incisions into longer statements. Pauses for breathing are leisurely, often before the last line in a terzina, and rarely are they short hesitations (as in *A Visit to the Louvre*, 2004). The Rai 3 Buti recordings show Passerone and Straub agreeing on the necessity of breathing in fully after the aforementioned *Paradiso*

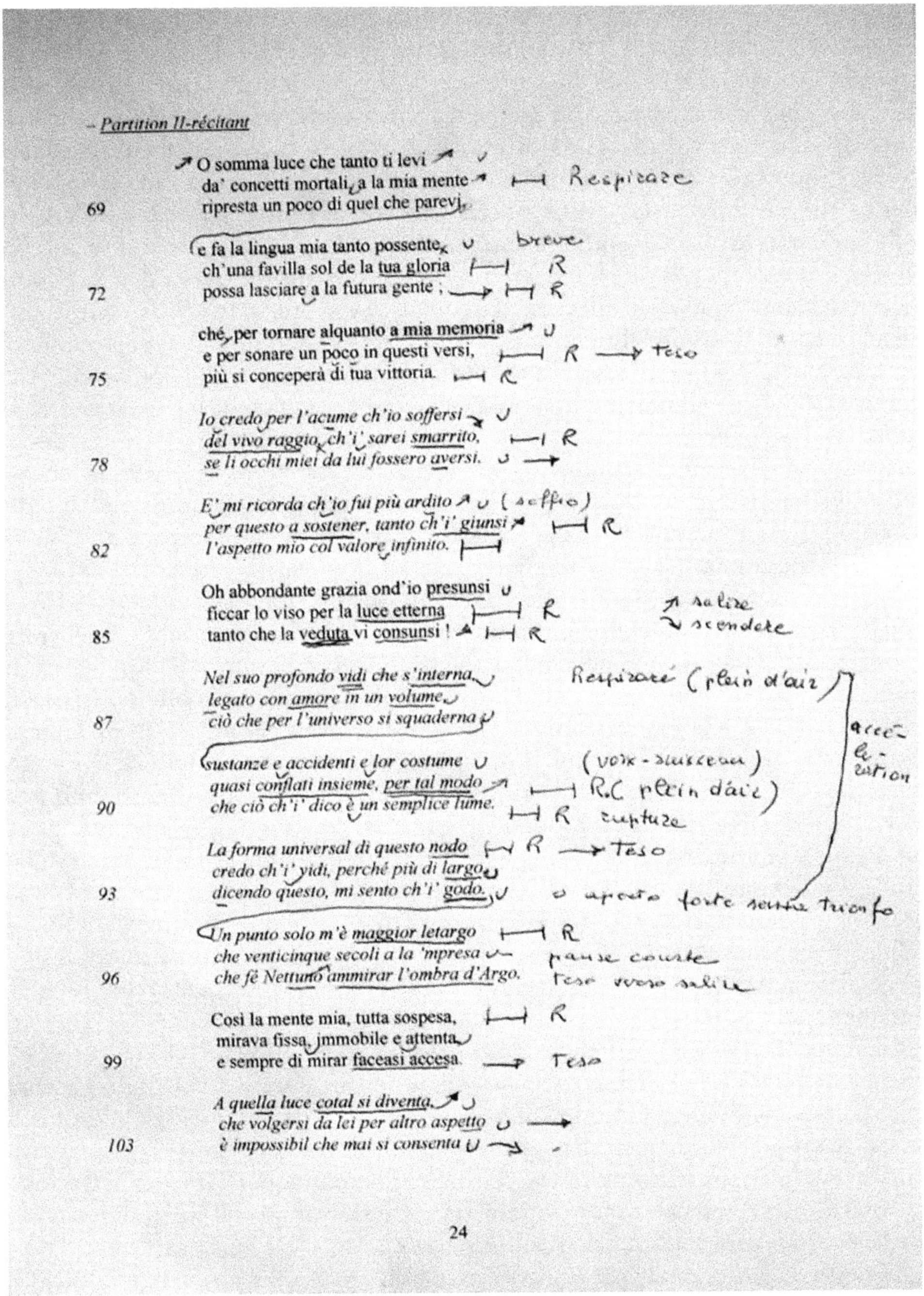

– *Partition II-récitant*

O somma luce che tanto ti levi
da' concetti mortali, a la mia mente   Respirare
69   ripresta un poco di quel che parevi.

e fa la lingua mia tanto possente,   breve
ch'una favilla sol de la tua gloria   R
72   possa lasciare a la futura gente ;   R

ché, per tornare alquanto a mia memoria
e per sonare un poco in questi versi,   R   Teso
75   più si conceperà di tua vittoria.   R

Io credo per l'acume ch'io soffersi
del vivo raggio, ch'i' sarei smarrito,   R
78   se li occhi miei da lui fossero aversi.

E' mi ricorda ch'io fui più ardito   (soffio)
per questo a sostener, tanto ch'i' giunsi   R
82   l'aspetto mio col valore infinito.

Oh abbondante grazia ond'io presunsi
ficcar lo viso per la luce etterna   R   salire
85   tanto che la veduta vi consunsi !   R   scendere

Nel suo profondo vidi che s'interna,
legato con amore in un volume,   Respirare (plein d'air)
87   ciò che per l'universo si squaderna

sustanze e accidenti e lor costume   (voix-ruisseau)   accé-
quasi conflati insieme, per tal modo   R.C plein d'air)   lé-
90   che ciò ch'i' dico è un semplice lume.   R rupture   ration

La forma universal di questo nodo   R   Teso
credo ch'i' vidi, perché più di largo
93   dicendo questo, mi sento ch'i' godo.   o aperto forte sente trionfo

Un punto solo m'è maggior letargo   R
che venticinque secoli a la 'mpresa   pause courte
96   che fé Nettuno ammirar l'ombra d'Argo.   teso verso salire

Così la mente mia, tutta sospesa,   R
mirava fissa, immobile e attenta,
99   e sempre di mirar faceasi accesa.   Teso

A quella luce cotal si diventa,
che volgersi da lei per altro aspetto
103   è impossibil che mai si consenta

24

FIG. 9.1. Giorgio Passerone, annotated script of *O somma luce*
(© Giorgio Passerone, by permission).

XXXIII: 126 — it ends up clearly marked with an exclamation in Passerone's script: 'Respirare!' (see Figure 9.2).[41] Often the last word in the line is stressed, as designed by Dante's rhyme and end-of-line stresses. Words are mostly separated, especially when one ends with a vowel and the next begins with one. In the Buti rehearsals, Straub is seen fixing Passerone's pronunciation of 'secoli' and 'foco', concerned that they sound too French and that the first vowel in each word should be longer, truer to the measure of Italian. Straub is also concerned that *Paradiso* XXXIII: 123 (see Figure 9.2), which is another example of Dante's modest voice and relates how feeble the poet's speech is, is delivered by Passerone in 'too prosaic' a manner. It is clear that our equivalent modern statement 'my words fail me' is off the mark when attending to Dante's intentions. Straub wants Passerone to be more emphatic, in a metaphysical sense, because of the distance of man from the divine (the Light Supreme). Likewise, the didactic, post-factum aspect must not be sacrificed to the immediate and experiential.

Occasionally, terzine, statements, or sentences are brought together, such as in *Paradiso* XXXIII: 93 and 94 (Figure 9.1), maintaining momentum and avoiding pauses. This is an interesting passage since it is one of the most arcane and is often failed by translation. The first terzina speaks of how clearly the poet saw the all-present order of things within the light; the second terzina contradicts this by saying that this one moment brings more forgetfulness than ever in the twenty-five centuries since Neptune was startled by the ship Argo on its great endeavour to find the Golden Fleece.[42] In this paradox, Dante uses the degree of oblivion (measured in centuries and relating to a myth that persists even seven centuries after the *Comedìa*) to speak about how much was revealed to him in an instant.[43] Presence is described through absence. By bringing the two terzine together, Straub keeps the contradictions close to each other, rather than treating the second terzina as a commentary on the first. By stressing two of the three rhymes ('modo'/'nodo'/'godo' and 'largo'/'letargo'/'Argo'), Straub keeps the statements together. The third, weak, emerging rhyme of 'impresa'/'sospesa'/'accessa' naturally proceeds in the following statement (which is also a different shot) without any stresses on the rhyme. This is a general organizing principle of keeping the sections in the sequence set out above contained.

Straub, so fond of irregular rhythms (see, for example, *Every Revolution is a Throw of the Dice* (1977) and *A Visit to the Louvre*), ignores the commas within lines which, after all, were only introduced into Dante's verses by the printing press, preferring instead to group words and phrases using tone of voice or equal rhythm, rather than have hesitations standing in for commas. There is a general tendency to avoid the invitation to sing the text through strict control of ascending and descending words, and a few tremolo lines, such as ll. 96 and 108.[44] This last line is noted for its modesty, Dante stating that his words are as weak as the baby-talk of a suckling. It lends itself to a reduction to melody at the expense of sense.

Passerone's gestures flow through all the four performances and play on the relationship between speech and memory, reading and reciting (Figures 9.4-9.7), since the division in the sequence listed above is also one between Passerone

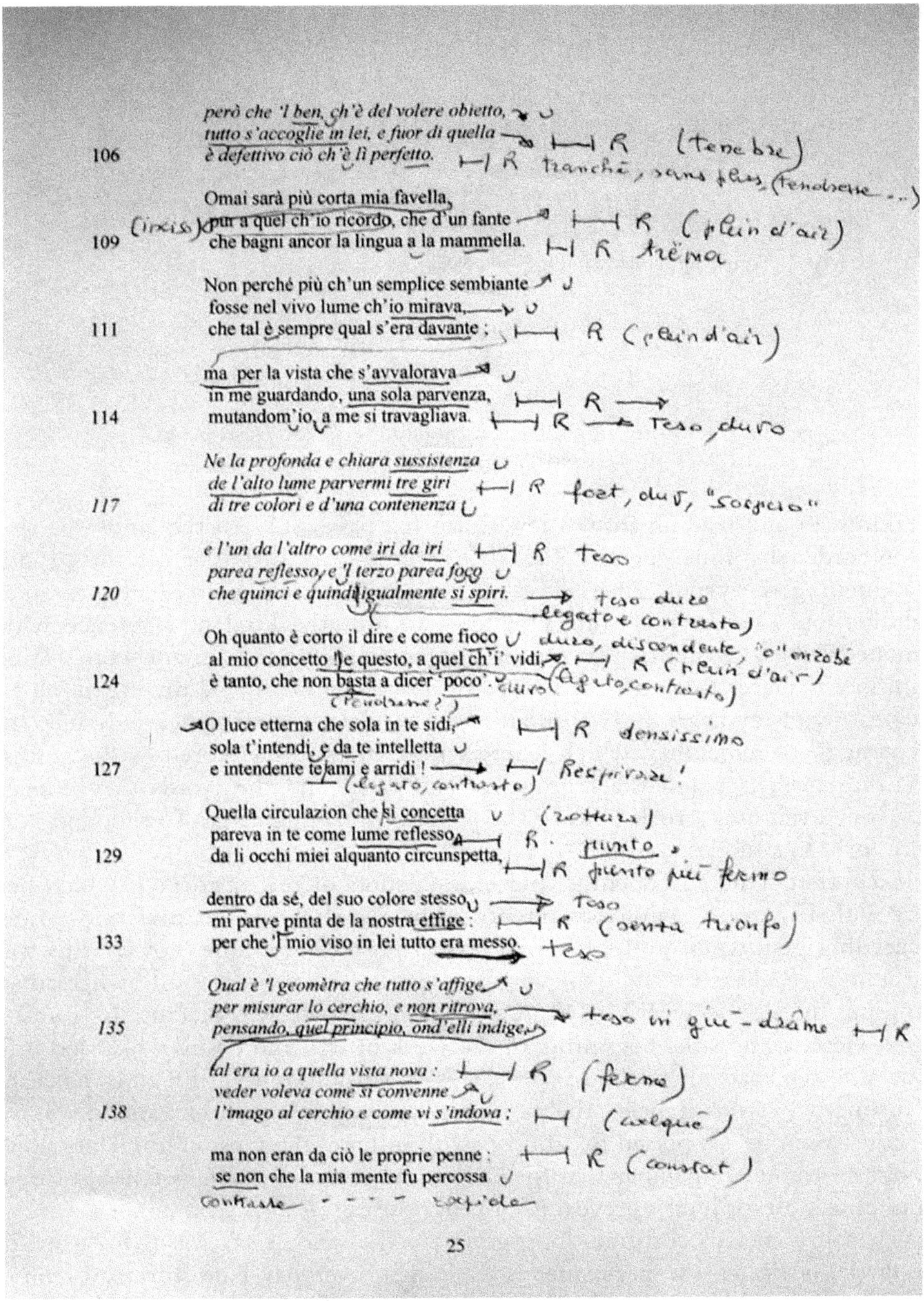

però che 'l ben, ch'è del volere obietto,
tutto s'accoglie in lei, e fuor di quella
106 è defettivo ciò ch'è lì perfetto.

Omai sarà più corta mia favella,
pur a quel ch'io ricordo, che d'un fante
109 che bagni ancor la lingua a la mammella.

Non perché più ch'un semplice sembiante
fosse nel vivo lume ch'io mirava,
111 che tal è sempre qual s'era davante;

ma per la vista che s'avvalorava
in me guardando, una sola parvenza,
114 mutandom'io, a me si travagliava.

Ne la profonda e chiara sussistenza
de l'alto lume parvermi tre giri
117 di tre colori e d'una contenenza;

e l'un da l'altro come iri da iri
parea reflesso, e 'l terzo parea foco
120 che quinci e quindi igualmente si spiri.

Oh quanto è corto il dire e come fioco
al mio concetto! e questo, a quel ch'i' vidi,
124 è tanto, che non basta a dicer 'poco'.

O luce etterna che sola in te sidi,
sola t'intendi, e da te intelletta
127 e intendente te ami e arridi!

Quella circulazion che sì concetta
pareva in te come lume reflesso,
129 da li occhi miei alquanto circunspetta,

dentro da sé, del suo colore stesso,
mi parve pinta de la nostra effige:
133 per che 'l mio viso in lei tutto era messo.

Qual è 'l geomètra che tutto s'affige
per misurar lo cerchio, e non ritrova,
135 pensando, quel principio, ond'elli indige,

tal era io a quella vista nova:
veder voleva come si convenne
138 l'imago al cerchio e come vi s'indova;

ma non eran da ciò le proprie penne:
se non che la mia mente fu percossa

25

FIG. 9.2. Giorgio Passerone, annotated script of O somma luce
(© Giorgio Passerone, by permission).

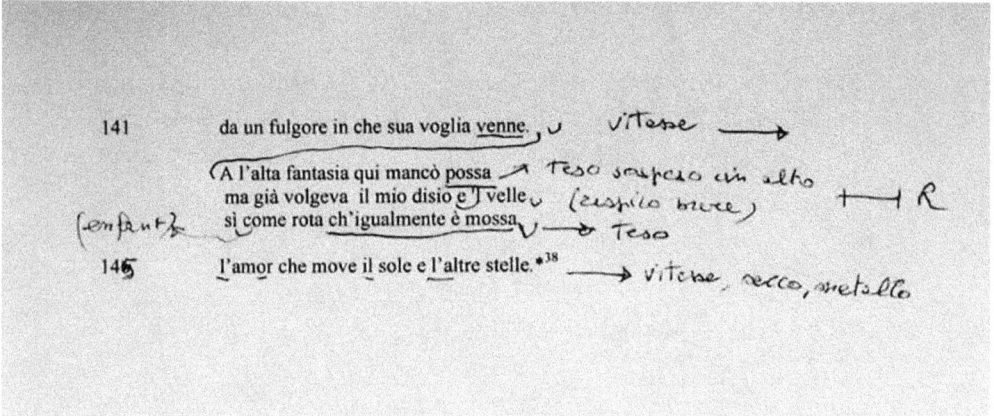

FIG. 9.3. Giorgio Passerone, annotated script of *O somma luce*
(© Giorgio Passerone, by permission).

speaking (P) and reading from a few fluttering pages (L). All the landscape shots are preceded by him opening the script, sometimes lifting it off the ground, straightening the pages. There is thus a strict separation between the speaker's sightline and the moving camera which performs the kind of reverence which Simone Weil also writes of: 'To see a landscape as it is when I am not there... When I am in any place, I disturb the silence of heaven and earth by my breathing and the beating of my heart'.[45] The unfailing sight of the gaze into heavenly light and the struggle to remember, which Dante writes of, are underscored by the gestures featuring spectacles and the fragility of the pages and the words they contain. Passerone even uses a rock to keep the pages from flying away. The modest voice finds form in a modest gesture.

In contrast stand the opening and closing shots of the performer, which both start with Passerone gazing out intently. The last shot also features two quickly succeeding gestures of poise, the first which precedes the line 'not for this were my wings' (*Paradiso* XXXIII: 139) with the speaker leaning forward as if ready to stand up, the second with him leaning back, chest out, as if bracing for a gust of wind. Here, then, is the beginning of the work of will and desire which has to be done after the heavenly vision has passed. Both versions of the film end with a shot in distinctly overcast light — the passing of the vision is palpable, and in the first version Passerone sits poised for almost a full minute, the tension unrelenting. We would do well to remember that for Dante, the cause of Lucifer's fall was that he would not wait for light to reveal itself progressively (*Paradiso*, IX: 46).

When it comes to costume, long gone are the sandals of *Othon* (1970) or *The Death of Empedocles*; the performer is dressed in everyday pale shirt and trousers which catch every change in the light, just as his scarf is caught by the wind.[46] The unpatterned fabrics stand out against the burnt grass of late summer and the rust of the excavator's arm. The red scarf teases our eye as a banner or standard would.

O somma luce dwells in the well-beloved vistas of Buti (think of the opening sequence of *These Encounters of Theirs* (2006) or the last shot of *Workers, Peasants*

FIGS. 9.4 & 9.5. Jean-Marie Straub, *O somma luce* (2010, courtesy of BELVA Film).

(2001)) with Passerone poised to recite in a quasi-amphitheatre, his back to the escarpment, facing what is probably Monte Aspro, covered in a lush canopy of trees. The poet's aria comes up against the reality of a humble spot of Tuscany with its hints of farms, worn-out machinery, and the traces of many generations who have lived on these hills.

O somma luce emerges from the tension between these different elements: costume, setting, props, camerawork, music, editing, actor's gestures, and actor's speech. This approach has parallels with what Brecht wrote about the theatre in 1930: '*Words, music and setting must become more independent of one another*'.[47] Two decades later, he would restate this by inviting the sister arts of the drama to 'alienate', that is estrange, each other, rather than losing themselves in an 'integrated work of art'.[48] This attitude whereby contradiction and friction help to maintain freedom

FIGS. 9.6 & 9.7. Jean-Marie Straub, *O somma luce* (2010, courtesy of BELVA Film).

and integrity of various elements which enrich each other, is one shared by Straub, Huillet, Dante, and Brecht. Similarly, every question as to a pure definition of 'the political' is for Straub to be answered only prismatically. To paraphrase him: there can be no political film without morality, theology, mysticism, and memory.[49] He might well have been talking about the *Comedìa*.

Binding all these elements together is the *longue durée* of remembrance, moved by will and desire to fulfil our human destiny. Cornel West, speaking of the relevance of Dante to the catastrophe experienced by African-Americans in the last four centuries, centres the long duration across past and future generations: 'a notion of temporality and historicity that cannot be snuffed out even in hell, and [...] the conception of the possibilities of transformation in the face of whatever kind of catastrophe is coming your way'.[50] In growing deserts and among ever-multiplying catastrophes of 'death, dogma and domination', there will also be revelation.[51] Here, the fate of the collective is bound to individual illumination, to knowledge, which the individual brings to the collective, and to works of art. However, as Eisenstein wrote in the depths of World War Two (in the lines which open this chapter), the paradox and scale of the catastrophe transcends individual consciousness and can only be grasped collectively. This connection between the individual and the collective is found in the content of what is revealed in the experience of illumination. Often (as in *O somma luce*), the experience of ecstasy, rapture, or apocalypse is represented through a tension between the raw experience and its content, be it Christian, pantheist, humanist, communist, etc. Here I want to draw on Eisenstein and Walter Benjamin (both of whom Straub repeatedly returned to). I believe they will also help us to reconcile the gradual and painstaking perfection of the soul (of the poet and the reader) which is integral to the design of the *Comedìa* (told in a stratified manner through the *longue durée* of lives dating back to Ancient Greece) with Straub's gesture in *O somma luce*: a tiger leap, a sudden, almost blasphemous, short, heavenly torrent.

In *Nonindifferent Nature*, Eisenstein's study of ecstasy as human experience and organized re-presentation in various artforms, we find a passage recounting the visions of Saint Ignatius of Loyola, based on a notebook the theologian forgot to burn.[52] Sometimes 'a symbolic image accompanies his vision, for example the image of the sun, but it is evidently only an accessory'. The passage then goes on to report Loyola's words about the experience of the divine Being or Essence in these terms: 'at first I saw the Being and then the Father, and my prayer ended with the Essence before arriving at the Father'.[53]

Eisenstein is fascinated that a zealot and master of psychotechnics such as Loyola would acknowledge the primacy of the universal form of ecstasy without binding it to its Christian content. This passage is mirrored by Dante's ll. 124-38 in *O somma luce* where he relates how gradually, deep in itself, the eternal light seemed to show him our human face, moving from pure light to an image. This tension between specific symbols and images which might be discovered through an ecstatic state and raw embodied experience is one which in Straub's film is felt through the tension between the text and the bodies of the performers (human or heavenly). It is also present in the decoupling of music from figuration. The body does not exist without language, which is our link to the past, and also the organ for engaging with the world. From here it is but one small step to Benjamin's fourth thesis on history:

> The class struggle, which is always present to a historian influenced by Marx, is a fight for the crude and material things without which no refined and spiritual things could exist. Nevertheless, it is not in the form of the spoils which fall to the victor that the latter make their presence felt in the class struggle. They manifest themselves in this struggle as confidence, courage, humour, cunning, and fortitude. They have retroactive force and will constantly call in question every victory, past and present, of the rulers. As flowers turn toward the sun by dint of a secret heliotropism the past strives to turn toward that sun which is rising in the sky of history. A historical materialist must be aware of this most inconspicuous of all transformations.[54]

The river-like virtues which Benjamin lists (confidence, courage, humour, cunning, fortitude) flowing from the past, are products and refinements of Dante's forces of desire and will, with which the poet concludes his poem, and starts again. Benjamin's virtues of class struggle are what remain after a battle lost or won: in strata, across generations. With Eisenstein (writing two years later, in 1942), there is an understanding that a catastrophe can only be met through communion with forces which are larger than a single consciousness, but which also manifest in the individual. And just as the individual can photosynthetically change through illumination or struggle, so can 'what has been' heliotropically grow in response to an illumination by the virtues of class struggle or Christianity. The past can turn to the future anew; to the past, it is of little relevance whether its future is our present or if it is our future. We find this framework in Dante, who encounters in *Inferno* and *Purgatorio* various virtuous proto-Christians who lived before Christ — for him they are imbued with the forces which follow Christ and which seem to have prepared the world for his coming. We can be illuminated differently by worlds which have ended. For Eisenstein it is the present which stretches out towards the light; for Benjamin it is the past (alive in all of us), which turns towards the sun. This is the same sun which we find in one of the poems which accompanied Babeuf's failed Conspiracy of the Equals (Conjuration des Égaux) in 1796: 'People, take hold of your rights, | The sun shines for all'.[55] Just as the sun gives to all, so should the earth, and learning from the sun we can redeem the earth and ourselves in paradise on earth or in communism. The personal illumination which sets this movement in motion could be termed 'communist photosynthesis'. I believe that this is the central gesture which Straub deploys in his work on Dante's text. With reverence, yet decisive editing and organizing of the different elements analysed above, Dante's words open out onto new worlds and opportunities for illumination.

If, however, we find ourselves in dark times, 'here, too, dead poetry will rise again' (*Purgatorio*, I: 7). Within us dwells our illustrious vernacular language, the mover of body and spirit: 'something that illuminates, and being itself illuminated casts forth its light... And this vernacular of which we speak is raised aloft in authority and power and raises its own followers in honour and glory'.[56] This is the attitude which permeates every line of Dante's poetry (and which has made it so beloved and desirable for all factions and projects: Left, Right, nationalist, humanist, cosmopolitan etc.). Straub, who devoted his life to the voicing of German, French, Italian, and English words (and their relationship to place), must be a fellow traveller. One cannot induce divine or communist photosynthesis, but one can put words into motion. Modestly and with maximum attention, this is what Passerone and Straub do with these verses. For a few minutes they dwell on the supreme moment of illumination, asking us to match the concentration of the poet and of the speaker.

Notes to Chapter 9

1. I am indebted to Lia Mazzari for a translation of the Buti audience discussion and rehearsals. I am grateful to Tag Gallagher for an extensive and generous polemic. Ian O'Sullivan and Eleanor Watkins from the BFI Library very kindly tracked down the Charles Tesson article during the library's closure to the public due to the Covid-19 pandemic.

2. Sergei Eisenstein, *Nonindifferent Nature*, trans. by Herbert Marshall (Cambridge: Cambridge University Press, 1987), p. 290. This text was written in Alma-Ata in October 1942 as part of a preface to an English edition of *The Film Sense* published in the same year. It was not included in that edition, but a revised version formed the preface for *Nonindifferent Nature*, first published in 1948.

3. This literal translation is taken from Robin Kirkpatrick, *Dante's Paradiso and the Limitations of Modern Criticism: A Study of Style and Poetic Theory* (Cambridge: Cambridge University Press, 1978), p. 161. I have chosen this word-for-word rendition on this single occasion for clarity. Henceforth, quotations from Dante's text are, unless otherwise indicated, from Dante Alighieri, *The Divine Comedy*, trans. by Robin Kirkpatrick (London: Penguin Classics, 2012), in the form canto: line(s). The original text reads 'Nel giallo de la rosa sempiterna, | Che si digrada e dilata e redole | Odor di lode al sol che sempre verna' (*Paradiso*, XXX: 124-26).

4. The first version is 17 minutes 50 seconds long, the second 16 minutes 53 seconds. There are multiple differences between them, as they are composed of different takes. The overall structure of the film is the same.

5. This is ground which Huillet and Straub have already covered with their adaptation of Arnold Schoenberg's *Accompaniment to a Cinematographic Scene*, Op. 34 in 1973. Other filmmakers have answered Varèse's call, notably Bill Viola in *Déserts* (1994) and Alain Montesse in *Étude pour Déserts* (1987).

6. Quoted in Paul Griffiths, *Modern Music and After* (Oxford: Oxford University Press, 2010), p. 140.

7. The transition from music to voice resembles the shifts between music and voice in Straub's beloved John Ford films. These moments — in *Cheyenne Autumn* (1964) at approximately 33 minutes or *The Searchers* (1956) at around 39 minutes — build up tension musically and relay it to the voice, but by keeping the two separate, with a brief pause in between. The two different versions of *O somma luce* illustrate the different effects of tension and rhythm that can be accomplished by pauses between the music and the voice: almost two seconds in version one and less than a second in version two. These approaches follow through in the two versions and predictably version two is significantly shorter.

8. Quoted in Griffiths, *Modern Music and After*, p. 140.

9. Friedrich Nietzsche, *Thus Spake Zarathustra: A Book for All and None* <https://www.gutenberg.org/files/1998/1998-h/1998-h.htm> [accessed 12 March 2021].

10. Friedrich Nietzsche, *Dionysian-Dithyrambs* <http://www.thenietzschechannel.com/works-pub/dd/dd.htm> [accessed 6 May 2021].

11. Jean Genet, *Prisoner of Love*, trans. by Barbara Bray (New York: New York Review Books, 2003), p. vii.

12. Dante Alighieri, *The Convivio Book 1*, quoted in Kirkpatrick, *Dante's Paradiso and the Limitations of Modern Criticism*, p. 53.

13. Kirkpatrick, *Dante's Paradiso and the Limitations of Modern Criticism*, p. 193.

14. Ibid., p. 192.

15. From Dante's *Convivio*, discussed by Eisenstein in *Nonindifferent Nature*, p. 275.

16. The full terzina runs like this: 'Eternal light, you sojourn in yourself alone. | Alone, you know yourself. Known to yourself, | you, knowing, love and smile on your own being'. The theatrical break of the line which someone like Vittorio Gassman makes (in *Legge una selezione di Canti della Divina Commedia*, Rubino Rubini, 1993 <https://youtu.be/BkVmum5l_3k> [accessed 6 May 2021]) works against the relentless drive of this line. As different an artist from Straub as can be, Roberto Benigni, who has spent years performing Dante, comes to the same conclusion that it is the minority of consonants which suffice in tempering the otherwise unbroken flow

of vowels, and that the line should be delivered in one expiration. See *Roberto Benigni: Tutto Dante — L'ultimo del Paradiso*, 2002 <https://youtu.be/sLxC56SjxHc> [accessed 6 May 2021].

17. See commentary on C. Segre in Kirkpatrick, *Dante's Paradiso and the Limitations of Modern Criticism*, p. 93.

18. Ibid., p. 85.

19. Quoted in ibid., p. 85.

20. See Robin Kirkpatrick, 'Introduction', in Dante, *The Divine Comedy*, trans. by Kirkpatrick, pp. ix–lvi (p. xliv).

21. Kirkpatrick cites Angelo Jacomuzzi in this context: Kirkpatrick, *Dante's Paradiso and the Limitations of Modern Criticism*, p. 37.

22. Ibid., p. 38.

23. Ibid., p. 30.

24. Ibid., p. 43.

25. Ibid.

26. Ibid., p. 16.

27. Ibid., p. 39.

28. Ibid., p. 75.

29. Ibid., p. 155.

30. Ibid., p. 82.

31. Ibid., p. 123.

32. For reasons of clarity and in order to distinguish between them, these words and phrases have been compiled from the translations of Henry Wadsworth Longfellow, Robert and Jean Hollander, and Kirkpatrick (see note 3). See: Dante, *The Divine Comedy*, trans. by Henry Wadsworth Longfellow <https://www.gutenberg.org/files/1003/1003-h/1003-h.htm> [accessed 16 November 2021]; and Robert and Jean Hollander, Princeton Dante Project <https://dante.princeton.edu/cgi-bin/dante/campuscgi/mpb/GetCantoSection.pl?LANG=2&INP_POEM=Par&INP_SECT=33&INP_START=52&INP_LEN=90> [accessed 16 November 2021].

33. See Byg, *Landscapes of Resistance*, p. 213. As Byg states, included in Straub's models for the ending of *Empedocles* are the final sequences of *Alexander Nevsky* (1938), *Foreign Correspondent* (1940), and *The Great Dictator* (1940), all of which feature voices addressing the People. This is based on Charles Tesson's report of a discussion after a screening of *Empedocles*: Charles Tesson, 'L'Heure de vérité', *Cahiers du cinéma*, 394 (1987), 50. See Byg, *Landscapes of Resistance*, p. 212.

34. See 'la vita futura' from *Inferno*, VI: 102. These two phrases are respectively translated by Longfellow and by Robert and Jean Hollander (see note 32).

35. Kirkpatrick, 'Introduction', p. xvi.

36. Passerone's annotated script is reproduced here <http://www.elumiere.net/exclusivo_web/internacional_straub/documentos/osommaluce.php> [accessed 28 January 2022].

37. After five decades of filmmaking, this is the first time Straub has explored the potential of a widescreen frame.

38. In their Buti work, Huillet and Straub started with the theatre performance and then proceeded to the film shoot a few weeks later; this is the one case where the sequence was reversed.

39. Carmelo Bene, for example, did a reading of Dante to commemorate the first anniversary of the Bologna massacre in 1981: Rino Caputo, 'Dante by Heart and Dante Declaimed: The "Realization" of the *Comedy* on Italian Radio and Television', in *Dante, Cinema, and Television*, ed. by Amilcare A. Iannucci (Toronto: University of Toronto Press, 2004), pp. 213–23 (p. 216).

40. Fieschi, 'Jean-Marie Straub and Danièle Huillet'.

41. See <http://www.elumiere.net/exclusivo_web/internacional_straub/documentos/osommaluce.php>. The line numbering in Passerone's script does not always match the conventional numbering used in this article.

42. Of course, Neptune was not around at the time, it would have been the Greek god Poseidon. This is just one of many examples of Dante's passion for the layers and palimpsests of history, shared by Huillet and Straub.

43. See George Ferzoco, 'Changes', in *Vertical Readings in Dante's Comedy*, ed. by George Corbett

and Heather Webb, 3 vols (Cambridge: Open Book, 2015-17), III, 51-69 (pp. 67-68) <https://books.openbookpublishers.com/10.11647/obp.0119.pdf> [accessed 8 March 2021].

44. For indications of ascending words see the arrows before and after the first line of Passerone's annotated script (Figure 9.1), and the end of l. 76 for an indication of a descending enunciation.

45. Weil, *Gravity and Grace*, p. 42.

46. Huillet and Straub have spoken about the many aspects of this shift away from period dress between their early and late treatment of Pavese in Emmanuel Burdeau and Jean-Michel Frodon, 'L'Important est l'éventail', *Cahiers du cinéma*, 616 (2006), 36-39; 'Encounter with Jean-Marie Straub and Danièle Huillet: Quei loro incontri', trans. by Ted Fendt <http://www.elumiere.net/exclusivo_web/internacional_straub/textos/interview_quei_loro_incontri.php> [accessed 8 March 2021].

47. Bertolt Brecht, 'The Modern Theatre is the Epic Theatre', in *Brecht on Theatre*, ed. by Willett, pp. 33-42 (p. 38).

48. Bertolt Brecht, 'A Short Organum for the Theatre', in *Brecht on Theatre*, ed. by Willet, pp. 179-205 (p. 204).

49. Albera, 'Sickle and Hammer, Cannons, Cannons, Dynamite!', pp. 109-11.

50. *African-American Interpretations of Dante's Divine Comedy*, hosted by Trinity College, 4 October 2020 <https://cdnapisec.kaltura.com/index.php/extwidget/preview/partner_id/2366381/uiconf_id/42684261/entry_id/1_0p4pdmee/embed/dynamic> [accessed 10 March 2021].

51. Ibid.

52. Eisenstein *Nonindifferent Nature*, pp. 165, 181-83.

53. Ibid., pp.172-74.

54. Benjamin, 'Theses on the Philosophy of History', in *Illuminations*, p. 246. Translation corrected to include 'confidence' [*Zuversicht*].

55. 'Peuple resaississez vos voix | Le soleil luit pour tout le monde', Charles Germain, 'Chanson des Égaux', 1796; 'Song of the Equals', trans. by Mitchell Abidor <https://www.marxists.org/history/france/revolution/conspiracy-equals/1796/song.htm> [accessed 11 March 2021].

56. Dante Alighieri, *De vulgari eloquentia*, quoted in Kirkpatrick, *Dante's Paradiso and the Limitations of Modern Criticism*, p. 64.

CHAPTER 10

❖

Relocating Kafka in Jean-Marie Straub's *Jackals and Arabs* (2011)

Helen Hughes

Introduction

In their many appropriations of literary works beginning with *Machorka-Muff* in 1963, Danièle Huillet and Jean-Marie Straub created distinctive relationships between texts and screens, engaging with literary sources as a form of reception, but particularly with the fluid status of the texts as living artefacts of cultural memory.[1] One of their methods, taking the text in the form of oral performance to a physical location connected with its genesis, does not so much return the text to its origin as — to adapt the words of the experimental ethnographic filmmaker Trinh T. Minh-ha — articulate it from a place nearby, so that the idea that the text carries within it a form of truth is, via the tradition of Brechtian estrangement, displaced into the gaps between the text, the *mise-en-scène*, and the bodies of the performers.[2] In the process, the critique of the text that can emerge is neither analytic nor deconstructive but synthetic and ecumenical, built up out of Huillet and Straub's use of the camera to close or rearticulate the gaps between physical landscapes and written words.

One of the most challenging and rich of the late films to thus displace a text is *Jackals and Arabs* (2011). This adaptation of a short story by Franz Kafka was first conceived by both filmmakers, and their translation of the text into French appeared in *Cahiers du cinéma* in 1987.[3] Continuing their interest in Kafka as 'the only poet of industrial civilisation', the text was published in a supplement to the four hundredth issue of the film journal, guest edited by the German director Wim Wenders.[4] Wenders had wanted to devote the pages of the journal to unrealized scripts by filmmakers he admired, but found, as he writes in a letter at the start of the supplement, 'happily there were many directors who had no "aborted" projects and no abandoned scripts in their desk drawers. So we extended our idea of the imaginary film to include the "roots", the sources of films'.[5] This is the sense in which Huillet and Straub contributed their translation, with the intention of rendering the German text more faithfully than was the case in existing French translations.[6] In Huillet and Straub's letter to Wenders about the contribution, reproduced alongside the script, they wrote:

So here, despite everything, is the text of a film that will perhaps never be made. But you absolutely must publish it. Please. Printed as is (*and please, with no notes*).

I don't know if these pages 'will inspire'; if it's so, it's because they are not by us: our films never pretended to inspire anyone, with each film we have tried to materialize a dream or a nightmare ('*materialize sensations,*' Cézanne used to say) — often the dream of another, for example Hölderlin's (communist) dream.[7]

Huillet's and Straub's interest in 'Schakale und Araber' brings Kafka together with several themes established in their other films.[8] They had already developed an approach to Kafka's prose in their adaptation of the fragmentary novel *The Man Who Disappeared (Der Verschollene)* for the film *Class Relations* (1984). Barton Byg has read the film as building on the novel's experiments with perspective to challenge the narrative conventions of cinema, analysing a shot-counter-shot sequence, for example, to show how one speaking character, Therese, connects with the listening principal character, Karl Rossmann, while showing them as separated. In his analysis of this shot sequence, Byg also shows how an open window lighting the face of the speaker offers a possibility for hope:

The window lights Therese's face, in a composition reminiscent of earlier films by Straub/Huillet. Far from frustrating visual pleasure, this shot uses the subjective point of view (so freely exploited in the empty promises of commercial cinema) to suggest unlimited possibility.[9]

The earlier films mentioned by Byg refer particularly to their body of German-language films *Machorka-Muff, Not Reconciled, or Only Violence Helps Where Violence Rules* (1965), *Chronicle of Anna Magdalena Bach* (1968), and *The Bridegroom, the Actress and the Pimp* (1968). These films established a cinematography that identified their style as Brechtian as well as developing a repertoire of distinctive shots — such as that of a face at a window — which can also be found in *Jackals and Arabs*.

Kafka's Jewish heritage and the first publication of the story in Martin Buber's journal *Der Jude* in 1917 also connect Straub's adaptation to their trilogy of films that reflect on Jewish history and culture: the discussion of anti-Semitism in *Introduction to Arnold Schoenberg's Accompaniment to a Cinematographic Scene* (1973, see Chapter 1); the Old Testament prohibition of (or ban on) images in *Moses and Aaron* (1975, see Chapter 2); *Fortini/Cani* (1976) and its engagement with the Arab-Israeli War of 1967 (see Chapter 4).[10] Equally pertinently, interpretations of Kafka's story which see it as about Zionism and the Arab world link it to *Too Early, Too Late* (1981) with its reflection on the relationship between Western Europe, North Africa, and colonialism.[11] The portrayal of the figure of the Arab in the story also evokes memories of Huillet and Straub's made-for-television *cinétract, Europa 2005, 27 October* (2006), commemorating the controversial death of two youths of Arab descent in Paris.

In her overview, Claudia Pummer has grouped three of the late films of Straub shot in a domestic interior space, as establishing a 'kind of signature setting'.[12] Alongside *Jackals and Arabs* these are *Corneille – Brecht* (2009) and *The Algerian War!* (2014). The domestic space can be understood as a theme in earlier films such as

En rachâchant (1983), or *Von heute auf morgen* (1997) which explore the politics of education and of marital relations respectively. While *Corneille – Brecht* is about the separation of public and private spaces, in *The Algerian War!* a ghost from the conflict in a sense revisits Straub, who fled France rather than be conscripted, in his apartment. For *Jackals and Arabs* something like the domestic space in which Kafka wrote his stories is created, where their intensity is surrounded by a kind of detachment noted by Brecht, who reluctantly acknowledged in conversation with Walter Benjamin, that 'suggestions *can* be extracted from them, if only because of their tone of superior calm'.[13] At the same time there is an interaction between the text, the space, and the lives of the performers, through whom the text is transmitted in the here and now.

Kafka's Animal Story and Literary Criticism

'Schakale und Araber' is a short story of around thirteen hundred words told in the first person by a European traveller in the desert who finds himself surrounded by a pack of jackals while resting overnight in an oasis. Two of the jackals pin him down while another, right in his face, explains they believe he is the chosen one from the north who will free them from their oppressors, the Arabs. After the European protests that their treatment of him is not helping their cause, the jackal goes on to lament, describing their hatred of impure Arab customs, particularly their treatment of animals, who are killed for their meat rather than left to die for the jackals to clean down to the bones. When the freed European is presented with a rusty pair of scissors, which are meant to free the jackals, their plot is abruptly interrupted by their Arab master, who scolds them, explaining that this story is told to all European travellers. The Arab is harsh with his whip but feeds the jackals with the meat of a recently deceased camel, acknowledging their hatred but declaring his love for the 'wonderful animals'.

The story is related in a way that is unusually visceral and threatening, even for Kafka's texts. Only a kind of slapstick humour around the alarmed European and the genial cheerfulness of the Arab relieve the tension created by the intense animals. The European describes the jackals' invasion of his personal space, their putrid breath, glinting eyes, howling, and unceasing circling around him. The jackal in turn portrays the Arabs as impure and immoral, with stinking armpits and unclean practices. Only the Arab seems to be at ease, laughing at the 'nonsensical animals', but controlling them viciously with his whip. Appreciating how the film realizes its versions of European, jackal, and Arab requires some understanding of the multivalence of the story and its journey through the history of literary criticism.

Kafka's story was first published in 1917 in the November issue of *Der Jude*, a journal described by Dimitry Shumsky as the 'intellectual organ of German-speaking Zionism', founded and edited by the Austrian philosopher Martin Buber.[14] It was placed alongside a second story by Kafka, 'A Report to an Academy' ('Ein Bericht für eine Akademie'), with both labelled 'animal stories', a designation that Kafka preferred to the terms 'parable' or 'allegory'.[15] The long and involved reception, which has continued to provoke new interpretations right up to the present day, began in a sense with its publication, as Kafka's friend and promoter Max Brod had written a critique in a previous issue of the same journal anticipating Kafka's stories as the 'most Jewish documents of our times'.[16] The reception of 'Schakale und Araber' in Western literary appreciation post-1945, however, took no account of its place of first publication. It had, after all, appeared several times afterwards in collections not connected with the Jewish community.[17] Dimitry Shumsky explains the ahistorical initial interpretations of Kafka's texts as the result of the vogue of 'text-immanent' practical literary criticism.[18] However, eminent scholars who wrote about Kafka after Max Brod included Hannah Arendt and Walter Benjamin, neither of whom wrote specifically about 'Schakale und Araber'. Gilles Deleuze and Félix Guattari, who published their highly influential *Kafka: Toward a Minor Literature* in 1975, saw it as one of a number of animal stories in which Kafka developed a writing style as a bid for freedom from the pressures of bourgeois expectation and marriage: 'Writing like a dog digging a hole, a rat digging its burrow. And to do that, finding his own point of underdevelopment, his own *patois*, his own third world, his own desert'.[19]

One scholar who has connected Kafka to his Jewish heritage for Western readers is Ritchie Robertson, who pointed out where the story was first published and related it to Buber's cultural Zionism.[20] To understand how Zionism might be a theme in the story, Robertson refers to the ideas expressed by Buber in a series of lectures in Prague which Kafka attended, and which were also published in an essay called 'The Watchword' ('Die Losung') in 1916. Buber saw the Jewish question being used as a political tool for the purposes of the warring nations and against this set out a vision which was no longer about the right to practice the faith, but about the development of Jewish people as subjects who were responsible for their own fate. He saw this as being achieved through creating a new kind of unity in which Jewish identity was not the goal but the starting-point:

> The function of Judaism as a binding force between peoples has a low and a high form today. The low form can be found among the roots of the people; it is practiced by the dispersed and debased, the masters and slaves of Capital. Contemporary nationalism is a legitimate revolt against this form of relationship between people. The higher form sweeps over the heads of the people; that is the rise of the enthusiastic cosmopolitan Jew who wishes to help in the preparation of a new humanity. The third form, the one we mean, the earthly one, which will not undermine or be beyond the reach of the people but will gather it up and bind it together, is not a reality but a mission. The directionless Jews of the West should step up to it as to a new self-confidence; the imprisoned Jews of the East should draw to it as their liberating vocation; the Jewish community in Palestine should dedicate its best strengths to becoming a binding force between Europe and the East and receive from this task its inner right to existence.[21]

In the context of this vision Kafka's story might unfold as follows: the jackal represents the imprisoned eastern Jews, the Arab represents the Jewish community in Palestine, and the European the directionless cosmopolitan Jew. Rather than affirming such a message, however, Kafka's story appears to exaggerate and perhaps satirize the failings of each and the aspiration for future co-operation along with it. 'Schakale und Araber' was published, then, in the midst of the discussion concerning the relationship between Jewish identity and Zionism. A significant historical point is that the story was written in February 1917 before the Balfour Declaration on 2 November of that year, so that the question of the nature of a Jewish state in Palestine was more open.[22]

The focus on Zionism from a European point of view brings out one understanding of the story's historical situatedness, directing debate to what the story might have meant in early twentieth-century Prague. Another direction for the reception of Kafka's works was taken, however, in scholarship in Egypt and the Arabic-speaking world more generally, that focused on the figure of the Arab in the story in a different way. A particularly resonant reception history for Straub's film is uncovered by Atef Botros, tracing the popularity of Kafka's works in Egypt from 1939.[23] His study of how the story came to be interpreted after the Six-Day War in 1967 shows how interpretation of the text changes once again if the Arab is not transposed into Kafka himself or into a Palestinian Jew, but is understood straightforwardly as an Arab. If the jackal is interpretable as a Jew, and the European as a European, this interpretation raises the question as to whether Kafka was anti-Semitic or anti-Zionist in associating Jewishness with the animal. Arab scholars after 1967 were particularly interested in Kafka's attitude towards Zionism and Arab culture.

The year 2011 was a significant year globally for Kafka reception and Straub's decision to return to the unrealized script can be seen as motivated by the 'Arab Spring'. At the same time, a public debate had been developing from 2010 around the deposit of Kafka manuscripts in the National Library of Israel, which had claimed in a court case to be the appropriate place to preserve these documents of Jewish literary history. In February of 2011 Judith Butler delivered a lively speech at the British Museum, full of irony about literary ownership, taking in the multiple identities of Kafka himself, the asset status of the manuscripts, and more general questions around politics and literary heritage, moving through Zionism, Israeli nationalism, and the varying positions of the Jewish diaspora with respect to the definition of exile.[24] In the article 'Kafka and Arabs' published in the journal *Critical Inquiry* the following year, Jens Hanssen followed up Butler's remarks with an interpretation of Kafka's 'Schakale und Araber', writing that the context for a new interpretation of the story had been set by the anti-government protests across North Africa: 'the current revolutionary moment in the Arab world allows us to rethink Kafka and Arabs and, at the same time, the Palestine conflict'. He captures the moment, stating simply, 'The reluctance of most Kafka scholars to acknowledge that "Jackals and Arabs" is about the question of Palestine is bewildering'.[25]

Developing a reading that considers the representation of the Arab in particular, Hanssen understands the story in terms of the early twentieth century: 'as a contrapuntal illumination of the historical moment in which Zionism turns from a movement of national liberation in Europe to a settler-colonial enterprise in Palestine'. He argues that reading it alongside fragments and diary entries demonstrates that Kafka was in favour of bi-nationalism, the idea pursued by his friends in the Brith Shalom movement. Hanssen goes on to explore the reception of Kafka in Egyptian and Iranian scholarship, arguing that Kafka helped to 'build a bridge to European culture'.[26] The bridge was full of traffic, led in many directions, sometimes by erroneous translations, a point that Huillet and Straub were concerned with, as well as by a false dating of the story.[27] Distinctive about the Arab reception was the agreement that it is set in Palestine and that the Arabs are really Arabs, and most important of all, 'Kafka's Arab feels, thinks, hesitates, and convinces'.[28]

In the process of claiming Kafka's story for bi-nationalism, Hanssen surveys European readings as either too abstract or too inflected by religious or Zionist perspectives. From this new perspective the story can be understood as critiquing not Zionism per se but a kind of Zionism that resembles European colonialism. In this interpretation the jackal is indeed a negative figure representing the desire to erase the culture of the Arab. Hanssen recognizes that in this reading the 'animal figure of the jackal invokes the objectionable dog metaphor in European anti-Semitism' and seeks to counter it with an analysis of Kafka's own attempts to persuade his community to appreciate rather than look down on the language and culture of eastern Jews.

The obviousness of the reference to Palestine has been since refuted by Jay Geller in a closely argued interpretation of the story that seeks to re-establish the location as unspecified:

> That a story includes 'Arabs' and desert might well have lead [sic] readers of *Der Jude* to think of Palestine and some of its inhabitants; yet no articles on Jew-Arab interaction in Palestine had appeared in the journal prior to the story's publication. Further if the setting is Palestine and the jackals are settler-colonizing Zionists, why do they characterize their location as one of exile? This does not disprove any claim for an association between the jackals and that species of Zionist, but it does call attention to how Kafka is destabilizing any attempt to set up one-to-one identifications.[29]

In the context of this absorbing body of scholarship, Straub's reading of the text might be understood as a new European reading that combines a different inflection of the figure of the Arab with a resituating of the text in Europe, where its relevance remains undiminished.

Straub's *Jackals and Arabs* 'de Franz Kafka'

In their 1987 version of Kafka's text, Straub and Huillet translated the entire text into French, including the descriptive passages that set the story in an oasis in the desert and describe the behaviours of the circling pack of jackals with their golden coats, glinting eyes, and threatening head movements. Their concern was with creating an accurate translation, closer to the original than previous versions in French. The film of the text, on the other hand, does not translate it except in subtitles and extracts only the dialogue, which reduces its length by a little more than half and focuses attention on the shifting registers of rhetoric: ceremonial introduction, attempt at conspiracy, diplomatic prevarication, ritualistic plea, command, and conciliation. There is nothing of the jackals' panting, their smell, their howling, plaintive tone, or of the delirium of their bloodthirsty devotion to devouring the camel meat, forgetting their hatred. The three speakers — the European from the north, the jackal, and the Arab — are created instead out of their own and each other's mouths.

Straub's film was shot in April and May of 2011 on MiniDV in two versions, lasting 10 minutes 43 seconds and 10 minutes 35 seconds. The first version begins with a pure white screen, followed by an opening credit combining French, English, and German: 'prèmiere version | straub huillet films | BELVA GmbH'. The title credit is in German and French: '*SCHAKALE UND ARABER de Franz Kafka*'. The name of the composer, Hungarian György Kurtág, appears just before the opening of the music — Part IV, no. 7, 'Once more, once more' from the *Kafka Fragments*, Op. 24 (1987) — played on the violin (by Hungarian András Keller) over the white screen (Figure 10.4) before the soprano voice (German Juliane Banse) enters and the words of the fragment appear on screen, again black on white. The text set to music is a late fragment, written by Kafka probably around 1922, some five years after the story was first published.[30] It sketches a landscape of repetitions and exile, framing Kafka's animal story at a far distance from Paris, the place where it is being imagined and set down on the page-turned-screen: 'Once more, once more, banished far, banished far. | Mountains, desert, a far land has to be wandered through'.[31]

This preface to Straub's story-turned-dialogue replaces Kafka's descriptive passage at the opening in which the European relates, 'we camped overnight in the oasis'. In Kafka's version an Arab is mentioned already in the first paragraph, described as 'tall and white', passing by as the European attempts to fall asleep. The jackals are introduced via their wailing howls first in the distance and then suddenly up close. A displacement of this passage can be found in the blank white screen (Figure 10.4) and the music, but it introduces a different kind of speaking nearby by putting Kafka's story as well as the fragment in dialogue with the Hungarian composer, highlighting his music of repetition and difference. The opening violin thus begins to articulate the space of the film as somewhere between Central Europe and North Africa, both avantgarde and oriental in its harmonies, gesturing towards the music of sub-Saharan Africa through the suggestion of a dominant Phrygian scale, and towards the movement of the jackals and perhaps the sand in the swirling motion of the triplets. The repetitions are insistent, as Stephen Blum writes, and the musical fragment 'opens with five repetitions of the word *wiederum* [once more], the first three in a triplet rhythm the violin has already played no less than 19 times (and will replicate many more times)'.[32]

The choice of the apartment and the casting transposes the story into the here and now. The intensity of the white screen cuts abruptly to the 'signature' interior space of the Paris apartment in colour and the dialogue begins with the eldest jackal's speech. In all, the dialogue is delivered in sixteen shots — six of the jackal, six black screens, three of the Arab, one of the scissors. Barbara Ulrich, playing the jackal, is represented kneeling throughout (Figure 10.1), with the cut to the close-up on the face, and slight movements to look left and right off-screen indicating the presence of the European, the other jackals, the imagined hated Arab, and then in the final sequence the actual Arab. 'Jubarite Semaran' (an anagram of Jean-Marie Straub), playing the European, exists only off-screen, with this perspective visually aligning with that of the spectator. When the European is first heard the image is still of Ulrich before the screen turns black in an implied reverse shot, which underlines a voice-of-God position of the voice. The jackal's understanding of the European as the longed-for Messiah or saviour and the prohibition of images both play into the use of the black screen (Figure 10.5). Giorgio Passerone (see also Chapter 9), Italian translator of Deleuze and Guattari, takes on the role of the Arab as a tall and authoritative male (Figure 10.2).[33] He is 'tall and white' as the story has it, but he is not dressed in white. He first appears in a close-up shot, his face against the window, which orients the viewer in the space generally. He looks down at Ulrich, displacing her, replacing her with himself in the gaze of the European and the viewer. The second shot of Passerone is a long shot against the window as he carries the imaginary whip and looks down to the left at the European, then up right, and finally at the camera as he delivers the line 'and how they hate us!'. The final shot is a close-up on Passerone's face as he looks down right (at the jackals) in a compassionate pose. While the delivery of the text is intense and the words are expressively violent, the domestic space creates a sense of intimate safety in which the three figures confront one another. Much as Kafka himself enjoyed reading aloud, each speaker appears to relish producing the words.[34]

Film, Space, and Polyvalency

In his article on Kafka's 'Schakale und Araber', Hanssen argues that the post-Cold War research into Kafka's attitude toward Zionism, and the Arab Spring, called for a new consideration of the text and the understanding of Zionism more generally, particularly on account of the representation, unusual for its time, of an Arab character with both a complex inner life and agency. Hanssen is concerned with resetting the debate about co-existence in a way that respects the Arab population in Israel and Palestine, considering the cultural framework in which Arab communities are represented as having a voice. Straub's decision to film a performance of 'Schakale und Araber' during the Arab Spring of 2011 is another act that has brought this text, which has become a kind of modernist legend, into close proximity with a new historical moment. It too poses questions about what has happened, particularly in the position of the people of Egypt who have overthrown the regime in the name of democracy. Here too there is a clear connection back to *Too Early, Too Late*. The exclusion of the more visceral passages of Kafka's story changes the feel of it somewhat, reflecting the changes in the nature of protest and revolution since the early twentieth century, and since the Six-Day War, particularly in the prominent use of social media and mobile screens in the demonstrations. The conditions — the time and the place — of Straub's realization of the script thus inevitably develops it beyond the translation published in *Cahiers du cinéma*. Not

FIG. 10.1. Danièle Huillet and Jean-Marie Straub, *Jackals and Arabs* (2011, courtesy of BELVA Film).

FIG. 10.2. Danièle Huillet and Jean-Marie Straub, *Jackals and Arabs* (2011, courtesy of BELVA Film).

filmed in the actual desert but rather in Europe, at most a metaphorical desert, it also speaks through different participants and places from those that might have been envisaged in the late 1980s.[35]

Hanssen argues that Kafka's jackal represented in the early twentieth century a critical portrait of the 'settler colonialist' of a European kind, rather than the humanist version of Zionism that imagined a peaceful co-existence of people of different faiths in Palestine. He bases this in part on a reading of the Arab as a respectful representation. What is important for Hanssen is the research into Kafka's diaries and letters that demonstrate his attitude towards Zionism as complex and humanist. Straub also emphasizes that the film is about Kafka's text. He gives it the expanded title SCHAKALE UND ARABER *de Franz Kafka* and the location of the film in an apartment echoes Kafka's own writing spaces. When it comes to an interpretation of the text as about Zionism, Straub's previous views would, however, indicate that the jackal is seen as oppressed. The opening posture of Ulrich, who speaks the words 'I am the oldest jackal' kneeling on the floor, is with head bowed, a pose described by Deleuze and Guattari as characteristic of the despairing animals of Kafka's stories, seeking a line of flight (see also Chapter 2).[36] She raises her head with words of faith, 'Glaube es!'. Speaking in response to questions about *Fortini/Cani* Straub expressed the opinion that 'it is not the Zionist or the Jew as such who becomes an executioner, he only does it in the role of the dog enslaved by American imperialism' (see Chapter 4).[37] In the film it is a Swiss speaker of German who voices the jackal. The French speaker, who voices the European, and who is hidden in the black screen (Figure 10.5), is, as Fortini was, the author/filmmaker reading his script. The Italian, representing the Arab, is the orientalized and yet still complex other, an 'angle' on this character which has something in common with Hanssen's position discussed above.[38] The focus on the Arab, his control of the jackals and his compassion for them, comes to a climax in the final statement to camera, which raises the question as to who 'they' are who hate, and also, in the present context, who precisely the object of hate or 'us', the Arabs, might be. That is, not only is there the simple assertion to be made that the Arab is indeed an Arab, but that the Arab also has a complex history, part of which was explored in the film *Too Early, Too Late*, and its engagement with *Class Conflict in Egypt: 1945–1971* by Mahmoud Hussein.[39] Is the Arab in the story the class that took control under the rule of Gamal Abdel Nasser, or is he the young person rebelling, or indeed the Muslim, with an attachment to eternal values and ritual not unlike that of the jackals? 'As long as there have been Arabs, these scissors wander through the desert and will wander with us until the end of days', is stated by the Arab.[40]

Taken together, all the decisions outlined about the cast, setting, and the framing of the characters make for a complex transposition of Kafka's story into a highly politicized present also for Arab affairs in France in 2011, where disputes over policing in minority communities, over visual references to the Prophet Mohammed, and the right of women to wear hijab, were compounded by the incident mentioned above in which two youths were killed and one severely injured with electrical burns after climbing over the wall of an electricity substation to avoid questioning by the police. Straub commemorated the deaths, which sparked three weeks of rioting throughout the country, with *Europa 2005, 27 October*. Divided into five sections each consisting of a pan right, a pan left, the sound of a dog barking, and the words '*Gas chamber. Electric chair*', the film exemplifies the practice of commemorating space in a dynamic relationship with film. In the case of *Jackals and Arabs* the apartment in Paris, with its parquet floor and floor-length

FIG. 10.3. Danièle Huillet and Jean-Marie Straub, *Jackals and Arabs*
(2011, courtesy of BELVA Film).

windows, adapts the text to a new context of intolerance. As with Kafka's text *The Man Who Disappeared* for the film *Class Relations*, and like the texts by Böll, Brecht, Fortini, Vittorini, and Barrès, but in contrast with those of Corneille, Schoenberg, Mallarmé, Hölderlin, and Pavese, which are unabridged, Kafka's animal story is cut and choreographed to the political moment.

Conclusion

The realization of *Jackals and Arabs* is an important late work, adding to the ways in which Huillet and Straub have resituated literary texts in the spaces of the present. It has a spontaneous and energetic feel and has benefited from its stop–start gestation and historical resituation. The oral performances of the cast lift Kafka's story out of its first publication context in *Der Jude*, its many reprints in different collections, its rediscovery through the debate about Kafka's relationship with his Jewish identity, all the way from Prague to the intimacy of an apartment in Paris. The riots in France, the uprisings across North Africa, the continued crises in Israel, and the question of where Kafka's manuscripts should be located, all form a context for a contemporary reading of the text as a European study in twenty-first-century multiculturalism and controlled intolerance. Straub's choice of actors and location is decisive. The gaps between the text, the *mise-en-scène*, and the bodies of the performers are large. In the process of filling them, the text emerges as a fascinating source of detailed disagreement, demonstrating its openness to resituating its verbal and visual meanings. In this film the sly if reticent European patriarch escapes from the clutches of the matriarchal jackal by siding with the controlling Arab patriarch. Only one moment of violence occurs when the scissors (Figure 10.3), grabbed from

FIG. 10.4. Danièle Huillet and Jean-Marie Straub, *Jackals and Arabs*
(2011, courtesy of BELVA Film).

FIG. 10.5. Danièle Huillet and Jean-Marie Straub, *Jackals and Arabs*
(2011, courtesy of BELVA Film).

the jackal as they are passed to the European, scratch the floor. Straub has quoted
Mallarmé to explain why location is so important to their works: 'nothing will take
place but the place'.[41] Only one scratch has been set down, but, as Kafka's story
goes, there will always be another iteration of the ritual, another desert, another
context for the text, and a variation that will produce difference.

Notes to Chapter 10

1. See the discussion of *Class Relations* (1984) in Nicola Albrecht, *Verschollen im Meer der Medien: Kafkas Romanfragment 'Amerika': zur Rekonstruktion und Deutung eines Medienkomplexes* (Heidelberg: Winter, 2006), pp. 219–54.

2. 'I do not intend to speak about | Just speak near by', Trinh T. Minh-ha, *Reassemblage* (1982). The script to the film is reproduced here: Trinh T. Minh-ha, 'Reassemblage', in *Framer Framed* (New York: Routledge, 1992), pp. 95-108 (p. 96).

3. The Kafka text appeared under the title 'Jean-Marie Straub', *Cahiers du cinéma*, 400 (supplement) (1987), 48. For the English translation, see note 6.

4. Blank, 'Wie will ich lustig lachen, wenn alles durcheinandergeht', p. 271.

5. Wim Wenders, *The Logic of Images: Essays and Conversations*, trans. by Michael Hofmann (London & Boston: Faber & Faber, 1991), p. 86.

6. Sally Shafto notes, 'Comparing DH and JMS's translation to Vialette's against Kafka's text also reveals the filmmakers' greater fidelity to the German original': Danièle Huillet and Jean-Marie Straub, 'Letter to Wim Wenders', in Straub and Huillet, *Writings*, pp. 196-200 (p. 200).

7. Ibid., p. 196.

8. In what follows Kafka's story is referred to by its German title to avoid confusion with Straub's film.

9. Byg, *Landscapes of Resistance*, pp. 174-75.

10. Franz Kafka, 'Zwei Tiergeschichten: 1. Schakale und Araber', *Der Jude: Eine Monatschrift*, 2.7 (1917-18), 488-90.

11. For an overview of such interpretations see: Jens Hanssen, 'Kafka and Arabs', *Critical Inquiry*, 39.1 (2012), 167-97. For an interpretation of the story specifically in the context of the politics of Arab-Jewish relations in Palestine in 1917, see Iris Bruce, 'Kafka's Journey into the Future: Crossing Borders into Israeli/Palestinian Worlds', in *Kafka for the Twenty-First Century*, ed. by Stanley Corngold and Ruth V. Gross (Rochester & New York: Camden House, 2011), pp. 222-36 (pp. 223-25).

12. Pummer, '(Not Only) for Children and Cavemen', p. 92.

13. Benjamin, *Understanding Brecht*, p. 110.

14. Dimitry Shumsky, 'Czechs, Germans, Arabs, Jews: Franz Kafka's "Jackals and Arabs" between Bohemia and Palestine', *AJS Review*, 33 (2009), 71-100 (p. 71).

15. See Jay Geller, 'Kafka's "Schakale und Araber" and the Question of Genre', in *Orientalism, Gender, and the Jews: Literary and Artistic Transformations of European National Discourses*, ed. by Ulrike Brunotte, Anna-Dorothea Ludewig, and Axel Stähler (Berlin & Boston: Walter De Gruyter/Oldenbourg, 2014), pp. 124-36 (p. 130).

16. Max Brod, 'Unsere Literaten und die Gemeinschaft', *Der Jude*, 1.7 (1916), 457-64 (p. 463). All translations are my own unless otherwise indicated.

17. Four publications appeared in Kafka's lifetime, see Franz Kafka, *Schriften: Tagebücher: Kritische Ausgabe*, ed. by Jürgen Born and others, 15 vols (Frankfurt am Main: Fischer, 2002), XIII (*Drucke zu Lebzeiten: Apparatband*), 332.

18. Shumsky, 'Czechs, Germans, Arabs, Jews', p. 72.

19. Gilles Deleuze and Félix Guattari, *Kafka: Toward a Minor Literature*, trans. by Dana Polan (Minneapolis & London: University of Minnesota Press, 1975), p. 18.

20. Ritchie Robertson, *Kafka: Judaism, Politics and Literature* (Oxford: Oxford University Press, 1985), p. 164.

21. Martin Buber, 'Die Losung', *Der Jude*, 1.1 (1916-17), 1-3 (p. 3).

22. See Kafka, *Schriften*, XIII, 332.

23. Atef Botros, *Kafka: ein jüdischer Schriftsteller aus arabischer Sicht* (Wiesbaden: Reichert, 2009).

24. Judith Butler, 'Who Owns Kafka?', *London Review of Books*, 3 March 2011 <https://www.lrb.co.uk/the-paper/v33/no5/judith-butler/who-owns-kafka> [accessed 17 June 2021].

25. Hanssen, 'Kafka and Arabs', pp. 168, 180.

26. Ibid., pp. 169, 170, 176.

27. Huillet and Straub, 'Letter to Wim Wenders', p. 200.

28. Hanssen, 'Kafka and Arabs', pp. 183, 186.

29. Geller, 'Kafka's "Schakale und Araber" and the Question of Genre', p. 130.
30. Kafka, *Schriften*, ed. by Born, Neumann, Pasley and Schillemeit, VII (*Nachgelassene Schriften und Fragmente II: Apparatband*), 128.
31. Ibid., VI (*Nachgelassene Schriften und Fragmente II*), 514. The translation in the film is credited to Misha Donat and Jean-Marie Straub.
32. Stephen Blum, 'Kurtág's Articulation of Kafka's Rhythms ("Kafka-Fragmente", op. 24)', *Studia Musicologica Academiae Scientiarum Hungaricae*, 43 (2002), 345–58 (p. 352).
33. See Gilles Deleuze and Félix Guattari, *Mille piani: capitalismo e schizofrenia*, trans. by Giorgio Passerone (Rome: Cooper & Castelvecchi, 2003).
34. See Lothar Müller, 'Performance and Recitation', in *Franz Kafka in Context*, ed. by Carolin Duttlinger (Cambridge: Cambridge University Press, 2018), pp. 100–08.
35. See Holl, *The Moses Complex*, p. 95.
36. See Deleuze and Guattari, *Kafka: Toward a Minor Literature*, p. 4. Deleuze and Guattari open their thesis with a repeated connection between the 'bent head' and the photograph in Kafka's work, which 'causes a functional blockage, a neutralization of experimental desire'. They interpret the 'head that straightens' as 'an answer to the bent head'.
37. Huillet, Straub, and Fortini, 'Pressekonferenz in Pesaro', p. 8.
38. Discussing the politics of the 1967 Arab-Israeli war Straub explained the Brechtian approach to realism: ' "to make a marked link between the specific and the general, to capture the particular within a general process, that is the art of the realists", says Brecht. And the reflection that leads to a film has to choose a certain angle'. Ibid., p. 6.
39. Mahmoud Hussein, *Class Conflict in Egypt: 1945–1971*, trans. by Michel Chirman and others (New York & London: Monthly Review Press, 1973).
40. Translation (by Misha Donat, Jean-Marie Straub) taken from the film.
41. 'Well cinema is, or should be, the art of space. Even though a film exists only if that space is able to become time. But the basic work is space. As Mallarme [*sic*] said: "Nothing will take place, but the place" ': Céline Condorelli, 'Speaking of Revolutions: Too Early, Too Late' [interview with Jean-Marie Straub], 20 March 2011 <https://lux.org.uk/writing/speaking-of-revolutions-too-early-too-late> [accessed 21 December 2021]. The reference is to Stéphane Mallarmé's poem 'Un coup de dés jamais n'abolira le hasard' (1897), which was adapted to film by Huillet and Straub (*Every Revolution is a Throw of the Dice*, 1977).

CHAPTER 11

❖

Interview with Danièle Huillet and Jean-Marie Straub apropos *The Death of Empedocles* and *Black Sin*: 9 April 1990, Goethe-Institut London

The following interview was held at the Goethe-Institut London on 9 April 1990 as the culmination of a retrospective of the films of Danièle Huillet and Jean-Marie Straub curated by Margaret Deriaz. The interview, which lasted about an hour, followed a screening of *The Death of Empedocles* (1987) and was conducted by Julian Petley (Brunel University) with Martin Brady interpreting. The interview was immediately followed by a screening of *Black Sin* (1989).

An extract of the interview (transferred from audio cassette) was played at the Goethe-Institut during the 2019 retrospective out of which this volume evolved. Many thanks to Margaret Deriaz, Julian Petley, and Barbara Ulrich for agreeing to the inclusion of the following transcript and, in part, translation.

Much of the interview was held in English and those parts in German and French have been translated (by the editors) and appear in italics. We have decided, as far as possible, to retain the dynamic of the interplay between Huillet and Straub, including occasional grammatical corrections and so forth, to give an impression of how they responded together to Petley's questions and developed a rapport with the audience.

All film titles are in small capitals.

Julian Petley: I think it's very difficult to think of any filmmakers who have pursued their own particular path as courageously and single-mindedly as yourselves, undaunted by what I should imagine were numerous difficulties. The only contemporary example I can think of like yourselves would be someone like Roberto Rossellini whose late films, whose television films in particular — in this country — seem to me to be still scandalously neglected. So, I'd really like to ask you how it is that you've been able to pursue this path of yours so single-mindedly. And I shall ask this question to both of you, so whoever wants to answer, please answer!

Danièle Huillet: Well, I think it's the biggest privilege to be able to do, to make, what you like.

Jean-Marie Straub: And only what you like. Who can say he has the possibility to do such a thing in our society? Fewer and fewer. So, if you have this privilege, you have to use it. And life is short, so it's better to do only what you like if you have the possibility to do only what you like.

JP: Could you give us some idea though of how you get your films funded? It might be interesting for instance to talk about how EMPEDOCLES was funded. It's almost impossible to imagine something like that being funded over here.

DH: Well, for the first time, we got some money from the French cultural...

J-MS: ...*Centre national de la cinématographie*

DH: ...but not directly from the *Centre national de la cinématographie* because the Commission President said there is no point asking the Commission to give money for this film. So, he took some money from a kind of private fund he had and for the first time we got some money from there...

J-MS: ...but only half of the usual...

DH: ...of the usual sum.

J-MS: Why half? Because Hölderlin is Hölderlin and because Hölderlin wrote in German. [*Laughter*]

DH: Even though it was a German-French co-production, the film was still shot in German and they knew it was not going to be translated.

J-MS: And for a film we made before in Italy, in Italian, from Pavese...

DH: ...FROM THE CLOUD TO THE RESISTANCE...

J-MS: ...we tried to ask for money from the same source...

DH: ...but it was not the same man...

J-MS: ...it was another man...

DH: ...and he said 'it's not possible, I won't. I cannot hinder you in bringing your script, but I won't give it to the Commission. If you want me to do the work you have to shoot the film in Corsica, in dialect, in Corsican'...

J-MS: ...and with French actors, because French cinema was in a crisis.

DH: And for EMPEDOCLES, when we got some money from German television, the Third Channel in Frankfurt — but only two thirds of the sum they had given for Kafka [CLASS RELATIONS, 1984] — Jean-Marie told them, 'for you the Jew Kafka has more worth than the German Hölderlin'. [*Laughter*]

JP: So, several of your films have been financed with television money...

J-MS: Yes, it's only possible like that, and for MOSES AND AARON. We had to wait ten years to find the money for CHRONICLE [OF ANNA MAGDALENA BACH]. We would be able to make the film...

DH: ...would have been...

J-MS: ...have been... ten years before, with Curd Jürgens as Johann Sebastian Bach [*laughter*] and then seven years later with Herbert von Karajan. And then we would have...

DH: ...we would have got twice as much money as we needed. [*Laughter*]

JMS: Because at that time when we went to every producer, distributor, even... I don't know... source of funding... and they would ask at the end, 'a very interesting film, but...

DH: ...project...

J-MS: ...but who will play the part of Bach?' And we said, 'Gustav Leonhardt'. They said, 'Who? Please?' Because Gustav Leonhardt at that time had only two records, only one in Vienna and the other one in the United States. And the same for Harnoncourt, who is in the film too.

DH: It's only possible to finance such films if you get money from many sources. You cannot hope to get the money from one.

J-MS: And so, for MOSES AND AARON we had six different funds to put together.

DH: You must build a finance system, a finance method for the film during two, three, four years.

J-MS: On the other hand, it is good that way, because that is *the only field where the saying 'diviser pour gagner' isn't just opportunistic, but necessary to retain your freedom.*

JP: ...'divide and rule'. Do you find that getting television money puts any particular kind of aesthetic limitations on you, makes you do things that you would rather not do, or do you find on the whole that it leaves you as free as one ever is?

J-MS: Us? Never. For us, until now, no! Because we come with something, and if they do not accept it, we have to wait one year, ten years, two years. I think we must say that this is the only justification for our work. *We're not stupid or naive, we know very well that even in the repertory cinemas in Germany there is only a very limited audience.* When we made MOSES AND AARON it was shown on television at eleven o'clock in the evening and they got 1,800,000 viewers. And they repeated the film three times afterwards and on other channels over the years ...

DH: ...and at better hours...

J-MS: ...and for this film [EMPEDOCLES] from this evening, they had only 800...

DH: ...800,000...

J-MS: ...but it was at 11.30. So, it is a little bit cynical, because they know very well that nobody working the next day can be...

DH: ...sitting at two o'clock in the night looking at a film on the television, it's not possible.

J-MS: But in a year they will show the film for the second time, maybe at nine o'clock or so.

JP: When EMPEDOCLES was released in Germany — I've just been looking at all the press coverage of it — I was quite impressed by the amount of press coverage and some of it was actually quite intelligent. Could you say something about the critical reactions to your films in Germany? Jean-Marie has already mentioned the fact that no British newspaper or magazine seems to have deigned to be interested in the fact that we have Jean-Marie and Danièle here, so things are pretty awful here. Perhaps you could say something about the state of film criticism, particularly vis-à-vis your own films, in Germany.

J-MS: May I add a small parenthesis about British information and newspapers? *It is really scandalous — and it's not about me, it's about Hölderlin — that there's no mention of it in any newspaper when a film of this kind is being screened. And I know, because you told me, that you tried* three newspapers and they refused.

JP: I spoke to *Time Out*, who I write for, the *Guardian*, who I write for, and the *Independent*, who I write for... and no interest. It is scandalous. It's scandalous for Hölderlin and for you.

J-MS: And we are talking about Europe, and what is Europe without Hölderlin? We are speaking about free expression. *Perhaps only three hundred people would have come. Perhaps one hundred would also have left. But at least it would have been known. I mean, a society which claims to be democratic should also, if it really is democratic, tolerate — only tolerate, I don't demand more — such products, let's just call them 'products'.*

DH: Not support, but tolerate them. *'Dulden'*.

Audience member: Suffer them.

J-MS: Suffer, yes, suffer... [*laughter*]

JP: As I'm sure you're both aware, there is absolutely no form of state support or anything for film distribution in this country. Everything is thrown open to the sheer brute forces of the market and if things can't, as Mrs Thatcher would say, 'pay their way', then they don't appear.

DH: As in America. It's exactly the same.

J-MS: It's only because you are in advance. The same thing is coming in Germany and in France. And you will be ital... how do you say...

DH: ...italianized...

J-MS: *'italianisiert'*. And the other countries, more in advance, will destroy what is not...

DH: ...already...

J-MS: ...destroyed.

JP: That's a very depressing thought, I always thought we were lagging behind everybody else, not in advance.

J-MS: And it will also happen on the 'other side' now, because the Wall is vanished.

DH: ...the Wall *has* vanished...

J-MS: and this is... *the free market economy*.

DH: I just wanted to say about Empedocles and the German press. The reason why we wanted to be in the official Competition in Berlin is because we well know that the newspapers and the journalists write on a film only if it's in the official Competition. And that's the only reason why there was anything in the German press. If you show such a film outside the official Competition, they won't run it. That was clear. And the reason why the film was in the official Competition in Berlin — nowadays it wouldn't happen anymore — is the same reason he said you are in advance in England. Also in Germany, all the spaces are closing. The reason why it was entered in the official Competition was that two years earlier the Kafka film was shown in the Competition, but only because Jean-Marie said to the Director of the Festival, 'either in Competition or not at all!'. 'So,' he said, 'I must think about it for three days after seeing the film'. And afterwards he said to Jean-Marie, 'I decided to take the bull by the horns and to show the film in the official Competition'. And it was a kind of success. So, two years later he accepted to take THE DEATH OF EMPEDOCLES. But for THE DEATH OF EMPEDOCLES it was different, there was nearly a fight in the auditorium. And it was very divided afterwards. Now he wouldn't take it anymore.

J-MS: This type of film is not possible.

DH: When you show a film such as the one you will see later [BLACK SIN] in Cannes, not in the official Competition, but in an official section such as 'Les Yeux fertiles', not only no newspaper ...

J-MS: ...film magazine...

DH: ...not even a single film review will be written on the film.

J-MS: You must know, even if you are right with the German newspapers and THE DEATH OF EMPEDOCLES, that for example, until now, with the exception of the *notorious* Berlin Festival

DH: ...reviews...

J-MS: the only newspaper who...

DH: ...which...

J-MS: ...could help such a film...

DH: ...to get an audience or to make people aware that it exists is *Die Zeit*.

J-MS: And *Die Zeit* refused to write about the film — even a text from Handke, and even a text from Wenders, and even a text from their own theatre critic because... [*to DH:*] ...*you explain why*...

DH: Because in Berlin the man who saw the film was against it, so he wrote about it because of the official Competition, but afterwards he made a... [*visual gesture, not recorded*].

JP: I take it from what you are saying that you don't seem to feel that the future for the kind of cinema which you bravely want to go on making is going to be any brighter in this new Germany that we see possibly coming along. Would I be right in saying that?

DH: It won't be easier!

JP: It won't be easier. Can I ask you finally, and then I think I'll throw it open to the audience, why is it that you've been, both of you, so drawn towards German culture? I know it's not only German culture, but you have been heavily drawn towards German culture. What is it about it that has fascinated you so much?

DH: *Caprice de l'histoire!*

JP: Caprice of history, right.

J-MS: I was born in Lothringen...

DH: ...Lorraine...

J-MS: ...and after joining up with Mr Goebbels, Lothringen belonged for a time to 'Groß-Germany' and so I had to learn German. But I refused to learn German. And after the war the other caprice was that the first film we wanted to make was CHRONICLE OF ANNA MAGDALENA BACH and it was a German film.

DH: It was the film that we wanted to make as Jean-Marie refused to join the Algerian War. So he had to escape, he had to get away from France. And since we had this project, we went first to Holland to see Leonhardt, and then to Germany. We went to East Germany because most of the manuscripts from Bach were in East Germany and then we established ourselves in Munich...

J-MS: ...settled [*laughter*]...

DH: ...because we thought maybe it would be easier to get some money to produce the film in Munich than in Hamburg, where we wanted more to live, but which was, at that time, very far away.

J-MS: I am proud to be registered in Wiesbaden as a 'German filmmaker'. I think no German filmmaker made such a gift to people born in the German language as this one. So, I am proud of it.

JP: We keep on coming back to CHRONICLE OF ANNA MAGDALENA BACH, so I wanted to ask you one last question: did you feel yourselves to be part of something which has since come to be called the 'New German Cinema' or was it very much a kind of historical accident that the Bach film came out at the same time as other stirrings were starting to happen within the German cinema?

DH: Well, it was an accidental happening because if we had got the money to shoot the film, it would have been shot, let's say...

J-MS: ...at the beginning of the sixties...

DH: ...eight or nine years earlier.

JP: Right! Let's take some questions from other people now.

Audience 1: I want to ask you about the method of making a film like EMPEDOCLES. I wondered how much the structure of the film is formed before you start shooting. Is there also improvisation during the shoot?

J-MS: Both. *We work things out on paper and then I have to decide, as every filmmaker should, who is going to be seen and when and at what distance, and whether to show the person who is speaking or those who are listening or someone else etc.*

DH: ...whom you show, if it's the one speaking or the one listening or, as a third possibility, for example, the landscape. And we decide all that on paper, before beginning shooting and even before beginning to look for people and for places.

J-MS: And even decide who is sitting, who is not sitting and when and why. What distance one actor has to stay in relation to another and so on.

Audience 1: Is there one stage that would be more prominent than another stage? So, when you come to edit is there a lot of material you have to discard?

DH: No. What is very difficult when we edit is not the editing itself, but to choose. Because we have — at least for this film we had — at least four takes for every shot which were very good. And it's often a torture to choose. That's the biggest work with editing.

J-MS: Because to get four takes that are very good you have to shoot...

DH: ...sometimes thirty-five, sometimes only sixteen. Sometimes seven or nine. And... since the light was always changing, always moving, when we had the first good one, we always made a second one because of the laboratories. Because something can always happen, and it happens more and more that you get something destroyed at the lab. So, we make a second one and since the light and the wind were so strong and changing, when we had the two which for us were very good, the cameraman said, 'well at the beginning it was right, but then in the middle it was very dark, and at the end I don't know how it will come out'. [*Laughter*] And sometimes the sound man, with whom we have worked since CHRONICLE, since '67, said 'Well it's OK, but the wind, so please listen...', and I go and hear the sound and I said, 'well, maybe we should try another one'. And since the actors were very well prepared, because we had worked for one and a half years with them, when we asked 'are you ready to try a third one?', they always said yes. But when we had the third one, very often we had to get a fourth because of the sun or the wind or... so in the end we had at least four very good ones for every shot. Sometimes five or six or seven even. And we had to choose. And from this film we have made four different versions with the same shots, but another take for every shot, another light, another sound, and even the actors are different, because every actor reacts differently if the wind is strong or not, if the sun is in his face or not, if the sun comes out suddenly, and so on. And we have made four versions and what you saw is the second one. Because it is the only one which is subtitled, either in French or in English or in Italian.

J-MS: *But with regard to the question about editing, I would just like to add that the editing work consists in deciding where to cut between two blocks, that is a twenty-fourth of a second or a single frame. So, we are working right down to a twenty-fourth of a second, sometimes even half a frame as the sound in 35mm is displaced by two counters.*

DH: Don't believe that it is easier to edit when you have long-lasting shots than when you have short ones...

J-MS: ...it has to be more precise then...

DH: Above all when you shoot with sound and you won't ever accept taking the sound off another take and putting it on another image, not even a word, which nearly every filmmaker does. What you hear is exactly the sound which was registered along with the image. There is nothing more and nothing less. So, when you edit with sound, you have not only to look at what the image says, if you have eyes going down or up, if you have a hand which is not quite down, but you have also to hear if you have a bird. You cannot cut in the middle of a ...

J-MS: ...of a 'queek queek' [*laughter*]. So, the last answer to your question: after this work on paper, on space, abstract space, we travel 30,000 kilometres...

DH: ...not always, but often...

J-MS: ...to find places. And after we found the places, we have to rediscover a concrete disposition. For example, here [*demonstrated on paper*] — only for the second reel of the film — here, you have five people [Figure 11.1]: the sheriff, the priest, the three...

DH: ...citizens...

J-MS: guys, puppets [Figure 11.2]. Like this [*shows the drawing*]. You have here a column, a broken column. That's the first one. You have here a bench, Empedocles was sitting here, and the young boy was sitting there. So. And

FIG. 11.1. Danièle Huillet and Jean-Marie Straub, *The Death of Empedocles* (1986, courtesy of BELVA Film).

FIG. 11.2. Danièle Huillet and Jean-Marie Straub, *The Death of Empedocles* (1986, courtesy of BELVA Film).

then the trial begins. So. Empedocles takes two steps in that direction. And the young boy. So. We had to know very exactly here if there was one step or two steps, or one and a half steps only, or three steps... to find exactly the right distance between *the accused and the accusers* and then to find a point from the camera...

DH: ...for the camera...

J-MS: ...for the camera a little closer to...

DH: ...the accused people

J-MS: ...than the prosecution. And this point was possible only here [*demonstrates on the drawing*] because we could not transgress the eyeline. And this point for the camera...

DH: ...from which we showed...

J-MS: ...from which we showed one here [*demonstrates on the drawing*], or both there... from there... one here, or both, or three, or one here... or three here...

DH: ...two...

J-MS: ...without moving the camera. And this point had to be the same for Empedocles coming from there. The five people came from there, like that [*demonstrates on the drawing*]. And they really came, they walked! And found their places normally. So. And then the young boy came from there and stood here and Empedocles came from here and stood here [Figure 11.3]. And then Empedocles went to the bench and the young boy to the bench. And so on. And when Empedocles was alone it was the same. So, we played with different lenses, lenses possible for five people in the same place, like that, so like that from here, this...

DH: ...angulation point...

J-MS: ...angulation point, or three for them, or two for them, or one for them. And then here the same and for him alone when he came and greets the new day. And then for both sitting and so on. So that is the work on space.

JP: It's an interesting insight into how shots are set up. The gentleman at the back.

FIG. 11.3. Danièle Huillet and Jean-Marie Straub, *The Death of Empedocles* (1986, courtesy of BELVA Film).

Audience 2: Why did you insist on the actors ending the verse so sharply at the end of each line? I found the film thrilling, but I couldn't help thinking at the same time of the little 'sub-play' at the end of *A Midsummer Night's Dream* with Pyramus and Thisbe where the verse is used deliberately by Shakespeare for comic effect. Clearly that was not your intention. And yet I wonder why you have arranged the delivery of the verse in just the way you did?

J-MS: Are you speaking as an English citizen or a German citizen? [*Laughter*] It's very important to me to know it.

Audience 2: I'm an English speaker.

J-MS: *Sprechen Sie Deutsch oder?* [You speak German, don't you?]

Audience 2: Ein bisschen. [A little.]

J-MS: *And why isn't Hölderlin allowed to be comic if Shakespeare is?* [*Laughter*] *And I believe...* the irony of Shakespeare is something very important, but I think the most ironic writers I know are Corneille, in his way, and Hölderlin in another way.

Audience 2: You can forget about Pyramus and Thisbe if you like! But I just wondered why in reading the verse the declamation is so much against the sense ...

DH: ...*contre le sens*.

J-MS: We tried for sixth months to make what they call an *enjambement*! But it was not working. That man wrote verse! I mean Hölderlin. And if you try to hide it, it makes no sense. No sense. If Hölderlin makes an affirmation in one line and the negation comes only at the end of the second line, you have to hear it...

JP: Can I ask a supplementary question there? Were you aiming at a particular, well-established German tradition of reading that kind of verse? I'm not a Germanist...

DH: Look. When we made the film, this question came up... and came up with much more violence in Germany than here, that's clear! And after six months, I think... after showing the film and so on, somebody said to us, 'But you know, until the beginning of the nineteenth century people spoke the lines of verse with a break at the end of the line. And only during the nineteenth century, as it became important to move towards naturalism, this break vanished'.

J-MS: So the real tradition...

DH: ...so we re-discovered something without knowing it...

J-MS: ...was destroyed. Destroyed. That was the tradition. What came afterwards was...

DH: ...*theatre de boulevard*. [*Laughter*]

J-MS: At the end of each verse we put, how do you say it, a simple caesura, which means half a second or a five to seven second pause. It depends.

DH: The breaks are very different. They can be very short, or they can be much longer.

J-MS: And so, within these blocks we sometimes chose *arioso*, sometimes *recitativo*, sometimes *accelerando*, sometimes *allargando*, depending on the blocks and the content.

Audience 3: The French and Egyptian landscapes and cityscapes in TOO EARLY, TOO LATE are filmed in a very open, airy, unpredictable way, visually, and on the soundtrack. By contrast EMPEDOCLES and to some extent MOSES AND AARON are much more tightly restricted and constrained films in their use of the settings. Presumably that is something that comes out of the text?

J-MS: One tries after one thing to make something different! [*Laughs*] I think it has a relation with the text, yes. Look... our society lives and dies on inflation. Art, so-called art, has to be the extreme contrast to inflation. *Moins on en montre, plus on en ressent.*

DH: The less you show, the more you feel.

Audience 4: I wanted to add that this 'cutting off' at the end of the verse was also done in the Italian film. [*Ends inaudibly*]

DH: Yes... but in the Italian film there were no verses. It was prose.

J-MS: That was an intervention from us. Not from the writer.

Audience 5: Did you want to make poetry out of that text?

J-MS: Yes.

DH: Look, when we begin to work on a text with somebody, it can be a professional actor or a non-professional, the first job is to let him read. We give him a paper with the text on it and he begins to read, and we just listen. And sometimes he does something and we say to him, 'There you have done that, can you do it again?'

J-MS: And our work consists in discovering how his... how do you say... works...? [*Taps his chest and breaths deeply*]

JP: ...heart?

DH: ...no...

J-MS: Heart too! [*Laughter*]

DH: ...heart and...

JP: ...lungs!

J-MS: ...breath. To find the connection between his breath and the *content of the text*. And to make out this connection...

DH: ...from this connection...

J-MS: yes, from this connection is better... a kind of *musical score*.

DH: And something which has to do with realism, but with a very deep one which you can also find again in dreams...

J-MS: ...or on the street...

DH: when you hear people speaking on the street and they are not aware that you are listening, you often hear things which you yourself... we ourselves... would not think possible, which go further than the things we try with people and the text.

J-MS: When we hear children on the street crying... *crient*...

DH: ...saying...

J-MS: ...saying '*beißt, der Hund*?' that is something else from '*beißt der Hund*?'. 'Bites, this dog? it's something else from 'Bites this dog?'...

DH: ...does this dog bite?

J-MS: ...'Does this dog bite?'. *If we had not taken Hölderlin at his word and if the listener... I'm only talking about the listener... could not hear the ends of the lines, be it as a caesura or a long pause, then Hölderlin, or rather what he wrote, would have become* newspaper language. And it would have been without suspense. For example, when the uncle in the Kafka film says, 'Yes, yes... *that was also my... pause... opinion*', Mario Adorf did it perchance and afterwards I said, 'Try it again!' and he said, 'It's not possible to say it like that!' But we said, 'There are two of us, you said it like that', and he said, 'It's true?', and we said, 'Yes, there are two of us.' [*Laughter*] And he said, 'No, no, it's not possible. No actor can say it like that'. And I said, 'Excuse me, do it for us, only for our friendship's sake'. He tried. Afterwards he had to...

DH: ...he made something out of it...

J-MS: Yes, he made something with that, out of it and he had... *he had to integrate it as a rhythm and, as in a nightmare, keep going with it...*

Audience 5: I wanted to ask if, in the years after the War, you felt close to French cinema, to the *Nouvelle Vague*? And what do you think now about it?

J-MS: It was a little later than after the War, the *Nouvelle Vague*. So, I was a friend of Truffaut, of Godard, of Rivette, and of Rohmer. We knew each other, that's all I can say.

JP: Bresson? Were you friendly with Bresson?

J-MS: Bresson was not our generation.

DH: Bresson was the one responsible for him beginning to make films.

J-MS: He trapped me! [*Laughter*] Because I went to him with the project called CHRONICLE OF ANNA MAGDALENA BACH and I said to him that is a project for you to maybe try to make something, some continuation of JOURNAL D'UN CURÉ DE CAMPAGNE, but in another way. And he said, 'Ah ha, very interesting, but that's your project, you have to do it!'. So, I was trapped! [*Laughter*]

Audience 6: I came this evening because I read in the programme that you were employing non-professional, non-emotive actors. I liked the idea that I would be listening to people speaking the words, not pretending that they had invented them...

J-MS: ...that's very good...

Audience 6: ...some of the time I think I was listening to that, but I was disappointed at other times. I thought now and again there is an actor speaking and pretending to have the emotion. And that put me off.

J-MS: That's what we have in common with François Truffaut. I like, how do you say...

DH: ...mixtures...

J-MS: mixtures. So we try to not...

DH: ...not to...

J-MS: ...not to be fanatical. We try every time with a film to make a fan... as open as possible. Here is an actor and here... and in the way you said... we try to introduce as much contradiction as possible.

Audience 6: Sometimes you have an actor, if he is an actor, I don't know...

J-MS: ...which one, for example? That would be interesting, which one, for example?

Audience 6: I don't know if they were actors or not, but I came in when they were sitting on the steps with those funny hats.

J-MS: But none of those three is an actor. [*Laughs*] It's a complicated question... because... I think you are more fanatical than we are. [*Laughter*] You can say like Brecht, 'Instead...', Brecht said that the only... he said the distanciation... which is not distanciation in German... in the United States they say, how do you put it...

DH: ...'alienation'...

J-MS: ...'alienation' and I said, what! Alienation? Yes, '*Verfremdung*'! But in French they say 'distanciation', I don't know... Brecht at the end of his life said, 'These idiots will have forced me to invent something like that!' [*Laughter*] I think that was a reflection about a concrete work for the theatre. But he said — to resume this reflection — he said, 'Instead of wanting to create the impression that he is improvising, the actor should rather show what the truth is: he is quoting'. But you cannot work with theory, you have to work with real people, with real texts. What do you want to say about your question and my bad answer? [*Laughter*]

Audience 6: I was wondering if several of your actors were professional actors...

J-MS: Yes, it's a mixture.

Audience 7: The subtitles were very selective, not everything was translated. Was that your intention?

J-MS: I am innocent, yes! [*Laughter*]

DH: Well, I wanted to leave some spaces where the people are not obliged, when they do not understand a word of German, to read all the time. Where they are free or obliged to look at the people and the trees, and to just hear the sound without reading. Also, because maybe when the titles come again, it's also a kind of suspense, because it's beginning again. So, it's a possibility to have some rest and then go on.

J-MS: And maybe this film is a silent film. The last silent film. [*Laughter*]

JP: Well, I think on that enigmatic note... [*laughter*]... it's probably a good place to finish. I'd like to thank both of you very much, Danièle and Jean-Marie, I'd like to thank Martin as well for your excellent translations, thank you for all your questions, and let's now get on with the next fascinating part of the evening, BLACK SIN.

DH: Without subtitles!

JP: Without subtitles. [*Laughter*] Thank you very much.

J-MS: Thank you.

[*Applause*]

J-MS: I meant what I said about newspapers and information in England. It's not about our film and Hölderlin and so on, but I think English citizens must have...

DH: ...should have...

J-MS: ...the right to see a film like this and to know that it exists.

[*Applause*]

FILMOGRAPHY

❖

The following list of films has been compiled by comparing various published sources including the volumes edited by Ted Fendt and Sally Shafto (see the Bibliography). Duration is given, with the exception of *Joachim Gatti*, to the nearest minute and dates reflect the first public screening or broadcast.

Danièle Huillet, Jean-Marie Straub

1963   *Machorka-Muff*, FRG, 35mm, b&w, 18 mins
1965   *Not Reconciled, or Only Violence Helps Where Violence Rules* (*Nicht versöhnt oder Es hilft nur Gewalt, wo Gewalt herrscht*), FRG, 35mm, b&w, 55 mins
1968   *Chronicle of Anna Magdalena Bach* (*Chronik der Anna Magdalena Bach*), FRG/Italy, 35mm, b&w, 93 mins
1968   *The Bridegroom, the Actress and the Pimp* (*Der Bräutigam, die Komödiantin und der Zuhälter*), FRG, 35mm, b&w, 23 mins
1970   *Eyes Do Not Want to Close at All Times, or Perhaps One Day Rome Will Permit Herself to Choose in Her Turn* [Othon] (*Les yeux ne veulent pas en tout temps se fermer ou Peut-être qu'un jour Rome se permettra de choisir à son tour*), FRG/Italy, 16mm (blown up to 35mm), colour, 88 mins
1972   *History Lessons* (*Geschichtsunterricht*), Italy/FRG, 16mm, colour, 85 mins
1973   *Introduction to Arnold Schoenberg's Accompaniment to a Cinematographic Scene* (*Einleitung zu Arnold Schoenbergs Begleitmusik zu einer Lichtspielscene*), FRG, 16mm, colour/b&w, 15 mins
1975   *Moses and Aaron* (*Moses und Aron*), Austria/FRG/France/Italy, 35mm (two shots in 16mm), colour, 105 mins
1976   *Fortini/Cani*, Italy, 16mm, colour, 83 mins
1977   *Every Revolution is a Throw of the Dice* (*Toute révolution est un coup de dés*), France, 35mm, colour, 10 mins
1979   *From the Cloud to the Resistance* (*Dalla nube alla resistenza*), Italy/FRG, 35mm, colour, 105 mins
1981   *Too Early, Too Late* (*Zu früh, zu spat/Trop tôt, trop tard/Troppo presto, troppo tardi*), France/Egypt, 16mm, colour, 100 mins
1983   *En rachâchant*, France, 35mm, b&w, 7 mins
1984   *Class Relations* (*Klassenverhältnisse*), FRG/France, 35mm, b&w, 130 mins
1985   *Proposition in Four Parts* (*Proposta in quattro parti*), Italy, video, colour, 41 mins
1987   *The Death of Empedocles, or When the Green of the Earth Will Glisten for You Anew* (*Der Tod des Empedokles oder: Wenn dann der Erde Grün von neuem euch erglänzt*), FRG/France, 35mm, colour, 132 mins
1989   *Black Sin* (*Schwarze Sünde*), FRG, 35mm, colour, 42 mins
1990   *Cézanne: Conversation with Joachim Gasquet* (*Cézanne: dialogue avec Joachim Gasquet*), France/FRG, 35mm, colour, 51 mins

1992   *The Antigone of Sophocles after Hölderlin's Translation Adapted for the Stage by Brecht 1948 (Suhrkamp Verlag) (Die Antigone des Sophokles nach der Hölderlinschen Übertragung für die Bühne bearbeitet von Brecht 1948 (Suhrkamp Verlag))*, Germany/France, 35mm, colour, 100 mins

1994   *Lothringen!*, Germany/France, 35mm, colour, 21 mins

1997   *Von heute auf morgen* [From Today until Tomorrow] Germany/France, 35mm, b&w, 62 mins

1999   *Sicilia!*, Italy/France, 35mm, b&w, 66 mins

2001   *Workers, Peasants (Operai, contadini)*, Italy/France, 35mm, colour, 123 mins

2001   *The Wayfarer (Il viandante)*, Italy/France, 35mm, b&w, 5 mins

2001   *The Knife Sharpener (L'arrotino)*, Italy/France, 35mm, b&w, 7 mins

2003   *The Return of the Prodigal Son (Il ritorno del figlio prodigo)*, Italy/France/Germany, 35mm, colour, 29 mins [see note below on *Humiliated*]

2003   *Humiliated: ... that nothing produced or touched by them, coming from their hands, proves free from the claim of some stranger (Workers, Peasants — continuation and end) (Umiliati: che niente di fatto o toccato da loro, di uscito dalle mani loro, risultasse esente dal diritto di qualche estraneo (Operai, contadini — seguito e fine))*, Italy/France/Germany, 35mm, colour, 35 mins [For theatrical distribution this film was released together with its predecessor as *The Return of the Prodigal Son — Humiliated (Il ritorno del figlio prodigo — Umiliati)*]

2003   *Incantati*, Italy/France/Germany, 35mm, colour, 6 mins

2003   *Dolando*, Italy/France/Germany, 35mm, colour, 7 mins

2004   *A Visit to the Louvre (Une visite au Louvre)*, France/Germany, 35mm, colour, 48 mins (first version), 47 mins (second version)

2006   *These Encounters of Theirs (Quei loro incontri)*, Italy/France, 35mm, colour, 68 mins

2006   *Europa 2005, 27 October (Europa 2005, 27 octobre)*, France, MiniDV, colour, 10 mins

2008   *Itinerary of Jean Bricard (Itinéraire de Jean Bricard)*, France, 35mm, b&w, 40 mins

Jean-Marie Straub

2008   *Artemide's Knee (Le Genou d'Artemide)*, Italy/France, 35mm, colour, 26 mins (first version), 27 mins (second version)

2009   *The Witches — Women among Themselves (Le streghe — Femmes entre elles)*, France/Italy, 35mm, colour, 21 mins

2009   *Corneille — Brecht*, France, MiniDV, colour, 26 mins (3 versions)

2009   *Joachim Gatti*, France, HD, colour, 1 min. 30 secs

2010   *O somma luce* [Oh Supreme Light], Italy/France, HD, colour, 18 mins (2 versions)

2011   *Jackals and Arabs (Schakale und Araber)*, France, MiniDV, colour, 10 mins (2 versions)

2011   *The Inconsolable One (L'Inconsolable)*, Italy, MiniDV, colour, 15 mins (2 versions)

2011   *An Heir (Un héritier)*, France, MiniDV, colour, 20 mins (version 1), 21 mins (version 2)

2012   *The Mother (La madre)*, Italy, HD, colour, 20 mins (3 versions)

2013   *A Tale by Michel de Montaigne (Un conte de Michel de Montaigne)*, France, HD, colour, 34 mins

2013   *The Death of Venice (La Mort de Venise)*, France, HD, colour, 2 mins

2014   *Dialogue of Shadows (Dialogue d'ombres)*, France, HD, colour, 28 mins ['A film by Jean-Marie Straub and Danièle Huillet (1954–2013)', opening credits. Assistant director: Barbara Ulrich]

2014   *Concerning Venice (History Lessons) (À propos de Venise (Geschichtsunterricht))*, Switzerland, HD, colour and b/w, 23 mins [directed with Barbara Ulrich]

2014   *Communists (Kommunisten)*, Switzerland/France, HD, colour, 70 mins

2014   *The Algerian War!* (*La Guerre d'Algérie!*), France, HD, colour, 2 mins
2015   *The Aquarium and the Nation* (*L'Aquarium et la Nation*), France, HD, colour, 31 mins
2015   *For Renato* (*Pour Renato*), Switzerland, HD, colour, 8 mins
2015   *Homage to Italian Art!* (*In omaggio all'arte Italiana!*), Italy, DV, colour, 9 mins [installation at the 2015 Venice Biennale]
2016   *Where Are You, Jean-Marie Straub?* (*Où en êtes-vous, Jean-Marie Straub?*), France/ Switzerland, HD, colour, 15 mins
2018   *People of the Lake* (*Gens du lac*), Switzerland, HD, colour, 18 mins
2020   *France Against Robots* (*La France contre les robots*), Switzerland, HD, colour, 10 mins (2 versions)

BIBLIOGRAPHY

❖

ADORNO, THEODOR W., *Gesammelte Schriften*, ed. by Rolf Tiedemann and Klaus Schultz, 20 vols (Frankfurt am Main: Suhrkamp, 1970–86)

——*Minima Moralia: Reflections from Damaged Life*, trans. by E. F. N. Jephcott (London & New York: Verso, 2020)

——*Philosophie der neuen Musik* (Frankfurt am Main: Suhrkamp, 1978)

——*Quasi una Fantasia: Essays on Modern Music*, trans. by Rodney Livingstone (London & New York: Verso, 1998)

——'Transparencies on Film', trans. by Thomas Y. Levin, *New German Critique*, 24–25 (1981–82), 199–205

ADORNO, THEODOR W., and MAX HORKHEIMER, *Dialectic of Enlightenment*, trans. by John Cumming (London: Verso, 1979)

ALBERA, FRANÇOIS, 'Sickle and Hammer, Cannons, Cannons, Dynamite!' [interview with Danièle Huillet and Jean-Marie Straub], in *Jean-Marie Straub & Danièle Huillet*, ed. by Ted Fendt (Vienna: SYNEMA, 2016), pp. 109–25

ALBRECHT, NICOLA, *Verschollen im Meer der Medien: Kafkas Romanfragment 'Amerika': zur Rekonstruktion und Deutung eines Medienkomplexes* (Heidelberg: Winter, 2006)

ALIGHIERI, DANTE, *The Divine Comedy*, trans. by Robin Kirkpatrick (London: Penguin Classics, 2012)

ANDREW, DUDLEY, 'Adaptation', in *Film Adaptation*, ed. by James Naremore (New Brunswick, NJ: Rutgers University Press, 2000), pp. 28–37

[ANON.], 'Die Revolution ist kein Deckensticken: Wang kuang-me, Chinas erste Dame, im Rotgardisten-Verhör', *Spiegel* 14 (1968), 132–35 <https://www.spiegel.de/politik/die-revolution-ist-kein-deckchenstickeni-a-af8a64c6-0002-0001-0000-000046094011> [accessed 26 January 2022]

AUMONT, JACQUES, 'The Invention of Place: Danièle Huillet and Jean-Marie Straub's *Moses and Aaron*', trans. by Kevin Shelton and Martin Lefebvre, in *Landscape and Film*, ed. by Martin Lefebvre (London & New York: Routledge, 2006), pp. 1–18

BARNETT, DAVID, and TOM KUHN, eds, *Recycling Brecht*, Brecht Yearbook 42 (Rochester: Camden House, 2017)

BARR, BURLIN, 'Too Close, Too Far: Cultural Composition in Straub and Huillet's *Too Early, Too Late*', *Camera Obscura*, 53 (2003), 1–25

BARTHES, ROLAND, *Image Music Text*, ed. and trans. by Stephen Heath (London: Fontana, 1977)

——*The Rustle of Language*, trans. by Richard Howard (Berkeley: University of California Press, 1989)

BATES, DAVID, ed., *Marxism, Intellectuals and Politics* (Basingstoke: Palgrave Macmillan, 2007)

BECHER, JOHANNES R., 'Selbstzensur', *Sinn und Form*, 40 (1988), 543–51

BENJAMIN, WALTER, *The Arcades Project*, trans. by Howard Eiland and Kevin McLaughlin (Cambridge, MA, & London: Harvard University Press, 1999)

——*Illuminations*, ed. by Hannah Arendt, trans. by Harry Zohn (London: Bodley Head, 2015)

——— *One Way Street and Other Writings*, trans. by Edmund Jephcott (London & New York: Verso, 1985)

——— *Understanding Brecht* (London & New York: Verso, 1998)

BERGSON, HENRI, *Matter and Memory*, trans. by Nancy Margaret Paul and W. Scott Palmer (New York: Zone, 1991)

BERNAUER, BARBARA, WOLFRAM SCHÜTTE, and F. W. VÖBEL, 'Gespräch mit Jean-Marie Straub', *Filmstudio*, 48 (1966), 2–9

BERTA, RENATO, 'Portfolio: Photographs and Commentary', in Jean-Marie Straub and Danièle Huillet, *Writings*, ed. and trans. by Sally Shafto (New York: Sequence Press, 2016), pp. 525–43

BERTA, RENATO, and RINALDO CENSI, 'When the Image Doesn't Exist Yet', in *Tell It to the Stones: Encounters with the Films of Danièle Huillet and Jean-Marie Straub*, ed. by Annett Busch and Tobias Hering (London: Sternberg, 2021), pp. 424–32

BIETTE, JEAN-CLAUDE, 'Jean Marie Straub: "Le Fiancé, la comédienne et le maquereau"', *Cahiers du cinéma*, 212 (1969), 9–10

BLANCHOT, MAURICE, *The Infinite Conversation*, trans. by Susan Hanson (Minneapolis & London: University of Minnesota Press, 1993)

BLANK, MANFRED, 'Wie will ich lustig lachen, wenn alles durcheinandergeht', *Filmkritik*, 28 (1984), 269–82

BLUM, STEPHEN, 'Kurtág's Articulation of Kafka's Rhythms ("Kafka-Fragmente", op. 24)', *Studia Musicologica Academiae Scientiarum Hungaricae*, 43 (2002), 345–58

BÖLL, HEINRICH, *Billard um halbzehn* (Cologne & Berlin: Kiepenheuer & Witsch, 1959)

——— *Billiards at Half Past Nine*, trans. by Patrick Bowles (London: Marion Boyars, 1987)

BONSAVER, GUIDO, *Elio Vittorini: The Writer and the Written* (Leeds: Northern Universities Press, 2000)

BÖSER, URSULA, *The Art of Seeing, the Art of Listening: The Politics of Representation in the Work of Jean-Marie Straub and Danièle Huillet* (Frankfurt am Main: Peter Lang, 2004)

BOTROS, ATEF, *Kafka: ein jüdischer Schriftsteller aus arabischer Sicht* (Wiesbaden: Reichert, 2009)

BRADY, MARTIN, '"Du Tag, wann wirst du sein...": Quotation, Emancipation and Dissonance in Straub/Huillet's *Der Bräutigam, die Komödiantin und der Zuhälter*', *German Life and Letters*, 53.3 (2000), 281–302

BRECHT, BERTOLT, *Brecht on Art and Politics*, ed. by Tom Kuhn and Steve Giles (London & New York: Bloomsbury, 2003)

——— *Brecht on Theatre*, ed. by Marc Silberman, Steve Giles, and Tom Kuhn, 3rd edn (London: Bloomsbury, 2015)

——— *Brecht on Theatre: The Development of an Aesthetic*, ed. and trans. by John Willett (London: Eyre Methuen, 1964; 1978)

——— *Collected Plays*, ed. by Tom Kuhn and David Constantine, 8 vols (London: Methuen, 1970–2003)

——— 'Intellectuals and Class Struggle', trans. by David Bathrick, *New German Critique*, 1 (1973), 19–21

——— *Werke: Große kommentierte Berliner und Frankfurter Ausgabe*, ed. by Werner Hecht and others, 30 vols (Berlin, Weimar, & Frankfurt am Main: Aufbau, Suhrkamp, 1988–2000)

BRESSON, ROBERT, *Notes on the Cinematographer*, trans. by Jonathan Griffin (London: Quartet Books, 1986)

BROD, MAX, 'Unsere Literaten und die Gemeinschaft', *Der Jude*, 1.7 (1916), 457–64

BRUCE, IRIS, 'Kafka's Journey into the Future: Crossing Borders into Israeli/Palestinian Worlds', in *Kafka for the Twenty-First Century*, ed. by Stanley Corngold and Ruth V. Gross (Rochester & New York: Camden House, 2011), pp. 222–36

BUBER, MARTIN, 'Die Losung', *Der Jude*, 1.1 (1916–17), 1–3

BUCK-MORSS, SUSAN, *The Dialectics of Seeing: Walter Benjamin and the Arcades Project* (Cambridge, MA, & London: MIT, 1989)

BURDEAU, EMMANUEL, and JEAN-MICHEL FRODON, 'L'Important est l'éventail', *Cahiers du cinéma*, 616 (2006), 36-39

——'Encounter with Jean-Marie Straub and Danièle Huillet: *Quei loro incontri*', trans. by Ted Fendt <http://www.elumiere.net/exclusivo_web/internacional_straub/textos/interview_quei_loro_incontri.php> [accessed 8 March 2021]

BUSCH, ANNETT, and TOBIAS HERING, eds, *Tell It to The Stones: Encounters with the Films of Danièle Huillet and Jean-Marie Straub* (London: Sternberg, 2021)

BUTLER, JUDITH, 'Who Owns Kafka?', *London Review of Books*, 3 March 2011 <https://www.lrb.co.uk/the-paper/v33/n05/judith-butler-who-owns-kafka> [accessed 17 June 2021]

BYG, BARTON, *Landscapes of Resistance: The German Films of Danièle Huillet and Jean-Marie Straub* (Berkeley, Los Angeles & London: University of California Press, 1995)

CAFFONI, PAOLO, 'A Revolutionary Copywriter: Franco Fortini and his Relations to Film', in *Tell It to the Stones: Encounters with the Films of Danièle Huillet and Jean-Marie Straub*, ed. by Annett Busch and Tobias Hering (London: Sternberg, 2021), pp. 160-81

CAHIERS, 'Questions à Jean-Marie Straub', *Cahiers du cinéma*, 224 (1970), 40-42

CAPUTO, RINO, 'Dante by Heart and Dante Declaimed: The "Realization" of the *Comedy* on Italian Radio and Television', in *Dante, Cinema, and Television*, ed. by Amilcare A. Iannucci (Toronto: University of Toronto Press, 2004), pp. 213-23

CAVALLO, JOANN [*sic*], 'Where Have All the Brave Knights Gone? Sicilian Puppet Theater and the Tuscan-Emilian Epic *Maggio*', *Italian Culture*, 19.2 (2001), 31-55

CERTEAU, MICHEL DE, LUCE GIARD, and PIERRE MAYOL, *The Practice of Everyday Life: Vol. 2: Living and Cooking*, trans by Timothy J. Tomaskik (Minneapolis & London: University of Minnesota Press, 1998)

CHEVRIE, MARC, and HERVÉ LE ROUX, 'Site and Speech: An Interview with Claude Lanzmann about *Shoah*', in *Claude Lanzmann's Shoah: Key Essays*, ed. by Stuart Liebman (New York: Oxford University Press, 2007), pp. 37-50

CHION, MICHEL, *Audio-Vision: Sound on Screen*, ed. and trans. by Claudia Gorbman (New York: Columbia University Press, 1994)

CONDORELLI, CÉLINE, 'Speaking of Revolutions: Too Early, Too Late' [interview with Jean-Marie Straub], 20 March 2011 <https://lux.org.uk/writing/speaking-of-revolutions-too-early-too-late> [accessed 21 December 2021]

COSGROVE, DENIS E., *Social Formation and Symbolic Landscape* (Madison: University of Wisconsin Press, 1998)

DANEY, SERGE, 'Cinemeteorology', in *The Cinema of Jean-Marie Straub and Daniele* [*sic*] *Huillet* [Film at the Public brochure, 1982] <https://www.straub-huillet.com/wp-content/uploads/2016/05/brochure-cinema1.pdf> [accessed 20 December 2021]

——'A Tomb for the Eye (Straubian Pedagogy)', trans. by Stoffel Debuysere and others <http://sergedaney.blogspot.com/2014/09/a-tomb-for-eye-straubian-pedagogy.html> [accessed 7 August 2021]

DEBORD, GUY, *Society of the Spectacle* (London: Rebel Press/ AIM, 1987)

DELAHAYE, MICHEL, 'Entretien avec J.-M. Straub', *Cahiers du cinéma*, 180 (1966), 52-57

DELEUZE, GILLES, *Cinema 2: The Time Image*, trans. by Hugh Tomlinson and Robert Galeta (London: Athlone Press, 1989; Minneapolis: University of Minneapolis Press, 1997; London & New York: Continuum, 2005)

DELEUZE, GILLES, and FÉLIX GUATTARI, *Kafka: Toward a Minor Literature*, trans. by Dana Polan (Minneapolis & London: University of Minnesota Press, 1975)

DIDI-HUBERMAN, GEORGES, *The Eye of History: When Images Take Positions*, trans. by Shane B. Lillis (Cambridge, MA, & London: MIT, 2018)

——'The Site, Despite Everything', in *Claude Lanzmann's Shoah: Key Essays*, ed. by Stuart Liebman (New York: Oxford University Press, 2007), pp. 113-23

DILTHEY, WILHELM, *Introduction to the Human Sciences*, ed. by Rudolf A. Makkreel and Frithjof Rodi (Princeton, NJ: Princeton University Press, 1989)

——*Selected Writings*, ed. and trans. by H. P. Rickman (Cambridge: Cambridge University Press 1976)

DUBOIS, PHILIPPE, 'The Written Screen: JLG and Writing as the Accursed Share', in *For Ever Godard*, ed. by Michael Temple, James S. Williams, and Michael Witt (London: Black Dog Publishing), pp. 232–49

DURET, JEAN-PIERRE, 'At Work with Straub and Huillet: Thoughts and Reflections from their Collaborators', in *Jean-Marie Straub & Danièle Huillet*, ed. by Ted Fendt (Vienna: SYNEMA, 2016), pp. 127-38

ECO, UMBERTO, *The Open Work*, trans. by Anna Cancogni (New York: Hutchinson Radius, 1989)

EISENSTEIN, SERGEI, *Nonindifferent Nature*, trans. by Herbert Marshall (Cambridge: Cambridge University Press, 1987)

ENGEL, ANDI, 'Andi Engel Talks to Jean-Marie Straub, and Danièle Huillet is There Too' [interview with Jean-Marie Straub and Daniçle Huillet], *Enthusiasm*, 1 (1975), 1-25

FAIRFAX, DANIEL, *The Red Years of Cahiers du Cinéma (1968–1973)*, 2 vols (Amsterdam: Amsterdam University Press, 2021)

——'Straub/Huillet's Ecological Communism', *Senses of Cinema*, 92 (2019) <https://www.sensesofcinema.com/2019/jean-marie-straub-daniele-huillet/straub-huillets-ecological-communism/> [accessed 29 December 2021]

FAROCKI, HARUN, 'Stop Coughing!', in *Jean-Marie Straub & Danièle Huillet*, ed. by Ted Fendt (Vienna: SYNEMA, 2016), pp. 154-55

FENDT, TED, ed., *Jean-Marie Straub & Danièle Huillet* (Vienna: SYNEMA, 2016)

FERZOCO, GEORGE, 'Changes', in *Vertical Readings in Dante's Comedy*, ed. by George Corbett and Heather Webb, 3 vols (Cambridge: Open Book, 2015-17), III, 51-69

FIESCHI, JEAN-ANDRÉ, 'Jean-Marie Straub and Danièle Huillet', trans. by Michael Graham, <https://kinoslang.blogspot.com/2019/07/jean-marie-straub-daniele-huillet-by-j.html> [accessed 22 May 2022]

FORTINI, FRANCO, *The Dogs of the Sinai*, trans. by Alberto Toscano (London, New York & Calcutta: Seagull Books, 2013)

——*A Test of Powers: Writings on Criticism and Literary Institutions*, trans. by Alberto Toscano (London, New York & Calcutta: Seagull Books, 2016)

FREY, HANS-JOST, *Der unendliche Text* (Frankfurt am Main: Suhrkamp, 1990)

FRIED, MICHAEL, *Absorption and Theatricality: Painting and Beholder in the Age of Diderot* (Chicago: University of Chicago Press, 1976)

GELLER, JAY, 'Kafka's "Schakale und Araber" and the Question of Genre', in *Orientalism, Gender, and the Jews: Literary and Artistic Transformations of European National Discourses*, ed. by Ulrike Brunotte, Anna-Dorothea Ludewig, and Axel Stähler (Berlin & Boston: Walter De Gruyter/ Oldenbourg, 2014), pp. 124-36

GENET, JEAN, *Prisoner of Love*, trans. by Barbara Bray (New York: New York Review Books, 2003)

GRAMSCI, ANTONIO, *Selections from the Prison Notebooks*, ed. and trans. by Quintin Hoare and Geoffrey Nowell-Smith (London: Lawrence & Wishart, 2003)

GREENFIELD, LUISA, 'History Lessons by Comparison', in *Tell It to the Stones: Encounters with the Films of Danièle Huillet and Jean-Marie Straub*, ed. by Annett Busch and Tobias Hering (London: Sternberg, 2021), pp. 268-92

GRIFFITHS, PAUL, *Modern Music and After* (Oxford: Oxford University Press, 2010)

HALBWACHS, MAURICE, *On Collective Memory*, ed. and trans by Lewis A. Coser (Chicago & London: University of Chicago Press, 1992)

HALL, STUART, *Essential Essays*, ed. by David Morley, 2 vols (Durham, NC: Duke University Press, 2019)

HANSSEN, JENS, 'Kafka and Arabs', *Critical Inquiry*, 39.1 (2012), 167–97

HEBERLE, HELGE, and MONIKA FUNKE STERN, 'The Fire Inside the Mountain: A Conversation with Danièle Huillet', trans. by John Crutchfield, in *Tell It to the Stones: Encounters with the Films of Danièle Huillet and Jean-Marie Straub*, ed. by Annett Busch and Tobias Hering (London: Sternberg Press, 2021), pp. 250–64

HILL, LESLIE, ' "O Himmlisch Licht!": Cinema and the Withdrawal of the Gods (Straub-Huillet, Hölderlin, Godard, Brecht)', *Angelaki*, 17.4 (2012), 139–55

HILZINGER, KLAUS HARRO, 'Montage des Zitats: zur Struktur der Dokumentarstücke von Peter Weiss', in *Peter Weiss*, ed. by Rainer Gerlach (Frankfurt am Main: Suhrkamp, 1984), pp. 268–82

HÖLDERLIN, FRIEDRICH, *The Death of Empedocles: A Mourning-Play*, trans. by David Farrell Krell (Albany: State University of New York Press, 2008)

HOLL, UTE, *The Moses Complex: Freud, Schoenberg, Straub/Huillet*, trans by Michael Turnbull (Zurich & Berlin: Diaphanes, 2017)

HUILLET, DANIÈLE, and JEAN-MARIE STRAUB, 'Introduction to Arnold Schoenberg's Accompaniment to a Cinematographic Scene — Scenario', *Screen*, 17.1 (1976), 77–83

HUILLET, DANIÈLE, JEAN-MARIE STRAUB, and FRANCO FORTINI, 'Pressekonferenz in Pesaro', *Filmkritik*, 247 (1977), 4–13

HURCH, HANS, '*Too Early, Too Late*: Interview with Huillet and Straub', trans. by Ben Brewster <http://kinoslang.blogspot.com/2014/08/too-early-too-late-interview-with.html> [accessed 27 July 2021]

HUSSEIN, MAHMOUD, *Class Conflict in Egypt: 1945–1971*, trans. by Michel Chirman and others (New York & London: Monthly Review Press, 1973)

JAMESON, FREDERIC, 'Adaptation as a Philosophical Problem', in *True to the Spirit: Film Adaptation and the Question of Fidelity*, ed. by Colin MacCabe, Kathleen Murray, and Rick Warner (Oxford & New York: Oxford University Press, 2011), pp. 215–33

JENNINGS, JEREMY, and TONY KEMP-WELCH, eds, *Intellectuals in Politics: From the Dreyfus Affair to Salman Rushdie* (London & New York: Routledge, 1997)

KAFKA, FRANZ, *Schriften: Tagebücher: Kritische Ausgabe*, ed. by Jürgen Born and others, 15 vols (Frankfurt am Main: Fischer, 2002)

——'Zwei Tiergeschichten: 1. Schakale und Araber', *Der Jude: Eine Monatschrift*, 2.7 (1917-18), 488–90

KAMMERER, PETER, and PATRICK PRIMAVESI, 'Work, Progress: On the Resistance of Peasants in the Work of Straub, Huillet, and Heiner Müller', in *Tell It to the Stones: Encounters with the Films of Danièle Huillet and Jean-Marie Straub*, ed. by Annett Busch and Tobias Hering (London: Sternberg Press, 2021), pp. 196–217

KANT, IMMANUEL, *Critique of Judgment*, trans. by Werner S. Pluhar (Indianapolis & Cambridge: Hackett, 1987)

KIRKPATRICK, ROBIN, *Dante's Paradiso and the Limitations of Modern Criticism: A Study of Style and Poetic Theory* (Cambridge: Cambridge University Press, 1978)

——'Introduction', in Dante Alighieri, *The Divine Comedy*, trans. by Robin Kirkpatrick (London: Penguin Classics, 2012), pp. ix-lvi

LENIN, VLADIMIR ILYICH, *What is to Be Done? Burning Questions of Our Movement*, trans. by Joe Fineberg and George Hanna (New York: International Publishers, 1969)

LESLIE, ESTHER, 'Anti-Fascism, Anti-Art, Doubt and Despair', *Third Text*, 33.3 (2019), 293-313

LUKÁCS, GYÖRGY, *The Theory of the Novel: A Historico-philosophical Essay on the Forms of Great Epic Literature*, trans. by Anna Bostock (London: Merlin Press, 1978)

LUXEMBURG, ROSA, *The Rosa Luxemburg Reader*, ed. by Peter Hudis and Kevin B. Anderson (New York: Monthly Review Press, 2004)

LYLOV, MIKHAIL, and ELKE MARHÖFER, 'A Thousand Cliffs' [interview with Jean-Marie Straub], in *Tell It to the Stones: Encounters with the Films of Danièle Huillet and Jean-Marie Straub*, ed. by Annett Busch and Tobias Hering (London: Sternberg Press, 2021), pp. 364–90

LYOTARD, JEAN-FRANÇOIS, *The Inhuman: Reflections on Time*, trans. by Geoffrey Bennington and Rachel Bowlby (Stanford, CA: Stanford University Press, 1991)

MABEY, RICHARD, *The Unofficial Countryside* (Stanbridge: Little Toller Books, 2010)

MACCABE, COLIN, 'Introduction: Bazinian Adaptation: *The Butcher Boy* as Example', in *True to the Spirit: Film Adaptation and the Question of Fidelity*, ed. by Colin MacCabe, Kathleen Murray, Rick Warner (Oxford & New York: Oxford University Press, 2011), pp. 3–26

MADSEN, JANE, 'Cutting Through the Seventies to Find the Thirties: A Consideration of "Fortini-Cani" as Marxist Reflection', in *History on/and/in Film*, ed. by T. O'Regan and B. Shoesmith (Perth: History & Film Association of Australia, 1987), pp. 159–65 <https://fremantlestuff.info/readingroom/hfilm/MADSEN.html > [accessed 30 December 2022]

MALIGNE, ALICE, 'Questions à Harun Farocki', *Revue de recherche sur l'art du XIX au XXI siècle 2.0.1.*, 1 (2008), 61–70

MATTICK, PAUL, *Anti-Bolshevik Communism* (London & New York: Routledge, 2018)

McFARLANE, BRIAN, *Novel to Film: An Introduction to the Theory of Adaptation* (Oxford: Clarendon Press, 1996)

METZ, CHRISTIAN, 'Aural Objects', trans. by Georgia Gurrieri, *Yale French Studies*, 60 (1980), 24–32

MEYNIER, FABIEN, 'Dépaysements géographiques, perceptifs et historiques dans le film *Fortini/Cani* de Jean-Marie Straub et Danièle Huillet', *L'Entre-deux*, 4 (2018) <https://lentre-deux.com/index.php?b=58> [accessed 5 August 2021]

MEZZADRI, BERNARD, 'Interview: No Appeasement' [interview with Danièle Huillet], in Danièle Huillet and Jean-Marie Straub, *Writings*, ed. and trans. by Sally Shafto (New York: Sequence Press, 2016), pp. 252–53

MÜLLER, LOTHAR, 'Performance and Recitation', in *Franz Kafka in Context*, ed. by Carolin Duttlinger (Cambridge: Cambridge University Press, 2018), pp. 100–08

NARBONI, JEAN, 'Là', *Cahiers du cinéma*, 275 (1977), 6–14

NAREMORE, JAMES, ed., *Film Adaptation* (New Brunswick, NJ: Rutgers University Press, 2000)

NASH, MARK, and STEVE NEALE, 'Film: "History/Production/Memory"', *Screen*, 18.4 (1977), 77–91

NIETZSCHE, FRIEDRICH, *Dionysian-Dithyrambs* <http://www.thenietzschechannel.com/works-pub/dd/dd.htm> [accessed 6 May 2021]

—— *Thus Spake Zarathustra: A Book for All and None* <https://www.gutenberg.org/files/1998/1998-h/1998-h.htm> [accessed 12 March 2021]

NOWELL-SMITH, GEOFFREY, 'After "Othon", Before "History Lessons": Geoffrey Nowell-Smith Talks to Jean-Marie Straub and Danièle Huillet', *Enthusiasm*, 1 (1975), 26–31

—— 'Fortini-Cani: Introduction', *Screen*, 19.2 (1978), 9–10

OSBORNE, PETER, ed., *A Critical Sense: Interviews with Intellectuals* (London & New York: Routledge, 1996)

PEREZ, GILBERTO, *The Material Ghost: Films and their Medium* (Baltimore, MD: John Hopkins University Press, 1998)

——'The Modernist Cinema: The History Lessons of Straub and Huillet', in *The Cinema of Jean-Marie Straub and Daniele [sic] Huillet* [Film at the Public brochure, 1982] <https://www.straub-huillet.com/wp-content/uploads/2016/05/brochure-cinema1.pdf> [accessed 20 December 2021]

POLLMANN, INGA, 'Invisible Worlds, Visible: Uexküll's *Umwelt*, Film and Film Theory', *Critical Inquiry*, 39 (2013), 777-816

PRIMAVESI, PATRICK, 'Violence and the Stones', in *Tell It to the Stones: Encounters with the Films of Danièle Huillet and Jean-Marie Straub*, ed. by Annett Busch and Tobias Hering (London: Sternberg, 2021), pp. 478-93

PUMMER, CLAUDIA, 'Elective Affinities: The Films of Daniele Huillet and Jean-Marie Straub' (doctoral thesis, University of Iowa, 2011) <https://ir.uiowa.edu/etd/2761/> [accessed 27 August 2021]

——'(Not Only) for Children and Cavemen: The Films of Jean-Marie Straub and Danièle Huillet', in *Jean-Marie Straub and Danièle Huillet*, ed. by Ted Fendt (Vienna: SYNEMA, 2016), pp. 7-95

QUANDT, JAMES, 'Operatic Tenor: Straub and Huillet's *Sicilia!*', *Artforum*, 9 (2016) <https://www.artforum.com/print/201605/operatic-tenor-straub-and-huillet-s-sicilia-59536> [accessed 2 November 2021]

RAMOS-MARTÍNEZ, MANUEL, '"Actors Simply Explode": To Act in the Cinema of Jean-Marie Straub and Danièle Huillet', *Camera Obscura*, 31.2 (2016), 93-117

——'Marx Immemorial: Workers and Peasants in the Cinema of Jean-Marie Straub and Danièle Huillet', in *Marxism and Film Activism: Screening Alternative Worlds*, ed. by Ewa Mazierska and Lars Kristensen (New York: Berghahn, 2015), pp. 105-23

RANCIÈRE, JACQUES, *The Ignorant Schoolmaster: Five Lessons in Intellectual Emancipation*, trans. by Kristin Ross (Stanford, CA: Stanford University Press, 1991)

——*The Intervals of Cinema*, trans. by John Howe (London & New York: Verso, 2019)

——*Staging the People: The Proletarian and his Double*, trans. by David Fernbach (London & New York: Verso, 2011)

RANCIÈRE, JACQUES, and PHILIPPE LAFOSSE, 'Politics and Aesthetics in the Straubs' Films', trans. by Ted Fendt <https://mubi.com/notebook/posts/politics-and-aesthetics-in-the-straubs-films> [accessed 29 December 2021]

RAUH, REINHOLD, ed., *Machorka-Muff: Jean-Marie Straubs und Danièle Huillets Verfilmung einer Satire von Heinrich Böll* (Münster: MAkS Publikationen, 1988)

ROBERTSON, RITCHIE, *Kafka: Judaism, Politics and Literature* (Oxford: Oxford University Press, 1985)

ROGERS, JOEL, 'Jean-Marie Straub and Danièle Huillet Interviewed: *Moses and Aaron* as an object of Marxist reflection', *Jump Cut*, 12-13 (1976), 61-64 <https://www.ejumpcut.org/archive/onlinessays/jc12–13folder/moses.int.html> [accessed 20 December 2021]

ROSENTHAL, MICHAEL A., 'Art and the Politics of the Desert: German Exiles in California and the Biblical "Bilderverbot"', *New German Critique*, 118 (2013), 46-53

ROTHBERG, MICHAEL, *Multidirectional Memory: Remembering the Holocaust in the Age of Decolonization* (Stanford, CA: Stanford University Press, 2009)

ROUD, RICHARD, *Jean-Marie Straub* (London: Secker & Warburg/BFI, 1971)

RUSSELL, CATHERINE, *Archiveology: Walter Benjamin and Archival Film Practices* (Durham, NC, & London: Duke University Press, 2018)

SAID, EDWARD, 'Invention, Memory and Place', in *Landscape and Power*, ed. by W. J. T. Mitchell (Chicago: University of Chicago Press, 2002), pp. 241-59

SARTRE, JEAN-PAUL, *Being and Nothingness: A Phenomenological Essay on Ontology*, trans. by Hazel E. Barnes (New York, London, Toronto & Sydney: Simon & Schuster, 1992)

SCHÖNBERG, ARNOLD, *Letters*, ed. by Erwin Stein (London: Faber & Faber, 1987)

SCHÖNBERG, ARNOLD, MAX BLONDA, DANIÈLE HUILLET and JEAN-MARIE STRAUB, *Von heute auf morgen: Oper / Musik / Film*, ed. by Klaus Volkmer, Klaus Kalchschmid and Patrick Primavesi (Berlin: Vorwerk 8, 1997)

SCHOTT, WEBSTER, 'Elio Vitttorini's Hoping and Nonhoping', in Elio Vittorini, *Women of Messina*, trans. by Frances Frenaye and Frances Keene (New York: New Directions, 1973), no page numbers

SCHÜTTE, WOLFRAM, ed., *Klassenverhältnisse: Von Danièle Huillet und Jean-Marie Straub nach dem Amerika-Roman 'Der Verschollene' von Franz Kafka* (Frankfurt am Main: Fischer Verlag, 1984)

SHUMSKY, DIMITRY, 'Czechs, Germans, Arabs, Jews: Franz Kafka's "Jackals and Arabs" between Bohemia and Palestine', *AJS Review*, 33 (2009), 71-100

SIMMEL, GEORG, *Essays on Art and Aesthetics*, ed. and trans. by Austin Harrington (Chicago & London: University of Chicago Press, 2020)

——'The Philosophy of Landscape', trans. by Josef Bleicher, *Theory, Culture and Society*, 24.7-8 (2007), 20-29

——'The Picture Frame: An Aesthetic Study', trans. by Mark Ritter, *Theory, Culture and Society*, 11.1 (1994), 11-17

SKORECKI, LOUIS, 'Qui est Farocki?', in *Cahiers du cinéma*, 329 (1981), 8

STAM, ROBERT, 'Beyond Fidelity: The Dialogics of Adaptation', in *Film Adaptation*, ed. by James Naremore (New Brunswick, NJ: Rutgers University Press, 2000), pp. 54–76

STENDHAL, *Scarlet and Black*, trans. by Margaret Shaw (Harmondsworth: Penguin Books, 1978)

STRASCHEK, GÜNTER PETER, 'Filmkritik: Straschek 1963-74, West Berlin', in *Günter Peter Straschek: Film — Emigration — Politik*, ed. by Julia Friedrich (Cologne: Museum Ludwig, 2018), pp. 162-81

STRAUB, JEAN-MARIE, 'Der Bräutigam, die Komödiantin und der Zuhälter', *Filmkritik*, 10 (1968), 677-87

——'"Le Fiancé, la comédienne et le maquereau" de Jean-Marie Straub', *Cahiers du cinéma*, 205 (1968), 15

——'Jean-Marie Straub', *Cahiers du cinéma*, 400 (supplement) (1987), 48

STRAUB, JEAN-MARIE, and DANIÈLE HUILLET, 'Fortini-Cani: Script', *Screen*, 19.2 (1978), 11-40

——*Writings*, ed. and trans. by Sally Shafto (New York: Sequence Press, 2016)

SYMMONS ROBERTS, MICHAEL, and PAUL FAIRLY, *Edgelands* (London: Vintage, 2012)

THÉORIE COMMUNISTE, 'Much Ado about Nothing', *Endnotes*, 1 (2008), 154-206

TOSCANO, ALBERTO, 'The Non-State Intellectual: Franco Fortini and Communist Criticism', in Franco Fortini, *The Dogs of the Sinai*, trans. by Alberto Toscano (London, New York & Calcutta: Seagull Books, 2013), pp. 89-129

——'Translator's Introduction: The Labour of Division', in Franco Fortini, *A Test of Powers: Writings on Criticism and Literary Institutions*, trans. by Alberto Toscano (London, New York & Calcutta: Seagull Books, 2016), pp. 1-55

TRINH, MINH-HA T., *Framer Framed* (New York: Routledge, 1992)

TURQUETY, BENOÎT, *Danièle Huillet, Jean-Marie Straub: 'Objectivists' in Cinema*, trans. by Ted Fendt (Amsterdam: Amsterdam University Press, 2020)

——'Orality and Objectification: Danièle Huillet and Jean-Marie Straub, Filmmakers and Translators', *SubStance*, 44.2 (2015), 47-65

ULMAN, ERIK, '*A Corner in Wheat*: An Analysis', *Senses of Cinema*, 14 (2001) <https://www.sensesofcinema.com/2001/feature-articles/cornerwheat/#11> [accessed 20 December 2021]

ULRICH, BARBARA, '"Hast du nicht alles mir gesagt?" and Hölderlin's *Native Reversal* as Response', in *Tell It to the Stones: Encounters with the Films of Danièle Huillet and Jean-Marie Straub*, ed. by Annett Busch and Tobias Hering (London: Sternberg Press, 2021), pp. 140-57

UNGARI, ENZO, 'Interview on Direct Sound' [interview with Danièle Huillet and Jean-Marie Straub], in Jean-Marie Straub and Danièle Huillet, *Writings*, ed. and trans. by Sally Shafto (New York: Sequence Press, 2016), pp. 156-60

VITTORINI, ELIO, *Conversazione in Sicilia* (Milan: Bompiani, 1941)

—— *Conversazione in Sicilia,* ed. by Robert C. Powell (Manchester: Manchester University Press, 1978)

—— *Conversations in Sicily*, trans. by Alane Salierno Mason (Edinburgh: Canongate, 2003)

—— *Women of Messina*, trans. by Frances Frenaye and Frances Keene (New York: New Directions, 1973)

WALSH, MARTIN, *The Brechtian Aspect of Radical Cinema: Essays* (London: BFI, 1981)

WARNER, RICK, '*Contempt* Revisited: Godard at the Margins of Adaptation', in *True to the Spirit: Film Adaptation and the Question of Fidelity*, ed. by Colin MacCabe, Kathleen Murray, and Rick Warner (Oxford & New York: Oxford University Press, 2011), pp. 195–213

WEIL, SIMONE, *Gravity and Grace*, trans. by Emma Crawford and Mario von der Ruhr (London: Routledge, 2002)

WENDERS, WIM, *The Logic of Images: Essays and Conversations*, trans. by Michael Hofmann (London & Boston: Faber & Faber, 1991)

WILLIAMS, RAYMOND, *Keywords: A Vocabulary of Culture and Society* (London: Fontana, 1983)

WITTE, KARSTEN, 'Interview' [interview with Danièle Huillet and Jean-Marie Straub], in *Herzog/Kluge/Straub*, ed. by Peter W. Jansen and Wolfram Schütte (Munich & Vienna: Carl Hanser, 1976), pp. 205-18

WOLLEN, PETER, *Readings and Writings: Semiotic Counter-Strategies* (London: Verso/NLB, 1982)

EPILOGUE

❖

'Be gone, you image of powerlessness to enclose the boundless in an image finite!'
— Arnold Schoenberg, *Moses and Aaron* (Act ii, Scene 4)★

Fig. E.1. Ernesto: 'It's a football, a potato and the earth.'
Danièle Huillet and Jean-Marie Straub, *En rachâchant*
(1983, Courtesy of BELVA Film).

★ The music opening this scene, in which Moses descends from Mount Sinai with the tablets, is heard in four films of Huillet and Straub: *Moses and Aaron, Fortini/Cani, Too Early, Too Late,* and *En rachâchant* (twice).

INDEX

❖

acting (performance) 6, 13, 16, 17–18, 39, 61–62, 63, 65–67, 72, 91, 92, 100, 104–05, 111, 118, 121, 123–25, 127, 129, 130, 134, 137, 138 n. 14, 169, 170–74, 175, 180 n. 38, 192, 197–98, 202, 205–08
  see also recitation
action-theater (Munich) 69, 70
adaptation 2, 4, 6, 7, 8–12, 13, 16, 17–18, 19, 61, 62, 64, 65, 79, 91, 93, 102, 111, 122 n. 13, 179 n. 5, 182, 183
Adorf, Mario 13, 207
Adorno, Theodor W. 16, 19, 27, 28, 52, 74 n. 17
  'Transparencies on Film' 61, 67, 72
  and Max Horkheimer:
    Dialectic of Enlightenment 79
Afterimage (British film journal) 14
Albera, François 67, 74 n. 20, 109
Algerian War 200
  see also Straub, Jean-Marie, films: *The Algerian War!*
Alighieri, Dante 7, 18, 166–81
  The Divine Comedy 166–81
America 2, 67, 71, 86, 111, 138 n. 17, 145, 146, 176, 191, 198, 199, 208
Andrew, Dudley 9
Angelopoulos, Theo 14
anti-Semitism 35, 38, 183, 186
apparatus of cinema 6, 8, 18, 19, 33–35, 52, 94, 97, 98, 103
Aprà, Adriano 78, 79, 95
Apuan Alps 16, 38, 50, 77–90, 103, 104, 128
Arab Spring 14, 18, 186, 189
archaeology (excavation) 8, 49, 87, 88, 128, 165
  see also geology; stratification
ARD (German broadcaster) 102
Arendt, Hannah 185
Artificial Eye (British distributor) 14
auteurism 1, 12, 101
automatism 16, 62, 66–67
  see also somnambulism
Aze, Jules 153

Babeuf, François-Noël 178
Bach, Johann Sebastian 6, 11, 13, 15, 21 n. 13, 41 n. 14, 67, 70, 197–98, 201
  Ascension Oratorio 13, 68, 69
Balfry, Pamela 14
Banse, Juliane 188
Barr, Berlin 17, 91

Barrès, Maurice 7, 13, 41, 43 n. 52, 192
Barthes, Roland 8, 28, 29, 51, 133
Bartók, Béla:
  Sonata for Two Pianos and Percussion 63
Baumgärtel, Tilman 102
Bazin, André 9
Becher, Johannes R. 19
  'The Poetic Principle' 20
Beethoven, Ludwig van 13, 109, 115, 121
  String Quartet in A minor (Op. 132) 111, 121, 122 n. 32
  String Quartet No. 16 (Op. 135) 20
Bene, Carmelo 180 n. 39
Benigni, Roberto 179 n. 16
Benjamin, Walter 7, 16, 62, 63, 64, 65, 67, 68, 70, 71, 72, 74 nn. 17 & 24 & 40, 97–98, 177, 178, 184, 185
  Arcades Project 7, 16, 65, 72, 75 n. 58
  Jetztzeit (now-time) 8, 72, 97, 106
  'Theses on the Philosophy of History' 7–8, 11–12, 18, 64, 74 n. 24, 177–78
  'The Work of Art in the Age of Mechanical Reproduction' 7, 10
Bergson, Henri:
  Matter and Memory 110
Berlin 3, 101, 102, 103, 104, 106, 126
  International Film Festival (Berlinale) 199–200
Bernanos, Georges 9, 19, 41, 43 n. 52
Berta, Renato 84, 87, 90 n. 38, 124, 128, 129
Biette, Jean-Claude 70
birds (and birdsong) 38, 82, 84, 88, 94, 95, 98, 99, 103, 105, 111, 114, 130, 202
black screen 95, 97, 99–100, 103, 106 n. 23, 166, 188–89, 191
Blanchot, Maurice 57
  'Speaking is Not Seeing' 56
Blank, Manfred 41 n. 2
Bleicher, Josef 58 n. 17
Blum, Stephen 188
Böll, Heinrich 6, 9, 13, 16, 61–65
  Billiards at Half Past Nine 9, 62–65, 72, 75 n. 67
Book of Numbers (Bible) 78
Böser, Ursula:
  The Art of Seeing, the Art of Listening 21 n. 13
Botros, Atef 186
Brady, Martin 196, 208
breathing 6, 80, 112, 118, 119, 120, 166, 170–72, 174, 206
Brecht, Bertolt 3, 6, 7, 11, 15, 16, 19, 25, 26, 27, 35, 36,

38, 40, 47, 48, 49, 51, 62, 64, 65, 66, 67, 71, 72,
   74 nn. 20 & 24 & 40, 123, 131, 163, 175, 176, 184,
   192, 195 n. 38, 208
film:
   Kuhle Wampe or Who Owns the World? 94
writings:
   'Five Difficulties in Writing the Truth' 35, 49
   'Instructions to Actors' 62
   The Business Affairs of Mr Julius Caesar 7, 25
   Turandot or The Whitewashers' Congress 27
epic theatre 7, 63, 64, 66, 71, 72, 175–76, 208
separation of the elements 7, 92, 93, 95, 97, 98, 125
see also estrangement (*Verfremdung*); Weill, Kurt: *Rise
   and Fall of the City of Mahagonny*
Brechtianism 1, 2, 3, 4, 6, 7, 12, 16, 21 n. 5, 43 nn. 38
   & 46, 51, 62, 63, 64, 66, 67, 68, 71, 92, 93, 98,
   101, 102, 124, 125, 131, 182, 183, 195 n. 38
Bresson, Robert 9, 109, 115, 122 n. 26, 207
films:
   Diary of a Country Priest 109
   L'Argent 122 n. 26
   Les Dames du Bois de Boulogne 70
   Mouchette 9, 67
   Pickpocket 122 n. 26
writings:
   Notes on the Cinematographer 66
Brod, Max 185
Brouard, Michel 153
Bruckner, Ferdinand 6, 9, 13, 16, 69–71
   Sickness of Youth 9, 69–71
Buber, Martin 183, 184, 185
Buck-Morss, Susan:
   *The Dialectics of Seeing: Walter Benjamin and the
      Arcades Project* 7, 16, 65
Buscarino, Gianni 116
Butler, Judith 186
Byg, Barton 4, 183
   Landscapes of Resistance 3, 180 n. 33

Cabo, Ricardo Matos 3
Caffoni, Paolo 36, 80
Cahiers de doléances 48–49
Cahiers du cinéma (French film journal) 1, 2, 3, 14,
   21 n. 2, 61, 70, 102, 182, 189
Cannes Film Festival 14, 200
capitalism 27, 35, 40, 49, 50–51, 86, 127, 185
Carmelo, Maddio 112
Cavallo, Jo Ann 137
Centre national de la cinématographie 197
Cézanne, Paul 15, 17, 21 n. 13, 41 n. 14, 74 n. 17, 84,
   115, 116, 126, 128, 129, 138 n. 30, 183
Chaplin, Charlie:
   The Great Dictator 180 n. 33
Chion, Michel 17, 91–92, 96, 106 n. 7
cinematography 18, 30, 33, 35, 36, 48, 53, 54–57, 63,
   65, 66, 71, 82, 84, 85–86, 87–88, 94, 98, 102,

103–04, 105–06, 112, 113, 114, 115, 116, 119, 124,
   125, 128–30, 131, 133, 134–35, 174, 175, 182, 183,
   189, 191, 201–04
   pan 33, 55, 56, 57, 67, 77, 78, 82, 84, 86, 88, 97, 98,
      114, 115, 128, 129, 134, 135, 170, 191
   tracking shot 48, 50, 114, 128
class struggle 48, 86, 177–78
collective 11, 30, 36, 39, 52, 57, 126, 127, 129, 131, 177
Cologne (Köln) 62, 63, 101
colonialism 18, 20, 183, 186–87, 190
communism 4, 11, 12–13, 18, 19–20, 27, 31, 32,
   42 nn. 17 & 20, 78, 121, 127, 129, 130–31, 137,
   138 n. 39, 166, 177, 178, 183
contingency (chance) 13–14, 61, 82, 94–95, 96, 97–98,
   106, 133, 134
Corneille, Pierre 8, 9, 192, 205
   Othon 9, 91–92
Cosgrove, Denis E 58 n. 19
Costa, Pedro 12–13
   6 Bagatelles 7, 74 n. 17

Daily Mail (British newspaper) 78
Daney, Serge 17, 33, 35, 91, 93, 94, 98
de Hooch, Pieter 115
Debord, Guy:
   Society of the Spectacle 71
deconstruction 1, 9, 11, 21 n. 5, 62, 182
Delahaye, Michel 61, 65, 66, 67
Deleuze, Gilles 8, 10, 17, 19, 49, 86, 87, 88, 91, 92–93,
   98, 125, 128, 185, 189, 191, 195 n. 36
   Cinema II 49, 87
   see also stratification
   and Félix Guattari 189
   Kafka: Toward a Minor Literature 19, 185, 191,
      195 n. 36
Der Jude (German journal) 183, 184, 187, 192
Der Spiegel (German weekly magazine) 70
Deriaz, Margaret 196
deserts 4, 18, 29, 38, 50, 167, 176, 184, 185, 187, 188,
   190, 191, 193
Devos, Louis 13
dialectics 8, 9–10, 13, 15, 17, 30, 38, 43 n. 46, 46, 69,
   72, 79, 84, 96, 97, 106, 111, 121, 131
Didi-Huberman, Georges 74 n. 40, 85
Die Zeit (German weekly newspaper) 200
Dilthey, Wilhelm 110, 115, 120
dispositif 100, 131
Döblin, Alfred 7
documentary 1, 7, 8, 9, 65, 68, 70, 71, 72, 77, 93,
   96–97, 98, 104, 106
documentary film 2, 23 n. 51, 63, 65, 68, 70, 77, 79, 80,
   82, 85, 86, 96–97, 100, 101, 102, 103, 104, 105, 124
Donat, Misha 22 n. 19, 73 n. 10, 141, 195 nn. 31 & 40
Dreyer, Carl Theodor 12
Dreyfus Affair 26
dubbing 33, 91–92

Dubois, Philippe 10
Duras, Marguerite 13, 43 n. 51, 92
Duret, Jean-Pierre 94
Dwoskin, Stephen 14
Dziga Vertov Group 12

earth (soil) 4, 5, 8, 30, 31, 48, 49, 50, 51, 54, 55, 56,
    78–79, 87, 88, 92, 98, 124, 127, 128, 129, 130, 131,
    134, 160, 161, 164, 167
Eco, Umberto:
    The Open Work 126
ecology 3–4, 6, 31, 77, 84, 88, 89, 130, 131, 138 n. 39
    see also earth (soil); green politics
edgeland 18, 129, 133, 138 n. 36, 159
editing 11, 13, 63, 94, 101, 109, 126, 138 n. 14, 163,
    164, 165, 170, 174, 175, 178, 179 n. 7, 188, 201–02
    see also montage
Egypt 29, 43 n. 51, 48, 78, 94, 98, 128, 186, 187, 189,
    206
Eisenstein, Sergei:
    film:
        Alexander Nevsky 180 n. 33
    writings:
        Nonindifferent Nature 18, 166, 177–78, 179 n. 2
Eisler, Hanns 13, 19
    Serious Songs 20
emancipation 2, 12, 16, 27, 30, 69, 71, 72, 122 n. 31
Empedocles (Greek philosopher) 15, 26, 29, 30–32, 40,
    42 n. 25, 128
    On Nature 130
Engel, Andi 3, 9, 14
    see also Enthusiasm (British film journal)
Engels, Friedrich 11, 47, 48, 95–97
Enthusiasm (British film journal) 3, 9, 14
epic theatre, *see* Bertolt Brecht
essay film 2, 5, 93, 100, 101
estrangement (*Verfremdung*) 1, 7, 16, 54, 63, 66, 67–68,
    72, 87, 91, 123, 163, 175–76, 182, 208
Exodus (Bible) 30, 52–53, 56
explosives (dynamite, ecrasite) 1–2, 7, 19, 71, 72,
    75 n. 58, 109, 121

Fairfax, Daniel 2, 21 nn. 5 & 15, 130, 131–32, 138 n. 39
farms and farming 50–51, 78, 82, 86, 114, 118, 124,
    127, 131, 134, 138 n. 20, 149, 150, 151, 157, 161,
    175
Farocki, Harun 5–6, 17, 93, 101–06
    films:
        Between Two Wars 101, 102, 104
        Filmtip: Death of Empedocles 5–6, 104–05
        Inextinguishable Fire 102
        *Jean-Marie Straub and Danièle Huillet at Work on a
            Film Based on Franz Kafka's 'Amerika'* 102
        The People are Standing Forwards in the Streets 17,
            93, 101, 104–06, 105 fig. 5.7
        The Taste of Life 17, 93, 101, 102–04, 104 fig. 5.6

installation:
    Workers Leaving the Factory in Eleven Decades 102,
        107 n. 40
fascism 1, 16, 20, 35, 36, 79, 80, 86, 90 n. 26, 110, 123
Fassbinder, Rainer Werner 69, 101
Fendt, Ted 3
fiction 1, 2, 9, 15, 23 n. 51, 32, 62, 65, 70, 72, 113–14
    see also adaptation
Fieschi, Jean-André 1, 21 n. 4, 170
Filmkritik (German film journal) 101
Filmstudio (German film journal) 66
Fitoussi, Jean-Charles 109, 115
Florence 38, 84, 86, 104
food and drink 4, 38, 40, 50, 97, 112, 113, 116, 118,
    119–20, 121, 127, 143, 147, 148, 184, 188
Ford, John:
    Cheyenne Autumn 179 n. 7
    The Searchers 179 n. 7
Fortini, Franco 11, 15, 17, 25, 26, 36–38, 40, 77–90,
    103, 191, 192
    The Dogs of the Sinai 17, 36, 78, 87, 89, 90 n. 33
fragments and fragmentation 6, 7, 8, 9, 16, 20, 38, 64,
    71, 115, 126–27, 163, 183, 187, 188
    see also Kurtág, György *Kafka Fragments*
framing 12, 17, 30, 36, 46, 48, 49, 50, 51, 52, 53, 54,
    56, 57, 66, 82, 98, 105, 113, 114, 115, 116, 118,
    119, 129–30, 131, 133, 134, 135, 163, 164, 170,
    180 n. 37, 191, 203–04
French Revolution 8, 47, 97
    see also revolution
Frey, Hans-Jost 72
Fried, Michael 59 n. 30

Gallagher, Tag 179 n. 1
Gassman, Vittorio 179 n. 16
Geller, Jay 187
Genet, Jean 167
geology 8, 49, 57, 78, 80, 84, 85, 86, 87, 114
    see also archaeology (excavation); stratification
German Film and Television School (DFFB) 101
Godard, Jean-Luc 1, 10, 12, 14, 21 n. 3, 23 n. 51, 109,
    207
    Contempt 10
Goebbels, Joseph 200
Gorin, Jean-Pierre 12
Gramsci, Antonio 127, 138 n. 20
green politics 4, 6, 88, 130
    see also ecology
Griffith, D. W.:
    A Corner in Wheat 50–51, 58 n. 14

Hall, Stuart 36, 41
Hamburg 101, 201
Handke, Peter 200
Hanssen, Jens 186–87, 189, 190–91, 194 n. 11
Hargesheimer, Heinrich 62, 66

Harnoncourt, Nikolaus 198
Harvey, Sylvia 21 n. 5
Heidegger, Martin 4, 10
Heinisch, Christian 104
Heym, Georg 104, 105, 106
Hilzinger, Klaus Harro 71–72
history 7–8, 11–12, 13, 15, 16–17, 20, 26, 35–38,
    42 n. 18, 46, 49, 51, 52–53, 57, 58 n. 13, 62–63,
    64, 70, 71, 72, 74 n. 17, 77–90, 97, 100, 105–06,
    114, 123, 126, 128, 129, 135, 137, 158, 160, 161,
    176, 177, 180 n. 42, 183, 186, 189, 191, 192, 200,
    201
Hitchcock, Alfred:
    Foreign Correspondent 180 n. 33
Hitler, Adolf 42 n. 18, 35
Hochet, Louis 94
Hölderlin, Friedrich 4–6, 11, 14, 18, 20, 26, 30, 84,
    104–05, 126, 128–29, 131, 137, 183, 192, 197,
    198–99, 205, 207, 209
    The Death of Empedocles 4–5, 15, 30–32, 126, 196–209
    see also Huillet, Danièle, and Jean-Marie Straub,
        films: Black Sin; The Death of Empedokles
Hollywood 70
Holocaust 78, 88
Huillet, Danièle passim
    and Jean-Marie Straub
    films:
        A Visit to the Louvre 41 n. 14, 170, 172
        Black Sin 13, 15, 19, 20, 20 fig. I.2, 25, 126, 128,
            196, 200, 208
        Cézanne: Conversation with Joachim Gasquet 4, 6–7,
            115, 126, 128
        Chronicle of Anna Magdalena Bach 6, 9, 15, 19, 25,
            41 n. 2, 68, 70, 72, 91, 100, 109, 183, 200,
            201, 202, 207
        Class Relations 8, 14, 102, 104, 183, 192, 197
        En rachâchant 22 n. 16, 184, 223, 223 fig. E.1
        Europa 2005, 27 October 14, 183, 191
        Every Revolution is a Throw of the Dice 25, 92, 172,
            195 n. 41
        Fortini/Cani 6, 11, 15, 16, 19, 25, 28, 32, 36–38,
            37 figs 1.7 & 1.8, 50, 77–90, 81 figs 4.1 &
            4.2, 83 figs 4.3 & 4.4, 95, 95 fig. 5.1, 96 fig.
            5.2, 98, 100, 101, 102, 103, 104, 128, 135,
            137 n. 5, 183, 191, 223
        From the Cloud to the Resistance 2, 4, 13, 50, 130,
            133, 197
        History Lessons 6, 11, 14, 15, 25, 85, 94, 97
        Humiliated 13, 15, 17, 39, 40, 40 fig. 1.10, 123–37,
            132 fig. 7.3, 135 fig. 7.6, 136 figs 7.7 & 7.8
        Incantati 126, 131
        Introduction to Arnold Schoenberg's Accompaniment
            to a Cinematographic Scene 1, 14, 15, 19, 25,
            32–36, 33 fig. 1.4, 34 figs 1.5 & 1.6, 137 n. 5,
            179 n. 5, 183
        Itinerary of Jean Bricard 15, 18, 141–65

Lothringen! 22 n. 16, 43 n. 52
Machorka-Muff 1, 13, 61, 72–73, 182, 183
Moses and Aaron 9, 11, 12, 15, 16, 25, 26, 29–31,
    31 fig. 1.2, 50, 52–57, 54 fig. 2.1, 55 fig. 2.2,
    58 n. 22, 68, 78, 89, 100, 183, 197, 198, 206,
    223
Not Reconciled, or Only Violence Helps Where
    Violence Rules 6, 16, 19, 61–67, 63 fig. 3.1,
    70, 71, 72, 75 nn. 53 & 58, 101, 133, 183
Othon 9, 21 n. 5, 85, 91–92, 95, 174
Proposition in Four Parts 16, 50–51, 58 n. 14
Return of the Prodigal Son 15, 17, 39, 39–40,
    123–37
Sicilia! 15, 17, 19, 22 n. 16, 25, 26 fig. 1.1,
    75 n. 58, 109–22, 117 figs 6.1 & 6.2, 119 fig.
    6.3, 120 fig. 6.4, 123, 138 n. 14
The Antigone of Sophocles 13, 133
The Bridegroom, the Actress and the Pimp 6, 9, 13,
    16, 61, 65, 68–72, 68 fig. 3.2, 69 fig. 3.3,
    70 fig. 3.4, 73 fig. 3.5, 75 nn. 47 & 50 & 59,
    133, 183
The Death of Empedocles 4–6, 5 fig. I.1, 13–14, 15,
    19, 25, 28, 29, 30–32, 32 fig. 1.3, 104–05, 106,
    126, 128–29, 131–32, 132 fig. 7.4, 169, 174,
    196–209, 203 figs 11.1 & 11.2, 204 fig. 11.3
The Knife Sharpener 138 n. 14
The Wayfarer 138 n. 14
These Encounters of Theirs 174, 181 n. 46
Too Early, Too Late 6, 11, 15, 16, 17, 19, 43 n. 51,
    47–50, 58 n. 13, 92, 93, 94–100, 96 fig. 5.2,
    99 figs 5.3 & 5.4, 100 fig. 5.5, 102, 106,
    107 n. 40, 128, 163, 183, 189, 191, 195 n. 41,
    206, 223
Von heute auf morgen 19, 22 n. 16, 100, 184
Workers, Peasants 15, 17, 19, 25, 28, 38–40, 39 fig.
    1.9, 43 n. 46, 123–39, 125 fig. 7.1, 130 fig.
    7.2, 133 fig. 7.5, 174
    writings:
        Writings (ed. Sally Schafto) 3, 7, 194 n. 6
Humeau, David 164
Hussein, Mahmoud (Bahgat Elnadi, Adel Rifaat) 11,
    20, 43 n. 51, 96
    Class Conflict in Egypt: 1945–1971 48, 191

Ignatius of Loyola 177
improvisation 6, 61, 62, 124, 201, 208
insects 14, 88, 114, 126, 130, 131
intellectuals 15, 25–43
Interlandi, Giovanni 112, 113
Interlope la Curieuse (French journal) 18, 141, 164
Israel 16–17, 20, 78, 79, 86, 88, 183, 186, 189, 192,
    194 n. 11, 195 n. 38

Jameson, Frederic 10–11
Jews (Judaism) 18, 19, 29, 30, 35, 36, 42 n. 18, 65, 67, 78,
    79, 90 n. 33, 183, 184–87, 191, 192, 194 n. 11, 197

John of the Cross 12, 68, 69, 70, 71
Jump Cut (British film journal) 14
Jürgens, Curd 197

Kabbalah 1, 8, 16, 65
Kafka, Franz:
    'Jackals and Arabs' ('Schakale und Araber') 18–19,
        182–95
    The Man Who Disappeared 183, 192
    'A Report to an Academy' 184
Kandinsky, Wassily 35
Kant, Immanuel 58 n. 25
Karajan, Herbert von 197
Kautsky, Karl 42 n. 20, 47, 96
Keller, András 188
Kirkpatrick, Robin 167, 168, 169
Kratisch, Ingo 105
Kurtág, György 13, 188
    Kafka Fragments 19, 188

L'Unità (Italian newspaper) 78
labour 25–28, 30, 38, 39, 40, 41, 49, 50–51, 111, 112,
        121, 123, 127, 131, 134, 138 n. 20, 154
Lack, Roland-François 75 n. 50
landscape 3, 15, 16–17, 17–18, 45–59, 68, 77–90, 97–100,
        111, 114, 115, 120, 122 n. 25, 123, 128–29, 134,
        137, 138 n. 30, 160, 170, 174, 182, 188, 201, 206
    see also deserts; ecology; mountains; nature
language 2, 3, 6, 8, 22 n. 16, 29–30, 38, 61–62, 65–68,
        71, 91, 92, 98, 100, 106, 167, 168, 177, 178, 187,
        197, 207
    English 6, 18, 26, 68, 80, 82, 112, 178, 188, 202, 205
    French 3, 43 n. 51, 172, 178, 182, 187, 188, 191, 197,
        202, 208
    German 3, 6, 16, 61, 178, 183, 188, 201, 202
    Italian 3, 79, 91, 111, 112, 172, 178, 189, 197, 202, 206
Lanzmann, Claude 85
    Shoah 85
Lao Tzu (Laozi) 158
Lautréamont, Compte de (Isidore Ducasse) 71
Le Nain brothers 116
Lenin, Vladimir Ilyich 42 n. 20, 78
Leonhardt, Gustav 13, 198, 201
Leslie, Esther 41 n. 12
Levi, Arrigo 78, 80, 86, 87
Levin, Bernard 78
lieux de mémoire (sites of memory) 16, 77–79, 85–87
light 1, 4, 14, 56, 69, 92–93, 94, 98, 105, 112, 116, 120,
        121, 166, 167, 169, 172, 174, 177, 178, 201–02
Linke, Armin 124
literary adaptation 2, 4, 6, 7, 8–12, 13, 16, 17, 18,
        19, 22 n. 31, 61, 62, 64, 65, 79, 91, 93, 102, 111,
        122 n. 13, 179 n. 5, 182, 183
Littré, Émile 75 n. 53
lizards 14, 126
location scouting 47, 102, 163–65, 202
Lorrain, Claude 138 n. 29

Lorraine (Lothringen) 200
    see also Huillet, Danièle, and Jean-Marie Straub,
        films: *Lothringen!*
Lubtchansky, William 112
Lukács, György:
    The Theory of the Novel 52
Lumière brothers:
    Workers Leaving the Lumière Factory 96
Luxemburg, Rosa 42 n. 20
Lyotard, Jean-François 54–55, 56–57

Mabey, Richard 129
MacCabe, Colin:
    True to the Spirit 10
Madsen, Jane 82, 84, 86
maggio epico 18, 124, 131, 137
Mahler, Gustav 13
Mallarmé, Stéphane 13, 25, 192, 193, 195 n. 41
    'Un coup de dés jamais n'abolira le hasard' 195 n. 41
Malraux, André 13, 20
    Days of Contempt (*Days of Wrath*) 19
Mao Zedong 70
Marconcini, Dario 124
Marx, Karl 8, 68, 129, 177
    see also Marxism
Marxism 2, 3, 4, 6, 11, 12, 13, 62, 68, 82, 84, 129
Massard, Janine 43 n. 51
McFarlane, Brian:
    Novel to Film 11
Meynier, Fabien 77, 78, 79, 80, 83–84, 86, 88
Michelet, Jules 161
Milton, John 168
mise-en-scène 38, 52, 63, 158, 163, 182, 192
Mizoguchi, Kenji 14
modernism 1, 2, 6, 9, 10, 13, 62, 64, 101, 110, 189
modernity 26, 38, 51–52, 100, 105, 115
Momigliano, Luciana Nissim 78, 79, 95
Mont Sainte-Victoire 84, 126, 129, 138 n. 30
montage 7, 16, 50, 63, 64, 71, 72, 126, 128, 164, 165,
        167
    see also editing
Montesse, Alain:
    Étude pour Déserts 179 n. 5
Moses (prophet) 15, 26, 53, 55–56
Mount Etna 4, 20, 25, 31, 32, 84, 128–29
Mount Sinai 54, 223
mountains 4, 5, 38, 53, 54, 55, 77–90, 114–15, 120, 126,
        135, 188
    see also Apuan Alps; Mont Sainte-Victoire; Mount
        Etna; Mount Sinai
Munich (München) 68–69, 70, 101, 201
music 2, 7, 13, 17, 18, 25, 63, 65, 80, 93, 94, 100, 101,
        102–03, 104, 110, 111, 166–67, 175, 177, 179 n. 7,
        206
    see also Johann Sebastian Bach; Ludwig van
        Beethoven; Hanns Eisler; György Kurtág;
        Arnold Schoenberg

Musil, Robert 61
Mussolini, Benito 16, 36, 79
mysticism 4, 7, 13, 18, 49, 62, 65, 67, 68, 71, 72, 109,
    127, 167, 176

Naderi, Amir 6
Narboni, Jean 21 n. 5, 36, 43 n. 38
Naremore, James:
    Film Adaptation 10
Nash, Mark 36, 77, 79, 82, 83
Nasser, Gamal Abdel 191
nature 4–5, 16, 18, 29, 32, 45–57, 88, 89, 98, 114, 123–37
    see also ecology; landscape; mountains; rivers; earth
        (soil); wind
Nazi and Fascist massacres in Italy 50, 77, 81–85, 88,
    90 n. 26, 128
Neale, Steve 36, 77, 79, 82, 83
Nestler, Peter 15, 25, 33, 35, 36
New German Cinema 14, 101, 201
Nietzsche, Friedrich 167
Nora, Pierre 77
Nowell-Smith, Geoffrey 80
Nugara, Angela 111, 116, 118, 119, 120

Oberhausen Manifesto 14
Oberhausen Short Film Festival 1
opera dei pupi (Sicilian puppet theatre) 124

Palestine 18, 185–87, 189, 191, 194 n. 11
Paris 7, 14, 18, 95–97, 126, 148, 166, 183, 188, 191, 192
Pasolini, Pier Paolo:
    Canterbury Tales 9
    Decameron 9
    Medea 9
Passerone, Giorgio 18, 167, 170–76, 178, 180 nn. 36 &
    41, 181 n. 44, 189
Pavese, Cesare 2, 4, 11, 20, 123, 130–31, 181 n. 46,
    192, 197
    Dialogues with Leucò 14
    The Moon and the Bonfires 2
peasants and peasantry 4, 18, 25, 27, 31, 38–39, 47, 48,
    50, 58 n. 13, 86, 97, 116, 123–37
    see also Huillet, Danièle, and Jean-Marie Straub,
        films: *Workers, Peasants*
Perez, Gilberto 17, 68, 71, 91, 94, 96, 104
Petiteau, Jean-Yves 18
    Itinerary of Jean Bricard 18, 141–65
Petley, Julian 14, 196–209
photosynthesis (and heliotropism) 18, 169, 177–78
Plato:
    Theaetetus 163
Politkino (British distributor) 14
Pollmann, Inga 97–98
Positif (French film journal) 3, 14
post-humanism 77, 79, 88
Poussin, Nicolas 138 n. 29
Powell, James (Jimmy) 69, 71, 72

prohibition of images (Old Testament) 30, 42 n. 18,
    183, 189
Pummer, Claudia 79, 85, 88, 128, 137 n. 5, 183
Pythagoras 160

quotation 3, 4, 6, 7, 8, 10, 11, 15, 16, 19, 35, 50, 61–75,
    78, 96

RAI (Radiotelevisione italiana) 86, 170
Ramos-Martínez, Manuel 39, 135
Rancière, Jacques 2, 3, 4, 10, 12–13, 38, 39, 43 n. 46,
    67, 122 n. 31, 125, 127, 130–31, 138 n. 39
    Intervals of Cinema 2, 43 n. 46, 67, 122 nn. 13 & 31
Rauch, Andreas von 6, 105, 106
realism 3, 12, 47, 61, 64–65, 67, 74 n. 20, 96, 115,
    138 n. 14, 195 n. 38, 206
recitation 6, 17, 18, 48, 58 n. 13, 61, 62, 66, 69, 78, 79,
    80, 84, 87, 95, 96, 97, 100, 101, 103, 104, 104–06,
    123, 124–25, 134, 170–74, 175, 182, 205–08
    see also acting
Rees, A. J. 21 n. 3
Rehm, Werner 13
Reich, Günter 13
resistance 17, 19, 30, 35, 50, 53, 78, 79, 87–88, 92, 97,
    128, 155, 164
    see also Huillet, Danièle, and Jean-Marie Straub,
        films: *From the Cloud to the Resistance*
revolution 2, 8, 13, 15, 20, 27, 30, 32, 41, 42 n. 20, 47,
    64, 71, 74 n. 17, 78, 97, 99, 121, 186, 189
    see also French Revolution
rivers:
    Loire 143–62, 164
    Nile 48, 50, 98–99, 100
    Rhine 63
Rivette, Jacques 207
Robbe-Grillet, Alain 64
Rogger, Adelheid 104, 105
Rohmer, Eric 207
Rolland, Isabelle 18, 141, 158–62
Rome 8, 35, 92, 95
Rossellini, Roberto 196
Rothberg, Michael 82–83
Roud, Richard 21 n. 4, 64, 65, 68, 70, 95
    Jean-Marie Straub 3, 22 n. 19, 73 n. 10
Rubbens, Désiré Florentin 153
Rubini, Rubino 179 n. 16

Said, Edward 128
Salter, Richard 13
Sartre, Jean-Paul:
    Being and Nothingness 62
Schlöndorff, Volker:
    Young Törless 61
Schoenberg, Arnold 9, 11, 13, 15, 19, 21 n. 13, 25,
    32–36, 38, 40, 41 n. 2, 42 n. 18, 52–57, 126, 192
    'Accompaniment to a Cinematographic Scene'
    32–36

Kol Nidre 1
Moses and Aaron 12, 26, 29–31, 52–57, 78, 223
Von heute auf morgen 19
see also Huillet, Danièle, and Jean-Marie Straub, films: *Introduction to Arnold Schoenberg's Accompaniment to a Cinematographic Scene*; *Moses and Aaron*; *Von heute auf morgen*
Scholem, Gershom 7
Schott, Webster 126
Schwarz, Libgart 13
Screen (British film journal) 3, 14, 77, 79, 80, 89 n. 13
Séguin, Louis 1
Sender Freies Berlin (German broadcaster) 102
Shafto, Sally 194 n. 6
Shakespeare, William 205
Shoard, Marion 138 n. 36
Shumsky, Dimitry 184, 185
Sicily 106, 109–22, 124, 126, 128, 137
silence 17, 31, 69, 71, 77, 79, 84, 93, 111, 113, 124, 164, 165, 167, 170, 174, 208
see also sound
Simmel, Georg 16, 45–47, 51–52, 58 n. 17
'The Philosophy of Landscape' 16, 45–47, 51–52
Six-Day War (1967 Arab-Israeli War) 20, 36, 78, 86, 88, 183, 186, 189, 195 n. 38
Socrates 163
somnambulism 61, 66, 67, 72, 125
see also automatism
sound:
  direct sound 6, 7, 13, 17, 33, 48, 80, 84, 91–107, 110–11, 114, 128, 130, 164, 166, 191, 202, 206, 208
  sound recording 93, 94, 96, 97, 100, 101, 106
  see also silence
Stalinism 12
Stam, Robert 11, 22 n. 31
Stendhal:
  Scarlet and Black 114, 122 n. 19
Straschek, Günter Peter 15, 25, 33, 35, 36
stratification 8, 16, 17, 49, 79–80, 84, 87, 97, 100, 101, 104, 105, 106, 125, 128, 134, 137, 161, 177, 178
  see also archaeology (excavation); Gilles Deleuze; geology
Straub, Jean-Marie *passim*
  films:
    An Heir 53 n. 52
    Artemide's Knee 13
    Communists 4, 7, 13, 19–20
    Concerning Venice (History Lessons) 6, 7, 19, 43 n. 52
    Corneille — Brecht 7, 183, 184
    Dialogue of Shadows 19, 43 n. 52
    France Against Robots 6, 19, 43 n. 52
    Jackals and Arabs 6, 13, 14, 15, 18–19, 65, 182–95, 190 figs 10.1 & 10.2, 192 fig. 10.3, 193 figs 10.4 & 10.5
    O somma luce 6, 7, 13, 15, 18, 22 n. 16, 65, 166–81,

171 fig. 9.1, 173 fig. 9.2, 174 fig. 9.3, 175 figs 9.4 & 9.5, 176 figs 9.6 & 9.7
The Algerian War! 183–84
The Aquarium and the Nation 19
installation:
  Homage to Italian Art! 6, 19, 103
subtitles 80, 91, 138 n. 17, 141, 187, 202, 208
Südwestfunk (German broadcaster) 104
surrealism 68
Syberberg, Hans Jürgen 92
synchronization 92, 93, 98, 103–04

Teatro Francesco di Bartolo (Buti) 4, 15, 17–18, 111, 123–25, 128–29, 137, 138 n. 14, 170–72, 179 n. 1, 180 n. 38
television 5, 38, 50, 78, 80, 91, 93, 102, 104, 183, 196, 197, 198
Tell It to the Stones (film retrospective 2017) 3, 93
Tesson, Charles 180 n. 33
Thales (of Miletus) 159, 160
Thatcher, Margaret 199
The Other Cinema (British distributor) 14
theatre 12–13, 53, 175, 205
  see also action-theater; Brecht, Bertolt; *maggio epico*; *opera dei pupi*; Teatro Francesco di Bartolo (Buti)
theology 7, 18, 29–32, 52–57, 62, 65, 67, 109, 127, 176, 177–78
Théorie Communiste (political group) 42 n. 17
Thome, Rudolf:
  Jane Shoots John Because He is Cheating on Her With Ann 101
Toscano, Alberto 27
traffic (and vehicles) 38, 69, 80, 82, 92, 94, 95, 97, 98, 102–03, 104, 105
translation 6, 10, 29, 39, 75 n. 59, 71, 182–83, 187, 189, 194 n. 6, 197, 208
Trinh, Minh-ha T. 182, 194 n. 2
Truffaut, François 207
Tsao, Ming 35
Turquety, Benoît 3, 17, 91, 98

Uexküll, Jakob Johann von 97
Ulrich, Barbara 129, 188–89, 191, 196
Umwelt 97–100, 106
Ungari, Enzo 91
Ungerer, Lilith 69, 71, 72
utopia 4, 12, 20, 26–27, 28, 41, 72, 127, 129, 138 n. 29

Varèse, Edgard 13
  Déserts 18, 166–67, 179 n. 5
Venice Biennale 6, 103
Verdi, Giuseppe 111
Vernon, Howard 13
Vigneri, Vittorio 121
Viola, Bill:
  Déserts 179 n. 5

Virgil 168

Vittorini, Elio 11, 15, 17–18, 20, 25, 109–22, 123–39,
        192
    Conversations in Sicily 25, 109–22
    Women of Messina 38, 123–39

voice 3, 6, 16, 18, 29, 30, 36, 38, 48, 50, 52, 55, 56,
        62, 71, 80, 84, 87, 88, 92–93, 94, 96, 97, 98, 103,
        110–13, 121, 124, 125, 128, 129, 164, 168, 169, 172,
        174, 179 n. 7, 180 n. 33, 188, 189, 191
    dialect 6, 123, 197

voiceover 31, 43 n. 51, 91, 93, 96, 102, 103

Völker, Klaus:
    Brecht Chronicle 25

Walsh, Martin 68, 71

Warner, Rick 10

WDR (German broadcaster) 102

Webern, Anton:
    Six Bagatelles (Op. 9) 68

Weil, Simone 17, 88, 109–10, 174

Weill, Kurt:
    Rise and Fall of the City of Mahagonny 7, 33

Wenders, Wim 182, 200

West, Cornel 176–77

Whittlesey, Christine 13

Wiesbaden 201

wind 4, 12, 14, 69, 91, 94, 97–100, 105–06, 133, 174,
        202

Wollen, Peter 1

woodland 4, 14, 17–18, 78, 123–37

workers 18, 35, 38–39, 102, 103, 118, 123, 124, 127,
        131, 133, 134, 135, 137
    see also Huillet, Danièle, and Jean-Marie Straub,
        films: *Workers, Peasants*

World War Two 40, 62, 78, 123, 128, 129, 164, 177

Zimmermann, Bernd-Alois 13

Zionism 18, 183, 184, 185–87, 189, 190–91